The Dharma Master Chŏngsan
of Won Buddhism

SUNY series in Korean Studies

Sung Bae Park, editor

The Dharma Master Chŏngsan
of Won Buddhism

Analects and Writings

Translated and with an Introduction by

Bongkil Chung

Published by State University of New York Press, Albany

© 2012 State University of New York

For information, contact State University of New York Press, Albany, NY
www.sunypress.edu

Production by Eileen Meehan
Marketing by Michael Campochiaro

Library of Congress Cataloging-in-Publication Data

Chongsan, 1900–1962.
  [Selections. 2012]
  The dharma master Chongsan of Won Buddhism : analects and writings /
Chongsan ; translated and with an introduction by Bongkil Chung.
      p. cm. — (SUNY series in Korean studies)
  Includes translations from Korean.
  Includes bibliographical references and index.
  ISBN 978-1-4384-4023-1 (hbk. : alk. paper) — 978-1-4384-4024-8 (pbk. : alk. paper)
  1. Won Pulgyo (Sect)—Doctrines.   I. Chung, Bongkil.   II. Title.

  BQ9229.C363E55 2012
  294.3′42042—dc23   2011015559

                        10 9 8 7 6 5 4 3 2 1

Contents

Part Two: *The Dharma Words* (*Pŏbŏ*)

Part Three: Other Selected Writings

Preface

This book is an introduction to the teachings of Song Kyu (1900–1962; "Chŏngsan"), whose lifetime aspiration and plan was to help realize in the New World "one harmonious family under Heaven, with morality." Chŏngsan had begun to formulate this aspiration in childhood, when Korea lost its national identity under the Japanese occupation and the Korean people began to suffer much hardship. While wandering in search of a mentor, the young Chŏngsan encountered Pak Chungbin (1891–1943; "Sot'aesan"), who was in the process of establishing a new religious order following his spiritual awakening in 1916. Sot'aesan ushered Chŏngsan into the new order as its "chief codifier." As the order's chief codifier, Chŏngsan helped Sot'aesan systematize the central doctrine of the new order until Sot'aesan's death in 1943, when he succeeded Sot'aesan as head dharma master of the order. This book includes Chŏngsan's analects and some of his writings before and after his inauguration as the second patriarch of the order of Won Buddhism.

The translations in this book consist mostly of moral and religious discourses that Chŏngsan delivered during his tenure as head dharma master. In 1972, ten years after Chŏngsan's death, the *Chŏngsan chongsa pŏbŏ* (Dharma words of Master Chŏngsan) was published as one of the order's two sacred books. The book consists of *Sejŏn* (Canon of the world) and *Pŏbŏ* (Dharma words); the former is Chŏngsan's own writing, the latter a compilation of his analects. In 1982, a second collection of Chŏngsan's moral and religious discourses, the *Hanuran hanich'i-e* (With one truth within one fence), was published, which is an invaluable source for Chŏngsan's insights into the question of moral perfection.

In 2000, I translated the *Chŏngsan chongsa pŏbŏ* as *The Dharma Words of Master Chŏngsan* for use within the Won Buddhist order. For this volume, I have redacted that canonized version to present Chŏngsan's moral, religious, and philosophical thought in ways more suited to a general readership. I deleted three chapters of the *Dharma Words,* moving some sections from those chapters into other, thematically appropriate chapters. I have inserted more than eighty sections from the *Hanuran hanich'i-e* (With one truth within one fence) into the *Dharma Words* and added a new chapter, "Moral Culture," which comprises sections from the *Dharma Words* and the *Hanuran hanich'i-e.* This reordering of material better reflects Chŏngsan's teaching that moral culture is essential for the New World, a central theme that is scattered throughout *Dharma Words.* The provenance of each of these collected and rearranged sections is given in parentheses at the end of each section. The translation consists of three parts: Part One is the *Canon of the World* (*Sejŏn*) with no changes from the canonized version; Part Two, *Dharma Words* (*Pŏbŏ*), has been redacted as described above; and Part Three, "Other Selected Writings," includes sections that can help understand Chŏngsan's central thought. Chŏngsan's "Ode to the Consummate Enlightenment" (1937) reveals his views of the ultimate principle of the universe, and the natural laws governing the vicissitude of life. The section "On Irwŏnsang" (1937) outlines the central doctrine of Won Buddhism systematized in the *Pulgyo chŏngjŏn* (Correct canon of Buddhism), as can be seen in the section "Truth, Faith, and Practice of Irwŏnsang."

I had the rare fortune to be a student of Master Chŏngsan for seven years, from 1955 to 1962, at the headquarters of Won Buddhism in Iksan City, South Korea. It is my hope that this translation of his sayings and writings will serve to make his wisdom and insights better known to a general readership.

It is with great pleasure that I acknowledge my indebtedness to those who gave me such unstinting support for the publication of this work. I would like to express my sincere appreciation to Professor Sung Bae Park for his initial examination of this project and decision to make this volume a part of SUNY series in Korean studies. I also thank Nancy Ellegate at SUNY Press for her help throughout the process of the publication of this book. My appreciation goes to the University of Hawai'i Press for permitting me to reproduce two sections of *The Scriptures of Won Buddhism,* "Section One: The Truth of Irwŏnsang" and "Section Three: The Practice of Irwŏnsang" (pp. 120–122). Following the constructive criticism of the two anonymous readers for SUNY Press, I have done quite an extensive revision to the introduction; I express my sincere appreciation to them. I am grateful to Maura High, who has done a thorough copyediting of the manuscript for grammatical and stylistic improvement. I am grateful to the copyeditor for SUNY Press, who has made grammatical improvement to my work.

I thank Dr. Song Chun Eun, former president of Won Kwang University, for his numerous suggestions for the direction of the translation and several doctrinal issues in Chŏngsan's thought. I would like to acknowledge my indebtedness to Dr. Han Kidu, emeritus professor of Won Kwang University, for his clarification of numerous points in Chŏngsan's thought. However, I am responsible for any errors remaining in the book.

I should not forget to express my gratitude to Dr. Mark B. Rosenberg, provost and academic vice president of Florida International University (now president), and the Committee for Sabbatical Leave, for granting me one semester of leave, so I could write the introduction to the translation. I am grateful to the late Mrs. Kim Hyŏn'gangok in Seoul, Rev. Chang Kyŏngjin, Rev. Song Yŏngbong, and Rev. Song Sunbong in the headquarters of Won Buddhism for providing me with the generous subvention for the publication of this book. And I owe a special debt of gratitude to my wife, Shinok (Yŏnt'awŏn Yi Sŏnghun), for her unfailing support and to my two sons, Andrew and Daniel, for their sacrifices to help this book see the light of day.

Bongkil Chung

Abbreviations and Conventions

AGM	James Legge, *Confucius: Confucian Analects, The Great Learning, and The Doctrine of the Mean*
C	Chinese pronunciation
CN	*The Canon* in *The Scriptures of Won Buddhism*
CCC	*Chŏngsan chongsa chŏn* 鼎山宗師傳 (The biography of Master Chŏngsan)
CP	*Chŏngsan chongsa pŏbŏ* 鼎山宗師法語 (The dharma words of Master Chŏngsan)
CPS	*Chŏngsan chongsa pŏpsŏl* 鼎山宗師法說 (Sermons of Master Chŏngsan)
CW	*Canon of the World* in this book (Translations, Part One)
DW	*Dharma Words* in this book (Translations, Part Two)
HC	*Han'guk chonggyo* 韓國宗教 (Korean religions)
HH	*Hanuran hanich'i-e* 한울안한이치에 (With one truth within one fence)
J	Japanese pronunciation
K	Korean pronunciation
KAZ	*Korean Approach to Zen,* trans. Robert E. Buswell Jr.
PC	*Pulgyo chŏngjŏn* 佛教正典 (Correct canon of Buddhism; 1943)
S	Sanskrit pronunciation
SS	*Scripture of Sot'aesan* in *The Scriptures of Won Buddhism*
SW	*The Scriptures of Won Buddhism,* translation of 圓佛教教典 by Bongkil Chung
T	*Taishō shinshū daizōkyō* 大正新修大藏經 (The Taishō tripitaka)
WBC	*Wŏnbulgyo chŏnsŏ* 圓佛教全書 (Complete works of Won Buddhism)

WE   Won Buddhist era

WK   *Wŏnbulgyo kyosa* 圓佛教教史 (History of Won Buddhism)

WKC   *Wŏnbulgyo kyogo ch'onggan* 圓佛教教故叢刊 (Comprehensive publication of the earlier writings of Won Buddhism)

The *Canon* abbreviated as *CN* in this book refers to the "Canon" in *SW*; it does not refer to either of the two Korean original 1943 or 1962 versions.

If a book has not been published in English, its Romanized title is, for the sake of readability, given in parentheses after the translated title, e.g., *The Canon of the World* (*Sejŏn*).

The tags *CP* and *HH* in the parentheses at the end of each section of the *Dharma Words* refer to the *Chŏngsan chongsa pŏbŏ* (The dharma words of Master Chŏngsan) and the *Hanuran han ich'i-e* (With one truth within one fence) respectively, followed by the chapter and section numbers; e.g., (*CP* 1:1) refers to *The Dharma Words of Master Chŏngsan*, chapter 1, section 1.

The *Taishō* Canons are listed in the following fashion: title (with Sanskrit title, if relevant, in parentheses) and fascicle number: *T*(aishō), serial number, volume number, page, register (a, b, or c); e.g., *Jingang boruo boluomi jing, T* 235.8.748c–752c.

Whether a term in parentheses is a Chinese, Korean, or Sanskrit can be seen in the Chinese Character Glossary and the Glossary of Terms.

Transliterations of Asian languages follow the systems commonly used in the scholarly community: Pinyin system for Chinese, Revised Hepburn for Japanese, McCune-Reishauer for Korean.

Sanskrit terminology that appears in *Webster's Third International Dictionary* is left unitalicized; e.g., dharma, dharmakāya, dhyāna, karma, nirvāṇa, prajñā, samādhi, tathāgata.

Korean personal names follow the traditional Korean form, with family name first and given name last (e.g., Kim Taejung), except for names already known in the Western style (e.g., Bongkil Chung, in Korean Chŏng Ponggil).

"The Buddha" refers to Śākyamuni Buddha; "a buddha" refers to anyone who is enlightened like the Buddha.

"Irwŏn" and "Irwŏnsang" are not italicized because they appear frequently throughout the book as special technical terms of Won Buddhism. The "Ir" in Irwŏn is pronounced like the "ir" in "irrigation." Other Won Buddhist technical terms are defined in the Glossary of Terms.

Introduction

Background

A proper introduction to Chŏngsan's thought requires an account of the historical context in which new religions indigenous to Korea came into being. Around the turn of the twentieth century, in the final decades of the waning Chosŏn kingdom (1392–1910), Korea was going through what has been described as a degenerate age. The Chosŏn kingdom was plagued by internal corruption and a predatory Confucian ruling class that dominated both the capital of Seoul and the rural areas, and that had gained wealth at the expense of the common people. To make matters worse, different factions of the ruling class fought among themselves. Foreign powers took advantage of the kingdom's weakness and launched repeated attacks against the impotent Chosŏn court. The common people, especially the peasants, suffered grievously under oppression, exploitation, and extortion by the ruling class and by local government officials. They were made even more miserable by recurrent epidemics, floods, bitterly cold winters, and famine.

Under these deplorable conditions there arose a religious movement called Tonghak (Eastern Learning). Tonghak was founded by Ch'oe Cheu (1824–1864; "Suun") as a result of a divine revelation. In April 1860, "the Supreme Lord," appeared to Ch'oe Cheu, directing him to teach people "the Eastern way" as opposed to the Western way (Catholicism), which was spreading rapidly in the upper classes.[1] The religious doctrine of Tonghak was a synthesis of Buddhism, Confucianism, and Taoism, which Ch'oe Cheu thought should not be replaced with the Western learning. He claimed, however, that the three Eastern ways were exhausted and in need of reform.[2]

The central tenet of Tonghak theology is the belief that humanity is heaven. Human mind is none other than God's mind; heaven originates in the human mind. Thus, the Lord on High, or God, is enshrined in the human body. Hence, humanity should be treated as heaven. This tenet aims to restore the dignity, liberty, and equality of human beings and raise them from the abjectness of their condition under the Chosŏn kings. Tonghak divided history into "earlier heaven" and "later heaven"; past culture and civilization, Ch'oe Cheu claimed, had ended and the new culture of the future had opened: the period of the later heaven had begun. A universal, humanitarian culture would, he predicted, unfold through an opening-up of the spirit, of the Korean people, and society.

Because the ruling class suppressed open political discussion, the peasants turned to the religious movement of Tonghak to express their grievances. In June 1861, as the number of people following him increased, Ch'oe Cheu announced the new religion. He asserted that the era had come when the nation should be strengthened and the livelihood of the people be assured, and called for reform of the corruption-ridden government. The Chosŏn court viewed this millenarian claim as a serious threat and moved to stop the spread of the Tonghak faith. It started to oppress Tonghak followers just as it had persecuted Christians earlier. In 1863, Ch'oe Cheu was arrested on charges of misleading the people and sowing discord in the society, and he was executed the following year.[3] Tonghak did not, however, fade away, and the second patriarch, Ch'oe Sihyŏng (1829–1898; "Haewŏl"), systematized the doctrine of Tonghak as a new religion, collecting it in a volume, the *Tonggyŏng taejŏn* (Great canon of Tonghak).[4]

The peasants' deep hostility toward the aristocratic class helped the Tonghak movement to gain momentum. In 1894, a peasant revolt broke out against the local government in North Cholla province, and Chŏn Pongjun (1853–1895) organized a Tonghak army, overwhelmingly defeating the government army. Alarmed by this defeat, the Chosŏn court asked China, ruled at that time by the Qing dynasty, for military reinforcements. The Japanese government took the opportunity to invade Korea, claiming that it had sovereignty there, thus beginning the Sino-Japanese War (1894–1895). The Qing army was defeated by the Japanese forces, and the Chosŏn kingdom was dissolved, to be succeeded by the Taehan dynasty (1897–1910).[5] Now threatened by the Japanese presence in Korea, the new Taehan court turned to Russia for help. But the Russian presence in Korea led only to the Russo-Japanese War (1904–1905), in which the Japanese were again the victors.

Eventually, Korea was annexed to Japan (1910), thus losing its national identity, and endured thirty-five years of Japanese occupation. In 1945, at the end of World War II, Korea was liberated from Japanese colonial rule, but the Korean people soon realized the painful truth that freedom is not free. The country was divided into the North and South Koreas and suffered three years of civil war, starting in 1950, which devastated the Korean peninsula and ended with two million Korean people dead.[6] The people had suffered a hundred years of almost unbroken strife and misery between the mid-nineteenth and the mid-twentieth century, and numerous religions indigenous to Korea arose in this period to address the deep needs of the populace.[7]

Besides Tonghak, there was Chŭngsan'gyo (religion of Chŭngsan). Because the Tonghak rebellion (1894) had failed without achieving its goal, some of the activists from that rebellion were still searching for a way to bring about social reform. Kang Ilsun (1871–1909; "Chŭngsan") had followed the Tonghak army, watching the course of the rebellion but not participating in the fighting.[8] He observed the failure of war and the social chaos that ensued, and came to the conclusion that the situation could not be rectified by any existing religious or human power. He thought that only divine magical art could open up a New World. Hoping to attain such power, he studied Confucianism, Buddhism, and Daoism, as well as yin-yang philosophy, geomancy, divination, and medicine; he dabbled in such occult disciplines as calling down rain and hail and the magic art of shape-shifting (transforming his own body into something else). He then wandered about Korea for three years, beginning in 1897, in order to attain a clear understanding of national and social conditions.[9] Upon returning to his home village in 1901, he started ascetic practice at Taewŏn-sa, a Buddhist temple on Mount Moak in North Cholla province, with the aim of attaining omniscience, with which he would deliver the world.[10] He became spiritually awakened to "the great way of heaven and earth," and began to attract followers from 1902 onward. He gave sermons, claiming that he had the authority to rule heaven, earth, and humans. He said that he had come to the world in order to open a new heaven and earth, a paradise into which he would deliver all men and women suffering in the bitter seas of misery. Kang Ilsun was believed in as a messiah, the incarnation of God. The fact that so many people believed his claim to be the supreme lord of heaven has to be seen in the context of his times: first, the social chaos that followed the failure of the Tonghak rebellion; the anticipation among Christians that Christ would come again; the Buddhist belief in the coming of Maitreya Buddha; and the rumor that Ch'oe Cheu, the founder of Tonghak, had reincarnated.[11] Kang Ilsun propagated his teaching from 1902 to 1909 but never instituted a religious order. Still, he called his religious work "the reconstruction of heaven and earth," and this was the essence of his religious planning. Some of the followers, however, complained about the delay of the promised opening of the new heaven and earth. They frequently pleaded with him that the paradise be realized quickly. In the midst of these difficulties, in 1909, Kang Ilsun died, and those followers who were disillusioned at his death dispersed without even attending the funeral; only a few Chŭngsan'gyo followers were said to have remained to hold the funeral.[12]

The idea of "opening the later heaven" had undergone a drastic change in Kang Ilsun's thought. From an exclusive reliance on magic, he thought that the ideological foundation of "the later heaven" could be laid only with a new synthesis of the best elements of all religions.[13] His doctrine thus came to include Taoism and yin-yang philosophy as well as traditional shamanism and geomancy. The Confucian cardinal moral virtues were promoted as the moral ideals; to these were added Tonghak's moral virtues, and together, these virtues comprised the moral discipline of Chŭngsan'gyo.[14]

In the cosmology of Chŭngsan'gyo, the earlier and later heavens are divided in accordance with the "schedule of the universe" controlled by the authority and power of Kang Ilsun. The age during which the earlier heaven is replaced by the later heaven is identified with Korea's degenerate age. The earlier heaven is characterized by extreme inequality, disorder, and injustice (all abundantly evident in Kang Ilsun's time), and the later heaven by equality, justice, and prosperity. During the degenerate age, all the conditions accumulated in the earlier heaven were clearly exposed and all hidden antagonisms and conflicts surfaced, with violence, tension, struggle, and chaos. It was due to the "reconstruction of heaven and earth" performed by Kang Ilsun that the schedule of the universe was readjusted toward the opening of the later heaven; the promised paradise would eventually be constructed in the later heaven with all conflicts and antagonism dissolved. One of the salient features of Kang Ilsun's later thought is the "resolution of grudges and enmities." He identified the cause of continuing tension, enmity, and fighting as rooted in resentments characteristic of the earlier heaven, in which the principle of mutual opposition was in charge of human affairs. Consequently, the universe was full of grudges and enmity, so that resentful spirits maneuvered to cause all the cruelty and calamity in the human world. Kang Ilsun therefore intended to amend the blueprint of heaven and earth by correcting the actions of these myriad spirits—correcting, that is, nothing less than the way of divinity—so that all ancient resentments could be resolved and a government of creative transformation could be erected.

A third indigenous religion is Wŏnbulgyo (Won Buddhism), described in detail below. The founders of these three major religions were all aware that they could not rely on any one of the three ancient religions of Buddhism, Confucianism, and Taoism, although they did incorporate some of the tenets of these religions into their new doctrines. As Korean Buddhism, ostracized by the Confucian ruling class, had barely survived in remote mountain areas during the five centuries of the Chosŏn kingdom, it could not be relied on to correct the direction of the Korean destiny. Confucianism, as practiced by the ruling class of the Chosŏn kingdom was blamed as the direct cause of Korea's ruin, so it too could not be used as the leading principle for any new religion. Some Buddhist thinkers tried to reform the Korean Buddhist system so that it would be more relevant to the Korean secular world. Han Yongun (1879–1944) and Paek Yongsŏng (1865–1940) were two of the most active figures in this attempt.[15] It should be noted here, however, that Korean Buddhism has come a long way since the liberation of Korea in 1945 and is now arguably the soundest Buddhism of modern times.

The Life of Chŏngsan

In Search of a Mentor

Song Kyu (1900–1962), better known by his dharma title, Chŏngsan, would eventually become the head dharma master of Wŏnbulgyo, succeeding the founder, Pak Chungbin (1891–1943; "Sot'aesan"). As his biographer points out,[16] Chŏngsan lived through the Korean national tragedies of the first half of the twentieth century.[17] As a young child in North Kyŏngsang province, he was already aspiring to become a sage. At age six, he started learning the Confucian classics from his grandfather. At age eight, while studying the *Zizhi tongjian*,[18] he was already aspiring to be a great man. Two years later, in the year Korea lost its national identity to Japan, Chŏngsan was studying the Confucian classics;[19] he would become, he had decided, a great figure capable of correcting the ills of the Korean national destiny. Enshrining the name tablets of ancient heroes and sages in his room, Chŏngsan offered prayers in front of them. He was thirteen when he began studying Confucianism at a private school run by Song Chunp'il (1869–1943). After two years of study, however, Chŏngsan realized that Korea could not be saved with Confucian moral and social teachings, and he started to deepen his interest in inquiry into the metaphysical principles of the universe and in moral cultivation. At age seventeen, Chŏngsan searched the Mount Kaya region three times in search of a recluse named Ryŏ, who was alleged to be an enlightened person, only to be disappointed. Chŏngsan offered prayers on Mount Kaya with three other men for three months; they advised him to go to North Chŏlla province to meet there with Song Ch'ano (1874–1939), who they said would help him find a great mentor.

Chŏngsan decided to travel there. In 1917 he met, not Song Ch'ano, but Ch'a Kyŏngsŏk (1880–?), the founder of Pochŏn'gyo, a sect of Chŭngsan'gyo that was centered in North Chŏlla province. Ch'a Kyŏngsŏk did not have the qualities that Chŏngsan was looking for in a teacher, but Chŏngsan did decide to travel to the house of the founder of Chŭngsan'gyo, Chŭngsan. Chŭngsan had died in 1909, but at his house Chŏngsan found Ko P'allye (1880–1935), Chŭngsan's widow, and he stayed there for several months. Chŭngsan's only daughter, Kang Sunim, who was four years younger than Chŏngsan, regarded him as her elder brother. One day when they were alone, she told him that her father had hidden a small book in the ceiling and instructed her to give it to someone who would come to her later. She took Chŏngsan to a small back room and pointed to a spot in the ceiling that was patched with pieces of paper. Carefully tearing open the patched spot, he found the *Essential Secrets of Correcting the Mind (Chŏngsim yogyŏl)*. This book reflected the Daoist method of spiritual cultivation. Chŏngsan later incorporated part of this book in the section on "cultivation of spirit" in the *Correct Canon of Buddhism (Pulgyo chŏngjŏn).*[20] According to Chŏngsan's biographer, the widow Ko P'allye found, after a while, that Chŏngsan's spiritual power conflicted with her own religious practice; so she wrote Chŏngsan's father to take him back to North Kyŏngsang province.

In November 1917, Chŏngsan left Chŭngsan's house and entered the Buddhist temple Taewŏnsa on Mount Moak, where the great monk Chinmuk (1562–1633) had briefly stayed and where Chŭngsan had attained his spiritual awakening in 1901. It was common for those connected with Chŭngsan'gyo to visit it. Chŏngsan stayed at this temple accumulating spiritual power by reciting mantras.[21]

While Chŏngsan was dedicating himself to mind cultivation at Taewŏnsa, a middle-aged woman, Kim Haeun, stopped by the temple. She was a devout follower of Chŭngsan'gyo, thinking that Chŭngsan was truly a man of the Way but that he had simply appeared at the wrong time. Her maternal aunt had told her that she had seen a truly enlightened man at Taewŏnsa, and now Kim Haeun wished also to see him. According to the biographer, her first impression of Chŏngsan was that he was like the "full moon in the empty sky." The sight of the young Chŏngsan, with his clear countenance and mind like the moon rising high in the sky, inspired her deeply. From that time on, Kim Haeun visited the temple frequently and learned about Chŏngsan's aspiration and goals. She wanted to serve him and help him. She therefore asked her son, Kim Toil, to invite Chŏngsan to her house, which he did, and Chŏngsan accepted the invitation.[22] In January 1918, at the age of eighteen, Chŏngsan left Taewŏnsa for Hwahae-ri, in Chŏngŭp county. He stayed there, at Kim Haeun's house, developing his spiritual power by prayers and chanting, until such time as he would meet his long-awaited mentor.[23]

This description of Chŏngsan's life would not be complete without considering his position in his mentor's plan, so we will turn briefly to Sot'aesan and the development of the order that would become Won Buddhism.

The Chief Codifier

In South Chŏlla province, Pak Chungbin (1891–1943; "Sot'aesan") attained a spiritual awakening in 1916, six years after Korea lost its national identity to Japanese imperialist ambitions. Sot'aesan appeared to his villagers as a figure with extraordinary charisma. About forty men, most of them his seniors, became his followers. Sot'aesan saw that human beings could become enslaved by the powerful seductions and pressures of the material world. He thought that the world could be transformed from one of torment and misery into one that was safe and happy as long as the spiritual power of human beings was strengthened and expanded. He felt it urgent, therefore, to strengthen the spiritual power of humankind, and he believed that the only way to accomplish this end was through faith in truthful religion and training in sound morality. Sot'aesan's first step in opening his new religious order was to choose eight of his followers as disciples, who, with the addition of himself and one new disciple, would form a ten-member body; this became the first unit of the new religious order he was establishing. The ten members would correspond to the traditional "ten directions": the leader corresponding to heaven, the central member to the earth, and the eight other members to the eight cardinal directions. Sot'aesan kept the center position vacant, appointing a proxy to hold it until the arrival of the right person "from afar." Sot'aesan told his disciples that his aspiration and plan to open a new religious order could not be realized until he met the right person. And the right person was Chŏngsan, from North Kyŏngsang province. According to Chŏngsan's biographer, Sot'aesan located the young Chŏngsan by studying the stars. In April 1918, Sot'aesan went to Hwahae-ri to meet the person who would become, in Sot'aesan's words, the "chief codifier of the new religious order," and in July, Chŏngsan moved to Yŏngsan, South Chŏlla province, the cradle of Won Buddhism, where he was appointed to the center position of the ten-member body, the first supreme council of the order. In July 1919, Chŏngsan received his dharma name, Kyu, and the dharma title *Chŏngsan* shortly afterward.[24] When Sot'aesan ushered Chŏngsan into the new order, he meant Chŏngsan to be the creator of the doctrine. To an extent, the word *creator* is more correct than *codifier*, because the details of Won Buddhist doctrine were in fact defined and articulated by Chŏngsan, not Sot'aesan. The third patriarch, Kim Taegŏ (1914–1998; "Taesan") called Chŏngsan "the mother of Dharma of the new order," a description that was inscribed on the Chŏngsan Monument at the headquarters of Won Buddhism.

In order to compare the nature of his own enlightenment with those of ancient sages, Sot'aesan perused the classics of Buddhism, Confucianism, Daoism, Christianity, and Tonghak. Upon reading the *Diamond Sūtra*, Sot'aesan declared that Śākyamuni Buddha was the sage of all sages and that he would take the Buddha's teaching as the central tenet of the doctrine of the new religious order he was planning to establish.[25] He did so because he realized that the Buddha's teaching was best in explicating the fundamental truth of the universe. However, he could not advocate traditional Buddhism to his disciples because Buddhism in Korea by that time had been marginalized for five hundred years by the Chosŏn kingdom's national ideology of Confucianism, and Buddhist monks were treated as the lowest of the Korean society's eight low classes. In Sot'aesan's view, Buddhism as practiced in Korean society could not be relied on for unfolding the spiritual power for the new era. Because the spiritual lights of ancient sages had been dimmed for such a long time, thought Sot'aesan, they were not bright enough to illuminate the spiritual darkness of those troubled times. The light of wisdom and compassion was obscured by the three mental "poisons" of greed, hatred, and delusion, which in the Buddhist view are the ultimate cause of all human miseries. Sot'aesan thus set aside what no longer seemed effective and incorporated into the doctrine of the new religious order a selection of relevant tenets of the ancient sages, taking Buddha-dharma as the core of the teaching.

Before mentioning anything about Buddhism to his disciples, the young Sot'aesan accomplished several things as examples of a new religious life. In order to show the way in which the old world would be transformed into a new one, he set up such precepts as diligence and frugality, the abolition of empty formalities, doing away with superstition, and abstinence from alcohol and tobacco. First, he set up a savings association. He then ordered his nine disciples to construct an embankment to stop the seawater from the tidal estuary beside his village, so that what had been wasteland could be used for growing crops. He launched the reclamation project in March 1918 and had it completed after one year of hard labor. Although the land reclaimed was only twenty-five acres, Sot'aesan had set an example of the new religious life. The farmland thus created provided a financial foundation for the new religious order.

Upon completing the embankment project, he ordered his nine disciples, including Chŏngsan, to offer special prayers, citing the precedent of some ancient sages who wished to save the world and who had offered prayers to Heaven and Earth in order to obtain authentication of their sincerity. The prayers began on the twenty-sixth day of the third month (lunar calendar) of 1919 and ended on the twenty-sixth day of the seventh month.[26] As there was no sign that the numinous spirits of Heaven and Earth had been moved by their prayers, Sot'aesan quoted the saying "One sacrifices oneself in order to preserve one's integrity." The disciples understood this to mean that they should be prepared to sacrifice their lives for the well-being of all sentient beings, and this they resolved to do. Sot'aesan prepared a document inscribed with the words "Sacrifice with no regret" followed by their names, and asked all nine to "seal" it by pressing their thumbs on the paper. As the story goes, they used no ink or wax, just their bare thumbs. Before the nine disciples left for the nine mountain tops, Sot'aesan asked whether they wanted to say anything;

they said that they had nothing to say. The young Chŏngsan said, "We are going to sacrifice our lives with pleasure like this; however, we pray that you should not be troubled a bit by this matter of ours."[27] When the disciples were leaving for their prayer sites on the mountaintops where they planned to commit suicide, Sot'aesan called them back. Under the nine names on the sheet of white paper were nine fingerprints, the color of blood. The appearance of the fingerprints was taken to be the sign of authentication of their selfless devotion. Sot'aesan told them that they did not have to carry out their sacrifice since the numinous power of Heaven and Earth was moved by their selfless sincerity and devotion.[28] This demonstration of selfless devotion became the spiritual foundation of the new religious order and the standard of Won Buddhist priesthood for future generations, the standard that a Won Buddhist priest ought to serve selflessly for the well-being of all sentient beings.

In March 1919, when the embankment project was almost complete, Sot'aesan had traveled to Wŏlmyŏngam on Mount Pyŏn, in Puan county, North Chŏlla province, and stayed there for ten days. In August, after the dharma authentication, he told Chŏngsan that he was planning to return to Mount Pyŏn in order to give repose to his spirit and to avoid the suspicion of the Japanese. He expressed his intention to draft, while he was there, a doctrine and system that would renovate the past Buddhist doctrine and system, and to prepare to open the gate of a new order by building up affinities in the surrounding districts. He told Chŏngsan to go to Wŏlmyŏngam before him, to shave his head, become the senior disciple of Zen monk Paek Hangmyŏng (1867–1929), and pursue various inquiries; but not to read any Buddhist scriptures.[29] Chŏngsan went to Paek Hangmyŏng, who received him warmly. After a few rounds of Zen questions and answers, the Zen monk gave Chŏngsan a Buddhist name, Myŏngan (Bright eye). Chŏngsan, with the Buddhist name Myŏngan, did his duty as the chief disciple of the Zen monk, making inquiries into various areas on which Sot'aesan would test him upon his return.

On October 6, 1919, Sot'aesan renamed his group the Preparatory Association for the Establishment of the Society for the Study of Buddha-dharma and ordered that the phrase "Buddha-dharma" should enter all records. He said, "From now on, what we should learn is Buddha-dharma and what we should teach our followers is Buddha-dharma. Exert yourselves to be enlightened to the fundamental truth by inquiring into the gist of Buddha-dharma."[30] He explained that because Buddhism had been treated contemptuously in Korea for several hundred years, no one would respect anything bearing the name "Buddhism," and hence he had been reluctant to introduce Buddha-dharma lest it would not be respected by the world. He explained that Buddha-dharma was, however, the best means to discover fundamental truth and to lead sentient beings to the gate of merit and wisdom through correct practice, and that he would therefore take Buddha-dharma as the central teaching of the new religious order he was planning to establish. He predicted that Buddhism would be the major religion of the world in the near future, but declared that it should be renovated for the new age. For instance, the worship of the Buddha should not be focused on the Buddha statue, because people should realize that all things in the universe are none other than the Buddha. Hence, Buddha-dharma would not be separated from daily life; daily life would itself be Buddha-dharma.[31]

On October 20, 1919, Sot'aesan left for Wŏlmyŏngam. On his arrival, he was met by Chŏngsan and the head monk, Paek Hangmyŏng, who welcomed him to the temple. People began to arrive from Chŏnju and Kimje, the two towns in North Chŏlla province, to receive teachings from Sot'aesan, so he needed larger quarters to accommodate them. With Paek Hangmyŏng's help, Sot'aesan purchased a house and field four kilometers away from Wŏlmyŏngam for use as a cloister, paying for them by selling the pocket watches used by the nine disciples during their prayers and with a donation from one of his followers from Chŏnju, Yi Man'gap (1879–1960). Chŏngsan stayed at Wŏlmyŏngam for two more years, until the cloister, Sŏktuam, was completed.

In all, Sot'aesan spent five years developing his personal spiritual practice, retiring from public activity during turbulent times, and crystallizing his ideas for the new religious order. In 1920 Sot'aesan announced the outline of the doctrine for the new religious order. It consisted of two related ways: the "way of humanity" and the "way of practice."

The first way outlines the path we are to follow in the world: to honor the sources of Fourfold Beneficence (of heaven and earth, parents, brethren, and laws) and follow the four essential rules of social reformation (equal rights of man and woman, using wisdom rather than seniority or relationship as the standard, educating the children of others, and venerating those who devote themselves to the public cause). The second way concerns moral culture and comprises a Threefold Practice (cultivation of spirit, inquiry into facts and principles, heedful choice in karmic action) and eight prerequisites for the Threefold Practice (four to keep, namely, faith, zeal, doubt, and sincerity; and four to forsake, namely, faithlessness, greed, laziness, and delusion). These tenets are summarized below. It should be noted that the outline of the doctrine at this point does not mention Buddha-dharma. Nor does it mention the circular symbol.

Irwŏnsang, the symbol of the source of the two ways, is now the distinguishing emblem of Won Buddhism worldwide. The word *wŏn* meaning "circle," appears later in the history of the order, and becomes important enough a concept to give the order its final name, Wŏnbulgyo (literally, "circle Buddhism").

While staying at Sŏktuam, Sot'aesan shared his ideas for Buddhist reform with Buddhist monks. Eventually, he wrote the *On the Renovation of Korean Buddhism* (*Chosŏn pulgyo hyŏkshillon*)[32] and the *Essentials of Spiritual Cultivation and Inquiry* (*Suyang yŏn'gu yoron*). The main point of the former is that the outmoded and obsolete Buddhism should be modernized and renovated to be useful for the general salvation of sentient beings.[33] The latter contains the proper method of spiritual cultivation and articles of inquiry as the correct ways of discipline.

In 1924, Sot'aesan left Mount Pyŏn and temporarily rented Pogwangsa Temple in Iri (now Iksan), in North Chŏlla province. The name of the order at this time was Pulbŏp yŏn'gu hoe (the society for the study of Buddha-dharma). This name was used until the order was renamed Wŏnbulgyo (Won Buddhism) by Chŏngsan in 1947, two years after Korea was liberated and four years after Sot'aesan's death. In the fall of 1924, eight years after Sot'aesan's enlightenment, two straw-thatched houses were built at Shinyong-dong, Iksan, the first structures in what would become the order's general headquarters. When construction of these buildings was under way, the communal life of the devotees took shape. The nine disciples, as well as other disciples of the earlier years, were mostly poor peasants, and hence their communal life through the construction period was a continuation of poverty and hardship. However, by all accounts, according to Chŏngsan's biographer, they found their life full of joy and happiness as they were trained in the doctrine of the new religion. They were happy to know that they were the founders of a new grand religious order.

In 1935, the Taegakchŏn (great enlightenment hall) was built in the precinct of the general headquarters and, instead of a Buddha statue, the circle symbol Irwŏnsang was enshrined there as a symbol of both object of religious worship and the standard of moral culture. The first Irwŏnsang consisted of a wooden board with a circle drawn on it; two phrases were written below the circle: "The Buddha-nature of the Tathāgata" and "The Fundamental Source of Fourfold Beneficence." This simple Irwŏnsang was soon replaced with another, without the two phrases, and this is the form in which it is enshrined to the present day. Sot'aesan's reasons for selecting the circle image and Chŏngsan's role in codifying it are discussed in detail below. With the enshrinement of Irwŏnsang, Sot'aesan completed the foundation of the new religious order. By means of the new doctrine, Sot'aesan taught his disciples the way toward the realization of buddhahood in this mundane world and produced large numbers of enlightened disciples, who were sent to branch temples, where they taught the new religion to the public.

For twelve years after the establishment of the Iksan headquarters in 1924, Chŏngsan devoted himself to the preparation of the teaching material for the edification and cultivation of talented youth, both men and women. For the following six years, from 1936 to 1942, he resided at the Yŏngsan branch temple, putting his heart into the construction of what is now revered as a sacred place and into the education of younger generation. During that time, he wrote the *Founding History of the Society for the Study of Buddha-dharma (Pulbŏp yŏn'guhoe ch'anggŏnsa)*.[34] In 1942, he returned to the general headquarters, helping Sot'aesan compile the *Correct Canon of Buddhism (Pulgyo chŏngjŏn)* and manage the general administration of the order.

In 1943, two years before the liberation of Korea from Japanese occupation, Sot'aesan was ordered to pay homage to the Japanese emperor. Sot'aesan was obliged to prepare to visit Japan, as he had no choice in the matter. The Japanese colonial government in Korea saw Sot'aesan as Korea's Gandhi, fearing that he would organize the Korean people against the Japanese aggressors. For reasons that are unclear, the order to go to Japan was rescinded. Sot'aesan, however, understood that his Society for the Study of Buddha-dharma would be harshly repressed as long as he remained alive. On May 16, Sot'aesan, apparently still in good health, fell ill; he died on June 1 at a Japanese hospital in Iri (Iksan).

Head Dharma Master

In June 1943, upon Sot'aesan's sudden death, Chŏngsan succeeded Sot'aesan as the head dharma master of the order. Immediately after the liberation of Korea from Japanese occupation in 1945, he ordered relief for the Korean refugees returning from overseas. At that time, Chŏngsan expressed his ideas about Korean national reconstruction in his *A Treatise on National Foundation (Kŏn'gungnon)*.[35] In 1947, Chŏngsan changed the name of the order from Pulbŏp yŏn'guhoe (Society for the study of Buddha-dharma) to Wŏnbulgyo (Won Buddhism) and proclaimed it to the world as a new Buddhist order. If Chŏngsan had not renamed the order, the question would have arisen whether Won Buddhism was a sect of Chogye order of Korean Buddhism. The *Correct Canon of Buddhism* (*Pulgyo chŏngjŏn* [1943]), which was completed and published after Sot'aesan's death (1943), allows such an interpretation: books 2 and 3 of the volume consist exclusively of some Buddhist scriptures and only book 1 was a new writing, which was redacted as the *Canon* (*Chŏngjŏn*) of the *Scriptures of Won Buddhism* (*Wŏnbulgyo kyojŏn* [1962]).

In 1946, Chŏngsan established the Yuil Institute to educate the leading figures of the order and developed it into Wŏn'gwang Junior and Senior High Schools and Wŏn'gwang College (now Won Kwang University). He established Wŏn'gwangsa (Won Buddhist press) to publish the order's magazine, the *Wŏn'gwang* (Consummate light). When the North Korean military forces occupied the general headquarters of Won Buddhism in 1950 during the Korean War, Chŏngsan, while staying at a nearby dwelling, sent his followers to branch temples, instructing them not to take part in the communist activities. Despite the difficult circumstances before and after the Korean War in 1950, Chŏngsan ordered the construction of a pagoda and stele to commemorate Sot'aesan's work. Amid the ravages of war, he maintained the viability of the order and continued to guide the populace. He assessed the public service and other merits of the first founding members, for which they were assigned appropriate dharma ranks, and in 1953 he called for a general meeting to celebrate the first generation's work. At the meeting, he was proclaimed head dharma master of the order for a second term (six years).

Chŏngsan suffered a stroke in 1953, brought on by overwork, and people in and associated with the order were filled with great anxiety. His condition improved a little, though his right side remained paralyzed. According to his biographer, followers as well as visitors reported that, despite his illness, they found respite from their afflictions in his presence,[36] and he was able to lay foundations for numerous projects of religious edification, education, and charitable work, which is the threefold mission of the order. Chŏngsan established Tongsan Monastery, Central Monastery, and the Wŏn'gwang girls' junior and senior high schools. He established Chŏnghwasa (a press) to launch his publication project. The publications included the *Canon of the World* (*Sejŏn* [1972]) and the *History of the Order* (*Kyosa* [1975]). He also ordered the establishment of charitable organizations such as orphanages, asylums for the aged, and sanatoria.

In 1959, Chŏngsan was proclaimed head dharma master for a third term. He ordered his followers not to observe the traditional formalities on his sixtieth birthday in August 1960, establishing instead the Dharma Beneficence Foundation, the medical foundation for the Won Buddhist clergy, with contributions from his followers in celebration of his birthday. It was Chŏngsan who designated Sot'aesan "the new presiding Buddha for the New World," when Sot'aesan was recognized as one of the patriarchs of the Buddhist tradition. The title was subsequently engraved on the epitaph erected in memory of Sot'aesan.[37] It was Chŏngsan, also, who began to compile a new scripture for the Won Buddhist order: the analects and chronicles of Sot'aesan, in the *Scripture of Sot'aesan* (*Taejonggyŏng*). On December 25, 1961, he instructed the members of the order's supreme council to complete the compilation of the *Scripture of Sot'aesan* and to proceed with the redaction of the *Canon* (*Chŏngjŏn,* published posthumously in 1962) in the *Scriptures of Won Buddhism* (*Wŏnbulgyo kyojŏn*). By publishing the new scriptures of the order, Chŏngsan sealed Won Buddhism's identity as a new, independent religious order with Buddha-dharma as the central tenet of its doctrine.

Chŏngsan's health deteriorated, despite various medical treatments, and he became critically ill in the first days of January 1962. On January 22, a group of men and women, laity and priests, gathered around his sick bed. Chŏngsan asked someone to explicate "the ethics of triple identity" (*samdong yulli*), which states that all religions come from the same source, all sentient beings have the same vital force, and all enterprises have the same goal. Chŏngsan told the people around him to create "one household under heaven" through the great Way of Irwŏn, the Way of "great cosmopolitanism." Two days later, on January 24, 1962, he passed away. After his death, the supreme council of the order met and conferred on him the posthumous dharma rank of "tathāgata of great enlightenment."[38] In doing so, they recognized Chŏngsan's achievements and merits, and signaled to Won Buddhists and others how exemplary he had been as a spiritual leader and as an embodiment of the values of the order.

The Central Doctrine of Won Buddhism

The central doctrine of Won Buddhism that Chŏngsan helped Sot'aesan systematize is set out in the *Correct Canon of Buddhism* (*Pulgyo chŏngjŏn* [1943]). In this section, I offer a summary of that doctrine by way of background for an understanding of Chŏngsan's own contribution; in the section following this one, I will turn to Chŏngsan's own thoughts on the doctrine, which are presented in full in my translation of his writings.[39]

Four Pillars

Won Buddhist doctrine is determined by the ultimate goals of the order, which are to deliver sentient beings from misery and suffering and to cure the world of moral ills. The whole doctrine of Won Buddhism is structured in order to realize these two goals. The ways to realize the goals are presented as four "pillars."

The first pillar is expressed in the maxim "Correct enlightenment and right practice." This pillar has its ground in Buddhism. One should be enlightened to one's own Buddha-nature and practice in accordance with light of its wisdom. Since deluded beings are not aware of their own Buddha-nature, they are advised to be enlightened to and practice the truth of Irwŏnsang, which has been correctly transmitted as the mind-seal by buddhas and patriarchs. This first pillar is expounded in the tenets of Irwŏnsang and Threefold Practice in the *Canon*, and aims to deliver the sentient beings from suffering.

The second pillar is expressed in the maxim "Awareness and requital of beneficence." The purpose of this pillar is to change the life of resentment and grudges to that of gratitude. By "beneficence" is meant what gives you life. In Confucianism, filial piety is the most important moral duty. In Won Buddhism the idea of this Confucian moral duty is extended beyond one's own parents to include heaven and earth, brethren, and laws (the Fourfold Beneficence),[40] without which one cannot exist.

The third pillar is expressed in the maxim "Practical application of Buddha-dharma." In the *Correct Canon of Buddhism* (*Pulgyo chŏngjŏn* [1943]), the maxim was "Propagation of Buddhism." This reflects the fact that Buddhism in Korea at the time was confined to remote mountain valleys and had no religious impact in Korean society. Although the teaching of the Buddha embodies truth and skillful means to save sentient beings from misery, the Buddhist system was formed mainly for the life of monks in monastic orders, and was not suitable for people living in the secular world. Under such a system, the Buddha-grace, no matter how great it may be, could not reach the numberless sentient beings of the world. Thus, Won Buddhism teaches that Buddha-dharma should not be separated from daily life. The spirit of practical application of Buddha-dharma is expressed in such mottos as "Buddha-dharma is daily life, and daily life is Buddha-dharma" and "Timeless Zen and placeless Zen."

The fourth pillar is expressed in the maxim "Selfless service for the public." This pillar reflects the ideal of the bodhisattva who benefits himself or herself only by benefiting others. Sot'aesan could see that the pursuit of material good, without a concomitant increase in spiritual good, was fanning the fires of greed, hatred, and delusion, and, to use the classic Buddhist metaphor, plunging humanity into ever-worsening, bitter seas of misery. Sot'aesan felt it urgent to strengthen the altruistic moral sense. Sentient beings could not be delivered into "the limitless paradise" as long as they remained selfish and egotistic with the three poisons of greed, hatred, and delusion in their hearts. Though this ideal may seem too lofty to reach, it expresses a widely held truth that human beings will save themselves from misery only by transforming themselves. The spirit of this pillar is expressed in the motto "Everywhere is the Buddha-image; do all things as an offering to the Buddha."

Irwŏnsang (as the symbol of Dharmakāya Buddha)

As a way of reforming Buddhism, Sot'aesan had the Irwŏnsang (unitary circular form) enshrined as the symbol of the Buddha-nature or Mind-Buddha in 1935. The circular symbol is traditional to Buddhism; it had been introduced in Korea by Sunji (fl. 858), who studied in China under Yangshan Huiji (803–887), cofounder of the Guiyang school of the classical Chinese Chan tradition.[41] In the doctrinal chart of the *Correct Canon of Buddhism* (*Pulgyo chŏngjŏn* [1943]) it was noted that Nanyang Huizhong drew the circle and transmitted it to his disciples, but this phrase was deleted in the *Canon* (*Chŏngjŏn* [1962]). Sot'aesan did not explain what the Mind-Buddha was, except that the circle Irwŏnsang was its symbol. In 1937, Chŏngsan wrote a treatise, "On Irwŏnsang," which explains the whole tenet of Irwŏnsang.[42] A year later, Sot'aesan wrote "An Account of the Mind-Buddha-Irwŏnsang and Vow,"[43] in which he gives an account of what the ultimate truth is and how one should practice. In 1943, Chŏngsan wrote three sections of the chapter "Irwŏnsang," which Sot'aesan allowed to be inserted in the *Correct Canon of Buddhism* (*Pulgyo chŏngjŏn* [1943]).[44] Since there are significant differences between Sot'aesan and Chŏngsan on the truth and practice of Irwŏnsang, Sot'aesan's view is presented first, leaving Chŏngsan's view to the section below that is devoted to his thought.

Sot'aesan calls the ultimate reality of the universe "Irwŏn" and says that it is the ineffable realm of samādhi. He characterizes Irwŏn as transcending being and nonbeing, and calls it the gate of birth and death.

It is the fundamental source of the Fourfold Beneficence (heaven and earth, parents, brethren, and laws), later identified as the Dharmakāya Buddha. Thus, "Irwŏnsang" is synonymous with "Dharmakāya Buddha" for Sot'aesan. It is also the original nature[45] of all buddhas, patriarchs, ordinary humans, and all other sentient beings. This reflects the Mahāyāna Buddhist tenet that all sentient beings are endowed with the Buddha-nature. To this point, Sot'aesan is describing the essence of Dharmakāya Buddha-Irwŏnsang as the ultimate reality of the universe.

Sot'aesan then expresses his view of the function of Irwŏn, saying that it includes permanency and impermanency. A rough analogy is the permanency of the ocean, compared with the impermanency of the waves. Viewed as permanent, Irwŏn—being invariable, immutable, and spontaneous—has unfolded itself as an infinite world. Viewed as impermanent, Irwŏn has unfolded itself as a world in constant flux: first, in the formation, abiding, decay, and destruction of the universe; second, in the arising, abiding, decay, and extinction of all things; and, third, through the changes undergone by beings through many lifetimes in keeping with the operation of laws of karma. Sot'aesan then shows what a practitioner should do with the understanding of this principle of the universe.

Sot'aesan's goal of practice is to attain the mighty power of Irwŏn and be unified with Irwŏn,[46] because without it, one cannot be on the path of improvement, and one cannot keep oneself from demotion and harm. Sot'aesan's method of attaining such power lies in modeling oneself after the Mind-Buddha, Irwŏnsang, when one practices in the triple discipline: guarding one's mind and body perfectly, knowing facts and principles perfectly, and using one's mind and body perfectly. Here the model of practice is the well-roundedness of the circular form, which is employed to depict the pure, complete, and perfect mental state of a Buddha-bodhisattva.

The Ethics of Beneficence

The chapter "Fourfold Beneficence" in the *Correct Canon of Buddhism* (*Pulgyo chŏngjŏn* [1943]) is a discourse on the Won Buddhist religious ethics.[47] The chapter explains how one is indebted for one's life to heaven and earth, parents, brethren, and laws, conceived of as a single beneficence made up of four parts; and how and why one should requite them. The appearance of the Fourfold Beneficence in the *Correct Canon of Buddhism* (*Pulgyo chŏngjŏn* [1943]) has its origin in Sot'aesan's reflection on the source of his enlightenment in 1916, in which he realized his debt to these four things. This realization developed into the ethics of benefi-cence. Sot'aesan challenges us to consider whether it is possible for one to live without what heaven and earth provide, whether one could have brought oneself to the world without one's parents, whether one could survive without the help from brethren or fellow beings, and whether one could live without the protection of laws. He says that even a person of limited intelligence will recognize that to live without these is impos-sible; even a person of limited intelligence will know, for instance, that one cannot exist without air and water provided by heaven and earth, just as fish cannot live without the beneficence of water. He then declares that nothing can be a greater beneficence than that without which one cannot live. Just as the ocean is "the universal beneficence of nature"[48] for fish, the Fourfold Beneficence is "the universal beneficence of nature" for human beings. Because the concept of "the universal beneficence of nature" does not imply any transcendent, anthropomorphic deity, the Fourfold Beneficence does not imply anything like "divine grace." Once it is proven that one is indebted to the Fourfold Beneficence, no further argument is necessary to prove that it is one's actual duty to requite it; Sot'aesan thinks it a matter of necessity to requite the beneficence to which one owes one's life.[49]

The ethics of beneficence provides the deontological reasons for requiting the Fourfold Beneficence (because one owes one's life to it); beneficence requital also is an act of religious faith in the teleological efficacy of making an offering to Dharmakāya Buddha, the fundamental source of the Fourfold Beneficence.[50] Thus, the making of offerings to Buddha as supplication for blessings has undergone a drastic change in Won Buddhism; it is replaced by the requital of the Fourfold Beneficence. However, the question was raised how one can ever repay one's immense debt to the beneficence of heaven and earth, just as how a fish can repay its debt to the ocean. Sot'aesan's model for beneficence requital is that a disciple indebted to the beneficence of the mentor can pay the debt by putting into practice the virtues of the mentor, returning the honor to the mentor.[51] Since it is impossible for one directly to requite the Fourfold Beneficence, one can fulfill the duty to requite the beneficence by per-fecting one's moral virtues through observing the moral maxims derived from the principle of indebtedness to them.

Now the two principles, religious and moral, are assimilated to each other by the imperative that one ought to requite beneficence as a way of reverent offering to the Buddha. If, for instance, I treat other human beings on the basis of fairness required by the maxim of requital of beneficence of brethren, I will be treating them as buddhas and thus be blessed insofar as they have the power to bless or punish. If, however, I treat them unfairly, violating the moral principle of fairness, I will be punished by them, the living buddhas.

In the following paragraphs I summarize Sot'aesan's views on how one is indebted to, and how one ought to requite, the Fourfold Beneficence. He sets out the schema in an orderly analytic fashion, for each of the four aspects, progressing through a statement of the kinds of situations in which beneficence manifests itself, to statements of the principles of gratitude and ingratitude and their consequences, and the moral duties entailed by it.

Beneficence of Heaven and Earth (Ch'ŏnjiŭn)

First, Sot'aesan states as a matter of fact that all human beings owe their lives to heaven and earth: from the largest cosmic motions down to the phenomena of sunlight and rain. Heaven and earth have "ways" and "virtues," which we can follow in our requital of these beneficences, namely, that they are (1) extremely bright, (2) extremely sincere,[52] (3) extremely fair, (4) natural, (5) vast and limitless, (6) eternal, (7) not subject to good or evil fortune, and (8) free of thought in their bestowals of beneficence.[53]

The way to requite the beneficence of heaven and earth lies in one's moral improvement by modeling oneself after their ways. One can form one body with heaven and earth if one practices such virtues as wisdom (brightness), immutability (eternity), imperturbability in the face of one's good or ill fortunes, and benevolence (not harboring or "abiding in" the idea of doing favors to others). Once one has perfected one's moral character with these virtues, one's moral influence on other sentient beings will be like that of heaven and earth.

Ingratitude to heaven and earth, on the other hand, brings on punishment. Although heaven and earth are empty and silent to one's deeds, ingratitude will lead to unexpected hardships and sufferings in life and sufferings caused by one's deeds.

The fact that heaven and earth act without calculation or partiality implies the moral duty "to harbor no notion of rendering favors to others." To neglect this duty, Sot'aesan points out, may cause resentment. The point is not to act dutifully or morally in order to avoid these harmful consequences, but to do them in order to show gratitude to the extent we are able, and to become more like the Dharmakāya Buddha. Thus, the duty to requite the beneficence of heaven and earth is the duty to perfect one's moral virtues, which reflects the Confucian moral teachings in the *Doctrine of the Mean.*

Beneficence of Parents (Pumoŭn)

A child is indebted to parents because they gave the child life, because they have—at some personal cost—raised the child, and because they have taught the child his or her duties and responsibilities to human society.

As the way of recompensing the beneficence of parents, one should follow the Threefold Practice (described below) and show gratitude, to the extent one is able, by supporting one's parents when they lack the ability to help themselves, and by bringing them spiritual comfort. One should also protect the helpless parents of others as one would one's own; and after one's parents are deceased, one should honor and remember them.

Sot'aesan points out the consequences of failing to perform these filial duties: in receiving back, when one becomes frail, the same kind of care one has shown to one's own parents. And not only in one's present lifetime: in accordance with the causal law of karmic retribution, the consequences will redound for many lifetimes, bringing one support or abandonment in accordance with how careful one was in fulfilling the duties in this life.

Beneficence of Brethren (Tongp'oŭn)

The term *brethren* designates, besides one's own siblings and compatriots, all people, animals, and plants. One owes one's life to brethren in this sense of the term.

To recompense brethren, people of all occupations should exchange what they can offer with others on the principle of mutual benefit based on fairness. If they follow this principle, they will be blessed, and will live in a world that is, in effect, a paradise. The alternative road leads to hate and scorn, quarrels among individuals, ill will among families, antagonism among societies, and war among nations.

Beneficence of Laws (Pŏmnyurŭn)

The term *laws* covers religious and moral principles, social institutions and legislation, and civil and penal laws. The laws are based on the principle of fairness in human justice. One owes one's life to laws in this sense of the term.

One recompenses the beneficence of laws by cultivating one's personal moral sense and practice, regulating one's family, working for harmony in society and government, and bringing about peace in the world. One "does justice and forsakes injustice." Responsibility starts at the level of the individual, and expands systematically from there in ever-widening circles, from the family, society, and nation, to encompass the whole world.

Requiting this beneficence accrues blessings and punishment just as with the others. If one is grateful to the beneficence of laws, one will be protected; and conversely, if one is ungrateful, that is, if one does not requite it, one will be punished, bound, and restrained—either literally or figuratively—in this life or subsequent ones.

Requital of Beneficence as an Offering to the Buddha

In Won Buddhism, the traditional practice of supplicating Buddha statues for blessings has been replaced by the new practice of showing gratitude to the Fourfold Beneficence, which is the manifestation of the Dharmakāya Buddha. Thus, the ideal of the motto "Everywhere is the Buddha image; hence do all things as an offering to the Buddha" can only be realized by following the maxims for the requital of the Fourfold Beneficence. One helps others without abiding in the idea of having rendered favors, one protects the helpless, helps out of a sense of fairness and reciprocity, and acts justly.[54] The heart of Won Buddhist ethics lies in these four moral imperatives. Moreover, the central moral virtues of Confucius—benevolence (ren) and righteousness (yi)—are realized by putting into practice these imperatives: benevolence lies in not abiding in the idea of having rendered favors and in protecting the helpless; righteousness lies in benefiting oneself by benefiting others and in doing justice and forsaking injustice.

Threefold Practice

The Threefold Practice in Won Buddhism has its roots in the teaching of the Buddha; however, it is thoroughly renovated and reformulated as the way of attaining the three great powers of emancipation, enlightenment, and the mean. The three modes of one's original nature are concentration (samādhi), wisdom (prajñā), and precepts (śīla), as taught by Hui-neng

(638–713), the sixth patriarch of Chan Buddhism in China.[55] This teaching originates in the Buddha's Four Noble Truths: life is suffering; suffering
has its cause; suffering can be stopped; and there is a way to stop it.[56] The
triple discipline of śīla, samādhi, and prajñā fulfills the fourth truth, and
is effected in Won Buddhist practice through cultivation of spirit, inquiry
into facts and principles, and heedful choice in karmic action.[57]

Cultivation of Spirit (Chŏngsin suyang)

In order to maintain the mental state of samādhi, serene reflection, or
quiet illumination, which is free from any kind of disturbance, one must
do spiritual cultivation, that is, cultivate a mental state that, in being clear
and calm, is devoid of discerning or attachment to anything. This is the
substantial aspect of one's own nature, the Dharmakāya of one's mind.
"Cultivation" means nourishing the clear and calm spirit by removing
internal discrimination or attachment and by keeping the mind free from
external disturbance.

If one's spiritual power is so weak that one loses one's mental poise
in adverse conditions, one cannot but suffer. We live in a world where
our mind can easily be disturbed by adversity. Sot'aesan uses the classic Buddhist metaphor of "drowning in the sea of misery" to describe
how one becomes overwhelmed by anger, greed, and delusion and their
consequences.[58] Thus, the purpose of spiritual cultivation, he states, is to
strengthen one's spiritual power so that one's mental poise in any adverse
condition is as immovable as a huge mountain and as serene and calm
as the empty sky.

Inquiry into Facts and Principles (Sari yŏn'gu)

Great importance is placed on seeing into one's own nature, or enlightenment, since one will be unable to subdue and annihilate the three poisons
of vehement desire or greed, anger or hatred, and delusions or folly in
one's mind in adverse conditions unless one is enlightened to one's original nature. However, Won Buddhism does not encourage one to spend
a lifetime or even years of sitting in meditation in order to attain great
enlightenment. It teaches a practical way in terms of inquiry into facts
and principles.

The studies and investigations that constitute inquiry[59] lead one to
be able to distinguish right from wrong, and gain from loss, in human

affairs; through inquiry one comes to know the principle of the ultimate reality and its phenomenal appearance and the change of existence and nonexistence. It gives one the ability to analyze and pass prompt correct judgment on practical daily affairs. One cannot live a perfect life without such ability.

Thus, the Won Buddhist way of attaining wisdom by inquiry into facts and principles is quite different from the traditional Buddhist way of attaining wisdom solely by awakening to one's own original nature. Awakening to one's nature is not neglected in Won Buddhism, however: Sot'aesan also advised his followers to contemplate one of twenty *kongans* (*hwadu*), at the end of regular morning seated meditation.[60]

Heedful Choice in Karmic Action (Chagŏp ch'uisa)

The third aspect of the practice is to follow one's original nature, which, as Irwŏn, is perfect and complete, and utterly fair and unselfish. Being enlightened to one's original nature, while being a necessary condition for moral perfection, is not a sufficient one; for one may be unable to follow one's original nature when using one's six sense organs because of the habit force, even after one has seen one's original nature. Thus, one needs to pursue a course of gradual cultivation. This requires one to train oneself in choosing justice and forsaking injustice while creating karma by thinking, speaking, and acting.

The powers of spiritual cultivation and inquiry into facts and principles will be complete only if one attains the power of heedful choice in karmic action; otherwise, one's moral cultivation will be, as Sot'aesan describes it, like a fruit tree with good roots, branches, leaves, and flowers but no fruit. Depending on what kind of karma one creates, one creates a heavenly world or a hell, no matter where one is. An evil karma follows oneself wherever one goes, like a shadow, until one wears it out completely. Good karma, too, follows one wherever one goes, until it is exhausted.

We human beings do not always do the good because we do not always know right from wrong or good from bad, or we cannot control consuming greed or anger, or we are pulled by habit force even though we know the good is preferable to evil. Thus, this practice aims at changing the "sea of misery" into a paradise by training ourselves to create good karma and keep evil karma from being created.

The Thought of Chŏngsan

If we recall that Sot'aesan ushered Chŏngsan into his new religious order as its chief codifier, it would be an error to separate Chŏngsan's thought from the central doctrine of Won Buddhism, for the central tenets of the doctrine were systematized through Chŏngsan. However, in this section are introduced some of what I take to be the salient points of Chŏngsan's thought.

The Moral Norms of a Perfect Life

Chŏngsan expounded the ways (norms) that help "realize one family under heaven, with morality" in the *Canon of the World* (*Sejŏn*).[61] This treatise reminds us of the Confucian moral and political programs in the *Great Learning* (*Daxue*). Chŏngsan has synthesized the otherworldly philosophy of Buddhism with the worldly philosophy of Confucianism in the treatise. The Confucian text expounds the norms a superior person should follow in order to illustrate illustrious virtue throughout a kingdom;[62] Chŏngsan, on the other hand, is concerned with the perfect life of the average human as member of a family, society, state, and the world.

Chŏngsan starts his treatise by declaring that human life can be perfect both in this life and the eternal life only if there exist correct ways to learn and follow for each stage of life, from the moment when the numinous consciousness enters the mother's womb through the stages of one's birth, growing, adulthood, and entering into nirvāṇa.[63] Chŏngsan then explicates the norms for each stage of one's life.

Education

Chŏngsan takes education to be the foundation of human civilization and progress, and says that the rise and fall, prosperity and decline of an individual, a family, a society, a nation depend on education, both scientific and moral. Education, for him, begins before birth[64] and continues into infancy and one's later life. The pregnant woman must be careful with her feelings, keeping her mind always pure and her conduct right, as her feelings and actions will affect the child developing in her womb. The raising of infants, like the care a mother must take with her developing fetus, is based on observation of facts. In the case of infants, their consciousness is not thoroughly developed, so it can easily be affected by their environments. Thus, infant education should include the wholesome spiritual influence of religion and morality, so the child can develop a wholesome spirit; the small child should be taught with examples, maxims, and stories, and if needed, by sterner methods. Education for older children and adults, Chŏngsan writes, should include both science and morality. Throughout one's life, one should continue to study science, spiritual education, conduct, and trades or professional subjects. But he points out that an education of science alone, without moral education, would be like giving a sword to a burglar.

Family

Chŏngsan declares that family is the basis of human life and suggests that a family can be happy, comfortable, and progressive only if all members of the family follow ways appropriate for their position and role in the family.[65] So he sets out in detail the specific ways that spouses, parents, children, and siblings and other relatives should follow. The way of spouses includes love, respect, and harmony by understanding each other's idiosyncrasies; generosity and fidelity to share pain and pleasure; a spirit of independence based on diligence; and contribution to the public good. The way of parents requires one to raise, protect, and educate one's children, and guide them to contribute to the public good. Parents should do their duty lovingly and diligently, without minding how loyal or grateful the children seem to be. The way of children requires obeying parents and supporting them, but also doing justice and contributing to the public good. The way of siblings and relatives is based on the notion of natural justice or reciprocity and fairness, in which people enlighten one another to live an independent life.[66]

Religious Faith

Chŏngsan regards religious faith as the fundamental necessity of human spiritual life and emphasizes that one must have religious faith to keep the mind calm in any situation. He lays out systematically both the norms of faith and what is required of the believer. Faith, he says, should be realistic, and the object of faith should be true. The question then arises, what is a realistic faith, and what is the nature of its truth? Chŏngsan explains in detail: it will be balanced between faith in other-power and faith in self-power; it will revere the dharma ancestors, and acknowledge the unity of the fundamental truth of all religions. Believers should have faith in the doctrine and put it into practice.

Society

Chŏngsan says that a healthy society needs sound social norms, just as a healthy religion needs sound religious norms. In his view, society is based on the relationships between individuals, and social peace and conflict depend on the relations of the people; hence, he puts a great importance on the nature of social relations between men and women, the old and the young, and the strong and the weak, and among the public generally. For each of these categories, he sets out specific norms of behavior, each based on principles of justice, fairness, and reciprocity.

The Nation

Chŏngsan assumes that in a nation there are leaders and those who are led, and that the rise and fall of a nation depends on whether the two sectors follow appropriate ways.[67] He prescribes the "ways of the nation" for the leaders[68] and the people: leaders should look ahead to the destiny of the nation and the future of the citizens; the people should conduct themselves in such a way as to ensure the prosperity and happiness of everyone. The nation should be concerned with "edification"—Chŏngsan has in mind edification toward enlightenment to the "fundamental truth"—and should pursue edification by a variety of noncoercive means. Government, he underlines, should be by the authority of law and be transparent and open.

The World

Chŏngsan sees the world as a great household that encompasses the whole human race. The "way of the world" lies in all people doing their duties as individuals and as members of a family, a society, and a nation. People should understand one another and cooperate for world peace and the common interests of the human race. The way of the world is summarized in what he would later call "the ethics of triple identity,"[69] based on what he identified as certain truths: that all religions come from one source, that all races and nations are one people, and that all enterprises are essentially one single enterprise. From these truths, he derives the duties of the world's religions, of nations and peoples, and of those who work in business.

Rest

Having considered the characteristics and implications of the way for individuals in the context of their family, society, and nation, Chŏngsan turns to some other important features of the perfect life. The first feature that he addresses in the *Canon of the World (Sejŏn)* is the matter of "rest." Chŏngsan suggests that a necessary condition of a perfect life is a sound foundation for one's personality, and that the way to develop this foundation is through the cultivation of equanimity. Equanimity entails a radical impartiality and indifference based on a sense of emptiness, in the Buddhist sense of the word; and also on emancipation, or freedom, based on an understanding of the basic existential and metaphysical principles, familiar in Buddhism, of birth and death, self-nature, and emptiness. Modeling oneself on these principles and acting in accordance with them, one will be immune to gossip and opinion, unmoved by reversals in fortune, and fair in one's treatment of others.

Nirvāṇa

Nirvāṇa is the final goal of Buddhist practice, and Chŏngsan interprets it as "residing comfortably in the clear and calm self-nature." He suggests that one should train oneself in this way of nirvāṇa in ordinary times, so that one can rejoice in the bliss of nirvāṇa in daily life and attain the spiritual nirvāṇa at the time of one's bodily death. Chŏngsan adds the way of deliverance to the way of nirvāṇa, that is, of delivering sentient beings from suffering, both by spiritual guidance and by practical acts of charity.

One Pure Mind

Chŏngsan believed that the greatest dharma and the greatest treasure "throughout the eternal world" is to nurture and use the "pure mind," which he defines as the mind of mutual benefaction, and the mind of impartiality and public spirit. Just as the rectification of the heart (mind) is central to the whole moral and political program in Confucius's *Great Learning (Daxue)*, so the pure mind, perfect and complete, and utterly fair and unselfish, is central to the realization of a perfect life. One can develop this pure mind, namely, prajñā-wisdom upon seeing into one's own Buddha-nature, as Chŏngsan expounds in his account of the practice of Irwŏnsang.[70]

The Fundamental Principles of Won Buddhism

The most fundamental principle of the doctrine of Won Buddhism is contained in the tenet of Irwŏnsang as Sot'aesan identified it, first with the Buddha-nature, second with Mind-Buddha, and third with Dharmakāya Buddha. In the Vow to Irwŏnsang, Sot'aesan uses the expression "Dharmakāya Buddha, Irwŏnsang." On the question whether the Irwŏnsang drawn on a wooden board has mighty power, Sot'aesan said that the Irwŏnsang is used to refer to the "true Irwŏn" just as a finger is used to point to the moon.[71] Although Sot'aesan never explained what the true Irwŏn is, we can say that it is, simply, the Dharmakāya Buddha to which the Irwŏnsang refers. Sot'aesan said further that the Irwŏnsang is a picture or a blueprint of the Buddha-nature of Tathāgata and refers to the fundamental source of the Fourfold Beneficence. Chŏngsan's thought on Irwŏnsang is expressed in three works: the essay "On Irwŏnsang," and two chapters in longer works, "Truth, Faith, and Practice of Irwŏnsang" and "Fundamental Principles."[72] His commentaries, along with the texts we have by Sot'aesan, allow us to examine more closely the tenet of Irwŏnsang as the fundamental principle of the doctrine of Won Buddhism.

In 1937, two years after the Irwŏnsang was enshrined, Chŏngsan published his essay "On Irwŏnsang," in order to explain the tenet. Chŏngsan uses the Irwŏnsang to refer to metaphysical first principles found in Confucianism, Buddhism, and Daoism. In his view, the Irwŏnsang is used to refer to the totality of beings in the universe and the empty dharma realm. The Irwŏnsang refers to the original source of the Fourfold Beneficence (heaven and earth, parents, brethren, and laws), and the essence of our original mind, where there is no birth, death, discrimination, or attachment. It also signifies the middle way. Thus, the Irwŏnsang points to both being and nonbeing and identifies substance and function, so that myriad facts and principles are all found in it. In ancient times, Buddha attained sudden enlightenment to this truth and called it Buddha-nature, Dharmakāya, or True Mind, and enlightened masters of successive generations have elucidated Buddha-nature. Sot'aesan named it Irwŏn. Confucius's "one all-pervading principle,"[73] Mencius's theory of "nourishing the vital force,"[74] and Chou Tuni's "Explanations of Diagram of the Supreme Ultimate" (*Taiji dushuo*)[75] all refer to it in different terms. Thus, in Chǒngsan's view, the truth of Irwǒnsang was known long ago, being the same realm of the Buddha-nature to which all sages were enlightened. Therefore, we should be awakened to the essence that Irwǒnsang refers to in order to have faith in and to worship that essence, and also so that we may model ourselves after Irwǒnsang, using Irwǒnsang in all our daily activities. In Chǒngsan's view, this is the right way to practice Buddha-dharma.[76]

Truth of Irwǒnsang

In the *Correct Canon of Buddhism* (*Pulgyo chǒngjǒn* [1943]), Chǒngsan expresses his view of the truth of Irwǒnsang in Mahāyāna Buddhist terms, in the section that explicates the meaning of the first pillar of the doctrine of Won Buddhism (correct enlightenment and right practice).[77] The essence of this pillar is that one should be enlightened to the "mind-seal" that buddhas and patriarchs transmit, namely, the mind as Irwǒn, which Sot'aesan called the Buddha-nature or Mind-Buddha. When Sot'aesan had Irwǒnsang enshrined as the symbol of the Buddha-nature or Mind-Buddha, he saw no problem with this reifying of Irwǒn, though he did remark (in 1938) that the Irwǒnsang on the wooden board simply referred to "the true Irwǒnsang" (this phrase was changed to "true Irwǒn" in 1962).[78]

In a long sentence, almost a half-page long, Chǒngsan compresses the tenets of the nature of reality of all dharmas (*dharmatā*), the nature of all buddhas and patriarchs (dharmakāya), the Buddha-nature of all sentient beings (*buddhatā*), the emptiness (śūnyatā) of inherent essence of all dharmas, and the phenomenal world as the appearance of reality in accord with consciousness (*vijñāptimātratā*). Chǒngsan identifies them all as the truth of Irwǒnsang. Irwǒnsang is presented as a symbol of these concepts for the use and convenience of ordinary beings. In several sections of the *Dharma Words* one finds Chǒngsan talking about Irwǒn as if it has an ontological reality. However, Chǒngsan's final statement on the truth of Irwǒnsang is in the *Correct Canon of Buddhism* (*Pulgyo chǒngjǒn* [1943]). In this text, Chǒngsan expressed what he calls "the truth of Irwǒnsang" in four statements. My interpretations of each follow, in the order Chǒngsan presents them.

Statement 1. "Irwŏn is the inherent essence of all things in the universe, the original nature of all buddhas and patriarchs, and the Buddha-nature of all sentient beings."[79]

In the *Correct Canon of Buddhism* (*Pulgyo chŏngjŏn* [1943]), the statement "Irwŏn is the inherent essence of all things" implies that the inherent essence of all things is Irwŏn just as gold is the inherent essence of all gold ornaments.[80] If Chŏngsan had said that "Irwŏn" is a name used to refer to the inherent essence of all things, just as the name "Morning Star" is used to refer to the planet Venus, we would not have this implication. For there is no Irwŏn subsisting apart from the inherent essence of all things, the original nature of all buddhas and patriarchs, or the Buddha-nature of all sentient beings, any more than there is a planet called "Morning Star" subsisting apart from Venus.

Chŏngsan has used "Irwŏn" to refer to the inherent essence (*svabhāva*; *dharmatā*) of all things existing in the universe, but he does not explain what the inherent essence is. According to Śūnyavāda, nothing has inherent essence; according to Vijñānavāda, all things are manifestation of consciousness. Chŏngsan does not say which of these two theories of reality applies. In the doctrinal chart of the *Correct Canon of Buddhism* (*Pulgyo chŏngjŏn* [1943]), however, Irwŏnsang is identified with "consummate emptiness." One suggestion is that "the inherent essence" can be replaced with "the dharma realm of the one reality" or simply "One Mind," which is the Huayan Buddhist view of reality. And the statement that Irwŏn is the original nature of all buddhas and patriarchs, and the Buddha-nature of all sentient beings, is the common theme of several Mahāyāna Buddhist scriptures.[81] The statement that Irwŏn is the inherent essence of all things is thus consistent with Sot'aesan's view that the Irwŏnsang should be enshrined as a symbol of the Buddha-nature or Mind-Buddha. The term *Irwŏn*, then, is like the term *One Mind* in Hakeda, *The Awakening of Faith in Mahāyāna*.

Statement 2. "[Irwŏnsang refers to] the realm where there is no differentiation of noumenon from phenomenon and existence from nonexistence; the realm where there is no change of arising and ceasing, or going and coming; the realm where the karmic retribution of good and evil has ceased; the realm where the verbal, audible, and visual characteristics are utterly void."[82]

In the *Awakening of Faith*, the mind in terms of the absolute is described as truly empty and truly nonempty. "Truly empty" refers to the substance of the mind and "truly nonempty" to the function of the mind. Here, Chŏngsan has described the substantial aspect of the Buddha-nature, which Sot'aesan identified with the ineffable realm of samādhi. Saying that the truth of Irwŏn can be summarized in terms of emptiness, perfection, and rightness, Sot'aesan said, "In nourishing the nature (samādhi), to intuit the state of mind that transcends existence and nonexistence is emptiness."[83]

> Statement 3. "In accord with the light of [the mind-essence that is] empty and calm, numinous awareness, the differentiation of noumenon from phenomenon and existence from nonexistence, appears; wherewith the distinction between good and evil karmic retribution comes into being; and the verbal, audible, and visible characteristics become clear and distinct so that the three worlds in the ten directions appear like a jewel on one's own palm."[84]

In the *Awakening of Faith,* the appearance of the phenomenal world is attributed to nonenlightenment. Because it is not enlightened, the deluded mind produces three constructs: the activity of ignorance, the perceiving subject, and the world of objects.[85] In Chŏngsan's view, however, the phenomenal world with all its differentiations appears by virtue of the calm numinous awareness, so that the three worlds in ten directions appear as wonderfully as a jewel on one's own palm. The view that the appearance of the phenomenal world depends on the mind can be found in Western philosophy, particularly in Immanuel Kant's metaphysics and epistemology. For Kant, the phenomenal world depends for its appearance on the a priori forms of intuition, namely, space and time, and a priori forms of understanding, namely, the twelve concepts.[86] For Kant, the phenomenal world is totally dependent on the mind.[87]

> Statement 4. "And the creative transformation of true emptiness-cum-wondrous existence freely conceals and reveals itself through all things in the universe throughout incalculable eons with no beginning."

The term "true emptiness-cum-wondrous existence" appears in some Zen and Huayan classics. "True emptiness" refers to the absolute as described in Statement 2, while "wondrous existence" refers to the relative relational as described in Statement 3. The expression "true emptiness-cum-wondrous existence" is sometimes interpreted as the true emptiness of wondrous existence *and* the wondrous existence of true emptiness, such that the two are inseparable from each other. Any entity in the universe has this dual aspect, which the *Heart Sūtra* describes with the expression "form is emptiness and emptiness is form." Chŏngsan's initial expression "Irwŏn is the inherent essence of all things in the universe" must be referring to this nature: true emptiness-cum-wondrous existence.

Sot'aesan advised his followers to take Irwŏnsang as a *hwadu* for "seeing the nature and attaining buddhahood"; Chŏngsan follows by spelling out the content of seeing the nature and calls it "the truth of Irwŏnsang." It is clear that there is no separate reality or truth called "Irwŏn" subsisting between Irwŏnsang and the truth asserted by the four statements. Just as "Vairocana" is merely a name given to the law of conditioned origination or interdependent existence,[88] "Irwŏn" is merely a name given to the truth expounded in the four statements.

Faith in Irwŏnsang

As part of his renovation of Buddhism, Sot'aesan had Irwŏnsang enshrined in place of the Buddha statue as the object of faith and worship. Sot'aesan made it clear that Irwŏnsang is the symbol of the Buddha-nature or Mind-Buddha, implying that Irwŏnsang should be taken as a *hwadu* for seeing the nature and attaining buddhahood. Thus, faith in Irwŏnsang is not faith in the symbol Irwŏnsang any more than the finger pointing at the moon is the moon. So "faith in Irwŏnsang" really means the faith in the *truth* of Irwŏnsang. This point is made very clear by Chŏngsan in the section titled "Faith in Irwŏnsang," where he writes that faith in Irwŏnsang lies in believing in all the statements listed individually in the section "Truth of Irwŏnsang," as explained above. Chŏngsan starts by writing: "To believe in Irwŏn is: to believe in Irwŏn as the inherent essence of all things in the universe; to believe in it as the original nature of all buddhas and patriarchs; to believe in it as the Buddha-nature of all sentient beings; . . . to believe that the creative transformation of true emptiness-cum-wondrous existence conceals and reveals itself through all things in the universe throughout the incalculable eons without beginning." None of these statements implies that faith in Irwŏnsang lies in believing in some intangible circle, let alone the circular form Irwŏnsang.

"Deluded beings" are advised to have a firm faith in each of the statements expounded in the truth of Irwŏnsang. Thus, the object of faith in Irwŏnsang is not the circular form Irwŏnsang but the truth expressed by the statements in the truth of Irwŏnsang. There is nothing religious in the faith in the truth of Irwŏnsang as expounded by Chŏngsan, for it is presented as a means for the deluded to be enlightened to what the mind-seal of all buddhas and patriarchs transmit. The truth of Irwŏnsang is thus expounded not for its own sake but as a vehicle for content that deluded beings should be enlightened to; correct enlightenment requires the deluded to have a firm faith in the truth of Irwŏnsang.

Practice of Irwŏnsang

For Chŏngsan, the first step one should take in one's practice is to develop a firm faith in the truth of Irwŏnsang, especially the truth that Irwŏn is the Buddha-nature of all sentient beings; one should take this faith as the guide for practice. In Chŏngsan's view,[89] one can pursue the right practice only after one is awakened to the truth of Irwŏnsang, and once this is accomplished one can activate prajñā-wisdom (*panyaji*). Chŏngsan requires one to have an awakening to the truth expounded in the section "The Truth of Irwŏnsang" because practice without awakening is a corrupt practice, like trying to wash dirty hands in dirty water.[90] The essence of practice lies in knowing, nourishing, and using one's own mind, which is as perfect, complete, utterly fair, and unselfish as Irwŏn, namely prajñā-wisdom. Chŏngsan identifies this perfect mind with the prajñā-wisdom acquired upon awakening to the truth of Irwŏnsang.[91] Notice that for Chŏngsan the model for perfection is not the Irwŏnsang, which is visible, but Irwŏn, which is invisible to the deluded—that is, the original nature of all buddhas and patriarchs and the Buddha-nature of all sentient beings.

By contrast, for Sot'aesan the model of perfection is Irwŏnsang, which is visible even to the deluded. Sot'aesan said: "That circular figure is a model that is adopted to make the true Irwŏn known. This is analogous to the fact that the finger used to point at the moon is not itself the moon."[92] Since the true Irwŏn, that is, Buddha-nature, can only be known upon seeing one's self-nature, and since the deluded cannot see Buddha-nature (called "true Irwŏn"), Sot'aesan set up the visible Irwŏnsang for the deluded to model after. However, Chŏngsan makes it clear that the Buddha's mind is not round like the circle. He says, "Irwŏnsang is used to refer to the realm of the Buddha's mind. However, this does not mean that the Buddha's mind is round. We have used the circular form to express the pure, perfect mind of the Buddha. It is like the finger pointing to the moon."[93] In the 1962 edition of the *Canon*, however, one is directed to model oneself after Irwŏnsang instead of Irwŏn: Chŏngsan's method of practice has been replaced with Sot'aesan's method. Since the altered version does not require one to be awakened to the truth of Irwŏnsang as the necessary condition for right practice, one is left to know, nourish, and use one's mind as perfect and complete, and utterly fair and unselfish as the circular form Irwŏnsang, but not to develop prajñā-wisdom. This is like taking the finger for the moon, in spite of the fact that Chŏngsan warned against doing so. The difference is that the deluded being might try to model his or her mind on the circular form, Irwŏnsang, without being enlightened to the pure and perfect mind of the Buddha, namely, prajñā-wisdom. With the invisible Irwŏn as cue, one would have tried to be enlightened to the pure and perfect mind of the Buddha and to know, nourish, and use this mind upon enlightenment to the truth of Irwŏn.

In the three sections analyzed here, Chŏngsan does not include the tenets of the Fourfold Beneficence or Dharmakāya Buddha; he is concerned exclusively with expounding the pillar "Correct Enlightenment and Right Practice" as pointed out above. Chŏngsan wrote on the truth of Irwŏnsang as the content of enlightenment, on faith of Irwŏnsang as the necessary condition for enlightenment, and on the practice of Irwŏnsang as the method of knowing, nourishing, and using prajñā-wisdom upon awakening to the truth of Irwŏnsang.

Dharmakāya Buddha and Irwŏnsang

In the chapter "Fundamental Principles" of the *Dharma Words,* Chŏngsan expands his explication of the tenet of Irwŏnsang to include its religious, metaphysical, and moral implications.[94]

In Chŏngsan's view, the noumenal nature of Dharmakāya Buddha cannot be described in words or symbols; however, all beings in the phenomenal world are nothing but its manifestations.[95] Moreover, as Sot'aesan had said, all things in the universe are the content of the Fourfold Beneficence. Because deluded beings do not know this, the Irwŏnsang was enshrined as the symbol of the Dharmakāya Buddha, linked to the Fourfold Beneficence. Prior to the enshrinement of Irwŏnsang in 1935, four wooden tablets were set up at the altar in the fashion of the Confucian ceremony of ancestor worship. On the four tablets were written: "The place where heaven and earth watch over"; "The place where parents watch over"; "The place where brethren respond"; and "The place where laws respond." Even after the enshrinement of Irwŏnsang in place of the four tablets, prayers for supplication are offered, not to Irwŏnsang, but to the Fourfold Beneficence with the invocation: "Oh! Dharmakāya Buddha–Fourfold Beneficence!" Chŏngsan says,[96] however, that the purpose of enshrining Irwŏnsang is (1) to see that our mind is none other than the Buddha, (2) to believe that the principle of karmic causality cannot be deceived or violated, (3) to know the details of the Fourfold Beneficence that rule over the karmic retribution of blessings and punishment, and (4) to practice a "limitless worship" such that, since the Buddha is manifested everywhere, every act should be an offering to the Buddha.

The other purpose of enshrining the Irwŏnsang is to take it as the standard of practice, such that one becomes enlightened to one's own original nature, or the Buddha-nature, which one can see when one beholds one's own mind that is devoid of any delusive thought.[97] All beings, including the Buddha, sages, and ordinary sentient beings, have numinous awareness in their original nature. It is because of numinous awareness that there are differences between ordinary sentient beings and sages—differences that also account for the production of good and evil. The numinous awareness of sentient beings is swayed by habit force and karma in response to mental spheres to produce various delusions. The Buddha, however, illuminates situations with numinous awareness, reflecting light inward on the original nature without being drawn to external conditions, so that the light of wisdom shines forth. In response to activity in mental spheres the unimpeded functioning of our original nature becomes good, while obstructed functioning becomes evil. Its straight functioning becomes rightness; its crooked functioning becomes wrongness. Its obscured functioning becomes ignorance; and its clear functioning becomes enlightenment.

Another principle that the Irwŏnsang refers to is that of change and immutability, on which the universe is based. To the principle of change belong the cycle of arising, continuity, decay, and disappearance of the universe; the cycle of the four seasons; birth, old age, illness, and death of humans; and the vicissitudes of fortunes and misfortunes, and calamity and happiness of life. To the principle of immutability belongs the original essence of the true thusness (*bhūtatathatā*) that neither arises nor ceases, being permanent with no beginning or end. Chŏngsan suggests that, in comprehending the principle of change, we correct our old habits, renew our mind, reform an obsolete system, and develop all these into new ones. Awakening to the principle that what changes is based on what does not change, we will be enlightened to and establish our original true character, and myriad changes will follow.[98] These two principles are two aspects of the truth of nonduality.

Chŏngsan uses the principle of yin-yang to explain the phenomena of change as the result of yin-yang's mutual advancement and overcoming. When yang reaches its acme, says Chŏngsan,[99] it produces the three ten-day periods of the hottest weather that are called "triple yielding" (san-fu): yin attempts to rise but yields three times to yang, being suppressed by the dominant power of the latter. After the last yielding, however, yang weakens and yin gradually gains power. This is the universal principle of nature, namely, that a change takes place in whatever reaches its highest point and that whatever is minute can become enormous. Furthermore, the way in which yin and yang alternate in dominance is governed by the principle of causality. Actions in accordance with this principle produce the karmic reciprocity of mutual benefaction; actions against this principle produce the karmic retribution of mutual destruction. Sages, says Chŏngsan, understand this principle of causality and live in accordance with the "way of mutual benefaction." But ordinary sentient beings, being ignorant of this principle, are led by greed, fame, and power and accumulate evil karma in "the way of mutual destruction." The ups and downs of political power and prosperity and the rise and fall of an individual or an organization are due to this principle. Hence, those who understand the principle behave with modesty, defer to others, and help them.[100]

On Moral Culture

Chŏngsan encouraged his followers to develop a moral culture so they could become the masters of the New World.[101] The end of moral culture is to realize buddhahood and deliver sentient beings from suffering. One cannot attain buddhahood without subjugating the māra lurking in one's mind. The Buddha is said to have attained the perfect and unsurpassed enlightenment only upon subjugating māra, personified as Māra, the evil one that destroys all goodness. In Won Buddhism, māra is identified mainly with the three mental poisons of greed, anger, and delusion; the last three of the thirty Won Buddhist precepts warn the practitioner against being greedy, angry, and deluded.[102]

Chŏngsan says that ordinary humans live their lives mired in the three poisons, but they do not know that they do. Listening to the teachings of the enlightened masters, some people for the first time come to know that they have these poisons in their mind, and they begin to exert themselves to eradicate them.[103] Since the three mental poisons can be eradicated only if the light of prajñā-wisdom shines, one needs to be enlightened to one's own Buddha-nature. Whether one will be on a progressive or retrogressive path depends on the strength of one's aspiration and practice for the realization of buddhahood.[104]

The essence of moral culture, as Chŏngsan explains, is in the Threefold Practice, that is, in spiritual cultivation, inquiry into facts and principles, and heedful choice in karmic action; these will help one attain the three great powers of emancipation, enlightenment, and the mean.

While commenting on the first three articles of the essentials of daily practice,[105] Chŏngsan says that the "elixir of immortality" grows when the mind-ground is free from disturbances; the wisdom of self-nature shines when the mind-ground is free from delusions, and the precept of self-nature is preserved when the mind-ground is free from errors. The key to attaining such freedom is, first, to understand and practice emptiness.

Chŏngsan gives utmost importance to emptiness (śūnyatā) as expounded in the Wisdom Sūtras (Prajñāpāramitā), since emptiness is highly effective in daily life and only the empty mind devoid of defilement can emancipate one from the cycle of the six paths.[106] Chŏngsan says that the world divided into the six realms is created and revealed in differentiating human mental states. One will be in the realm of devas if one transcends all situations of suffering and pleasure; in the realm of humans if one can decide between good or evil and the progressive or retrogressive path; in the realm of animals if one has no sense of propriety and shame; in the realm of asuras if one is apathetic and does nothing, believing that it makes no difference after death; in the realm of hungry ghosts if one is selfish and greedy, struggling constantly for one's own material advancement; and in the realm of hell if one is always angry, stubborn, and opinionated.[107] In Chŏngsan's view, one can realize nirvāṇa in daily life transcending the six realms of existence only if one's prajñā-wisdom shines through the six realms of existence; and prajñā-wisdom is none other than the insight into the emptiness of inherent existence of all beings of the universe.

However, one cannot maintain the empty mind, the mind that is as perfect, complete, utterly fair, and unselfish as Irwŏn, namely, prajñā-wisdom, unless one is enlightened to one's Buddha-nature. Chŏngsan has explicated enlightenment or "seeing the nature" in terms of "awakening to the truth of Irwŏnsang" and demystified "seeing the nature" (enlightenment) by spelling out five steps of seeing the nature. These are (1) showing that "all dharmas return to the One";[108] (2) knowing the realm of true emptiness; (3) seeing the truth of "wondrous existence"; (4) keeping the one mind from internal disturbances and external temptations; and (5) applying this mind to all situations "magnificently."

The final goal of Sot'aesan's practice as stated in the Vow to Irwŏnsang is "to be endowed with the great power of Irwŏn" and "unified with the noumenal nature of Irwŏn," as analyzed above.[109] However, Sot'aesan left the impression that the true Irwŏn (invisible circle) has such power and noumenal nature in spite of the fact that he used Irwŏnsang as a symbol of the Buddha-nature or Mind-Buddha. It was Chŏngsan who explained the true meaning of the two phrases in the vow.[110]

According to Chŏngsan, "Being endowed with great power of Irwŏn" means that we gradually attain three great powers by disciplining ourselves with the Threefold Practice. By "three great powers" are meant the powers of samādhi, prajñā, and śīla of the self-nature, and emancipation, enlightenment, and the mean of the self-nature. By disciplining ourselves with the Threefold Practice (spiritual concentration, inquiry into facts and principles, and heedful choice in karmic action) we protect our mind and body from disturbances, delusions, and errors, eventually attaining the three great powers; we will be as steady as a steel pillar in any situation. It also means that we can go through the six paths freely, delivering all sentient beings with the three great powers. With a wholehearted concentration of mind, one can employ at will the awesome power of heaven and earth, says Chŏngsan.

By "being unified with the noumenal nature of Irwŏn" is meant, says Chŏngsan, that, upon attaining the three great powers of Irwŏn (the Buddha-nature), we practitioners enter, on the one hand, in times of "quietude," the perfect and complete samādhi that is devoid of wicked thoughts and foolish imagination. On the other, in motion, we have the utterly fair and unselfish mind, the one mind of no disturbance. Only if one has perfected the two modes of Irwŏn (samādhi and śīla), one can be said to have reached buddhahood. For an effective method of attaining such power and being unified as one with the noumenal nature of Irwŏn (the Buddha-nature), Chŏngsan suggests the tantric practice of chanting mantras.[111]

On Buddhism and Confucianism

Buddhism

If we recall that in 1919 Sot'aesan sent Chŏngsan to the Zen monk Paek Hangmyŏng at Wŏlmyŏngam in Mount Pongnae, to become the monk's chief disciple, and that Chŏngsan stayed there for five years, we can surmise that Chŏngsan became very well acquainted with the essence of the Buddha-dharma. The fact that Chŏngsan identified Sot'aesan as the second appearance of the Buddha Śākyamuni during the period of decay and termination of the Buddha-dharma[112] proves that Chŏngsan worked hard to help his mentor take the Buddha-dharma as the central tenet of the doctrine of the new religious order. The fact that Sot'aesan set up Irwŏnsang as the symbol of the Buddha-nature, the Mind-Buddha, and Dharmakāya Buddha also makes it clear that Sot'aesan's new order, the Society for the Study of Buddha-dharma, was a Buddhist order. It was Chŏngsan who renamed the order Wŏnbulgyo (Won Buddhism) in 1947, thus drawing a clear line between the existing Korean Buddhist orders and the new Buddhist order that Sot'aesan had established. Chŏngsan's teaching on personal spiritual discipline follows the Hīnayānist practice, while edification follows more the Mahāyāna line. Thus, Won Buddhism is a reformed Buddhism, as the term *Buddhism* implies, even though the central doctrine of Won Buddhism contains only a dozen or so Buddhist terms that connect it to the roots of Mahāyāna Buddhist doctrine.

Chŏngsan produced interpretative translations in Korean vernacular, with commentaries, of several short Buddhist scriptures, including the *Diamond Sūtra* and the *Heart Sūtra*, which he used to teach his students. Chŏngsan's lectures on the fundamental tenets of Buddhism were published in the *Sermons of Master Chŏngsan* (*Chŏngsan chongsa pŏpsŏl* [2000]).[113] Some of his discourses on Buddhist terms are included in the *Dharma Words* in this book.[114] In both of these works, one sees that Chŏngsan puts great emphasis on the tenets of emptiness (śūnyatā) and wisdom (prajñā); in his view, one cannot subjugate the mighty Māra (identified as the three mental poisons) without the light of wisdom, which one can activate only upon seeing into one's own Buddha-nature—the Buddha-nature that, for the sake of deluded beings, is signaled by Irwŏnsang. The most important contribution Chŏngsan made to the system of the Won Buddhist doctrine is that he expounded the truth and practice of Irwŏnsang exclusively in terms of the Mahāyāna Buddhist metaphysics. If one is enlightened to the Buddha-nature using Irwŏnsang as a pointer, one does not need many other terms. And prajñā-wisdom is the intuition of emptiness (śūnyatā) of the inherent essence of all things in the universe, which can be applied with great effectiveness in daily life, helping one realize nirvāṇa in saṁsāra. For Chŏngsan, nirvāṇa is one's own mind that is perfect, complete, utterly fair, and unselfish, like Irwŏn (the Buddha-nature), in other words, prajñā-wisdom. This is the culmination of Chŏngsan's application of the Mahāyāna Buddhist ideal of "seeing the nature" and attaining buddhahood. In the redacted version (1962) of the *Correct Canon of Buddhism* (1943), however, Chŏngsan's teachings on awakening to the Buddha-nature and prajñā-wisdom were heavily cut, so that the core of the Mahāyāna Buddhist practice has been lost. In order to restore the heart of Chŏngsan's teaching, I have translated his original writing in this book.

Confucianism

Chŏngsan was well aware of the obsoleteness of the Confucian moral norms; however, he was also aware of some enduring moral truth in Confucianism, and declared that benevolence (*ren*) and righteousness (*yi*) are the foundation of morality. Chŏngsan recognized that the Confucian cardinal moral virtues are benevolence (*ren*), righteousness (*yi*), propriety (*li*), wisdom (*zhi*), and faith (*xin*). Chŏngsan, however, has given new interpretations to benevolence and righteousness, saying that benevolence refers to the Buddha's compassion and Christ's love. Righteousness lies in the ways one ought to follow and in doing all things without violating heavenly principle. In practicing benevolence and righteousness in balance, one will demonstrate dignified calmness, even after subjugating a myriad evils as a result of the grand influence of one's edification.[115] Chŏngsan characterizes the great compassion and great pity (*maitrī-karuṇā*) of the Buddha as "cosmopolitanism," and uses the same term to characterize the spirit of benevolence and righteousness of Confucius, and the spirit of universal love of Jesus Christ. All these sages, regarding the whole world as one household and all humans as one family, advocated great moral principles with which to save the human race.[116]

Chŏngsan gives new definitions also to the central moral norms (duties).[117] The Confucian moral norms are expressed as the three bonds and the five relationships.[118] The moral duty of the subject to the sovereign is loyalty (*zhong*), that of the son to his father is filial piety (*xiao*), and that of the wife to her husband is chastity (*lie*). In Chŏngsan's view, these moral norms are unjust unless they are reformed.

He notes that the Chinese character for loyalty (*zhong*) is composed of two characters standing for central mind, and that the reference thus is to fidelity. When people associate with one another, they should serve society, contribute to the state, and exert themselves everywhere with this true mind; this is the application of loyalty. This loyalty-fidelity is different from the kind of loyalty that requires one to sacrifice oneself for a wicked ruler regardless of national interest. When people deceive their own conscience with no sign of remorse and cheat on society with no sense of shame, human life becomes compromised and social disorder is perpetuated. If this disordered world is to be turned to a wholesome and truthful one, the spirit of true loyalty should be promoted, says Chŏngsan.

For Confucius, filial piety was the most fundamental virtue, if a child was to be a true human being. In Chŏngsan's view, however, the traditional practices of filial piety cannot be promoted any longer.[119] For Chŏngsan, true filial piety lies in the requital of beneficence, and there are four beneficences: heaven and earth, parents, brethren, and laws. Certainly, the requital of the beneficence of parents is the most fundamental of these, for no one can know all other beneficences without knowing first the beneficence of parents. Therefore, the practice of filial piety lies in discovering all beneficence, starting with that of parents. When one discovers beneficence everywhere and sees even adverse conditions as opportunities to feel and express gratitude, this is precisely the application of filial piety. Chŏngsan points out that the general moral sentiment of today is lacking in filial piety in this new sense of the term. In the family, one resents one's parents; away from one's family, one resents heaven and earth, brethren, and laws. Consequently, the mood of society is depressed and human life becomes dangerous. For this critical situation to change so we realize a peaceful and comfortable world, suggests Chŏngsan, the spirit of filial piety in this new sense should be put into practice in the public sphere.

In an earlier canonical text of Won Buddhism published in 1932, the first article of the "Four Essentials" for social ethics is "Equal Rights of Man and Woman."[120] This article was changed to "Cultivation of Self-power" in the *Correct Canon of Buddhism* (*Pulgyo chŏngjŏn* [1943]). The point of the article is that Sot'aesan and Chŏngsan were clearly aware of male chauvinistic injustice against women for the two millennia under the Confucian moral system. In Chŏngsan's redefinition, chastity (*lie*) is the standard of moral integrity for both men and women, using women's chastity as the model for strict integrity.

Chŏngsan's redefinition of chastity is as follows. Chastity lies in not compromising with one's principles, or "righteous determination." One can be said to be chaste if one keeps to one's principles in all situations. This is so because one should value one's integrity as highly as a woman should value her chastity. A woman who does not regard her chastity as important would certainly not be sincere about the rest of her moral character. Thus, the practice of chastity lies in doing one's utmost to practice justice and avoid committing injustice, keeping a firm will and staying within the bounds of one's social position, says Chŏngsan. This is different from the narrow interpretation of chastity in the ancient world, in which a woman would grow old at the home of the dead man with whom she had only been engaged. Nor is this the foolish chastity a woman kept by immolating herself on the death of her husband, ignoring her other duties and obligations of humanity. Thus, the significance of chastity is truly broad and widely applicable to be the eternal moral principle of the world and the standard of humanity under heaven.[121]

On Korean National Destiny

Chŏngsan was concerned about the reconstruction of Korean nation upon the liberation of Korea from Japanese occupation in 1945; for this reason, he wrote the *Treatise on the National Foundation* (*Kŏn'gungnon*).[122] Right after liberation, several political parties announced their political platforms, but the leading figures could not unite themselves for reconstruction of Korea.[123] Chŏngsan wrote the treatise in hopes of correcting the political confusion and disorder that he observed after liberation. It contains outlines of his theory of national foundation, the correct way of government, and instructions on the construction of a nation. The gist of the treatise is to take the spiritual as the root; government and education as the trunk; national defense, construction, and economy as branches and leaves; and the way of improvement as the fruit, so that national power in Korea would have a healthy basis. The ethos of the national foundation consists of the following: (1) spiritual union, (2) establishment of the national self-sufficiency, (3) loyalty, justice, and dedication to the public, (4) regulation and rectification, and (5) an insightful view of the general situation. Chŏngsan puts emphasis on the importance of compulsory education and expansion of educational system since education is the great way of the national progress. He divides the way of progress into three branches: to honor those who serve the public altruistically, to encourage education, and to limit the system of heredity and inheritance.

Chŏngsan writes that at a time (1945) of cultural exchange it would be a senseless obstinacy to hold on to one's own culture only, and it also would be just as senseless to be fascinated by someone else's. One should be independent internally and harmonious externally, that is, with others, adopting another's good points and avoiding the other's weaknesses. Thus, Chŏngsan explicates a practical basic approach to adopting foreign culture. He puts emphasis on the importance of the leader's responsibility when he says, "If the head is disturbed, the end gets disturbed following the head; if the head is right then the end gets right accordingly. Hence, the leader takes the total responsibility." Chŏngsan's emphasis on the importance of the spiritual or moral integrity of the leaders seems as valid today as it was when he was writing, more than a half-century after the liberation of Korea.

On the Ethics of Triple Identity

On his deathbed, Chŏngsan allowed his definition of the "ethics of triple identity"[124] to be the *gāthā* (verse) of his dharma transmission. Chŏngsan believed firmly that the world was a global village and was slowly moving toward the realization of the "one family under heaven, with morality," and he proposed a set of norms to be observed for the realization of such a world.

At the midpoint of the twentieth century, the world was turning into a global village where peoples of different religions, races, and political and social ideologies all lived together. Chŏngsan saw the world as moving toward a truly civilized, bright future. However, there were no moral norms for this new world, no ethics that could be endorsed by all parties as the groundwork to build a harmonious, peaceful, and prosperous world. The way toward the realization of such a world was blocked by antagonism between the followers of different religions, by racial disharmony, and by individual and collective egoism based on ideological, economical, and political biases. In Chŏngsan's view, there would be no harmonious and peaceful world as long as these impediments were couched in the hearts of humankind as the world history attests. Thus, he proposed three moral norms that all religionists, all human races, and all political, social, and business leaders could honor and endorse as a global ethics, by which one harmonious family under Heaven would be realized "with morality." Chŏngsan named it the ethics of triple identity (*samdong yulli*).

The first norm is that all followers of religion ought to harmonize with one another in the knowledge that the fundamental origin of all religions and religious sects is unitary. If all the religions of the world were awakened to this fundamental truth and thus were in harmony with one another, all the religionists of the world would form one great household, adapting to one another and frequenting one another's places of gathering and worship.

Chŏngsan's view that all religions have one origin, and that they therefore ought to harmonize with one another raises two philosophical problems. First, whether it is in fact the case that all religions have one identical origin; and second, whether it therefore follows that they ought to harmonize with one another. For the first question, one may suggest all religions are generally of the identical origin just as the colors of the spectrum have an identical origin, namely, white light. However, even if the first statement is accepted by all parties, which is highly unlikely at the moment, there is no convincing argument for the inference that "they ought to harmonize one another." As enmities between certain religions have worsened for centuries, there does not seem to be any hope for reconciliation and peace. In Chŏngsan's view, however, the world is still in the midst of the last phase of the "earlier heaven" so that the world is still dark. When the world enters the "later heaven," which is bright and just, enmities, conflicts, and wars that have been afflicting humanity for centuries will be driven away.

The second norm is that all races and all sentient beings should unite in harmony by awakening to the truth that they are all bonded by one identical vital force. Although we recognize races of various colors living in different parts of the world, and various nations as comprising one race, and various sectors comprising one nation, there is just one fundamental life source. To those who see heaven and earth as their parents and the universe as their own household, Chŏngsan argues, all people are brethren; even birds, beasts, and insects are related to us by the single great vital force.[125] Thus, says Chŏngsan, when all people in the world are awakened to this relationship and harmonize together, all races and all nations will unite as one family and cultivate universal friendship and harmony, influencing all sentient beings by virtuous example.

As with the first norm, the proposition is open to philosophical questioning: Even assuming that people accept fundamental interrelatedness of all life, will this necessarily entail harmony? Chŏngsan's answer would be the same: in the "later heaven" it will be achieved. Parallel arguments and counterarguments hold for the third norm.

The third and final norm is that all enterprises should harmonize because they all have one identical aim. In Chŏngsan's view, all enterprises and ideologies aim to make a better world, and hence, all should unite in grand harmony. When Chŏngsan proposed this principle, the world was divided into huge political and ideological power blocs; but, wherever they could, entrepreneurs launched all sorts of enterprises within their areas of specialty and within the boundaries of business. Although some of these enterprises are questionable in their ends and means while others are fully supportable, he argues, their fundamental aims are to make this world a better place. In this situation even evil has the power to help one awaken to the good. Thus, all enterprises are essentially in one identical line of business. When all the entrepreneurs in the world, being awakened to this relationship, understand each other and harmonize together, all the enterprises of the world will form one household, encouraging each other and making advances side by side, and eventually being united into the way of fairness.

Chŏngsan's ideal here is admittedly unrealistic: too lofty a goal to reach in a free-for-all, capitalist, global economy where greed seems to be the primary moving force. The ideal can only be realized when people follow the principles of beneficence requital: working toward mutual benefit based on fairness toward brethren and by doing justice and forsaking injustice. In Chŏngsan's view, however, humans would eventually improve and become bodhisattvas in the later heaven, realizing a paradise in this very world.

Concluding Remarks

Won Buddhism (Wŏnbulgyo), now the fourth major religion in Korea, with branch chapters overseas, owes its identity to Chŏngsan. If he had not promulgated Wŏnbulgyo as the new name of the order but had kept the old name, *Pulbŏp yŏn'guhoe* (Society for the Study of Buddha-dharma), which was the name given by Sot'aesan, the new order would have been regarded only as a sect of Korean Buddhism both in Korea and overseas. And if Chŏngsan had not compiled the order's new scriptures, the *Scriptures of Won Buddhism* (*Wŏnbulgyo kyojŏn* [1962]), the order's principal scripture would have been the *Correct Canon of Buddhism* (*Pulgyo chŏngjŏn* [1943]), keeping the door open for more arguments that Won Buddhism is just a sect of Korean Buddhist order. Thus, it was Chŏngsan who with these dual achievements laid the foundation of Won Buddhism as an independent religious order.

Chŏngsan's vision of the "later heaven" or the New World, as expressed in the *Canon of the World* (*Sejŏn*) reflects a reformative synthesis of the Confucian moral and political programs with the Buddhist way of emancipation from the cycle of birth and death. In Chŏngsan's view, human perfection cannot be realized unless one takes the Buddhist emptiness (*śūnyatā*) as the substance of the Way and the Confucian moral virtues of benevolence (*ren*) and righteousness (*yi*) as its function. Chŏngsan has thus spelled out the norms of social ethics to be followed by an individual, the family, the society, and the nation for the perfect life in the New World. It should be noted here that Chŏngsan is concerned with showing the ways for a person to follow for a perfect life that can only be realized as a full member of a family, society, state, and the world.

While fulfilling his duty of "the chief codifier of the new order," as designated by Sot'aesan, Chŏngsan did more than help Sot'aesan systematize the central doctrine of Won Buddhism. In expounding "the truth of Irwŏnsang," Chŏngsan drew on some quintessential terms of Mahāyāna Buddhism to explicate the secret of the mind-seal (symbolized, in Won Buddhism, by the circle symbol), which, it is alleged, has been transmitted from the Buddha to the patriarchs. By saying that Irwŏn (unitary circle) is the original nature of all buddhas and patriarchs and the Buddha-nature of all sentient beings, Chŏngsan has brought the heart of Buddha-dharma to the secular world. In the section "The Practice of Irwŏnsang" in the *Correct Canon of Buddhism* (*Pulgyo chŏngjŏn* [1943]),

Chŏngsan connects the practice to Mahāyāna Buddhist enlightenment by saying that the practice of Irwŏn lies in knowing, fostering, and using one's own prajñā-wisdom, upon enlightenment to the truth of Irwŏnsang. The *Dharma Words* (*Pŏbŏ*), which takes up most of this volume, consists of Chŏngsan's explanations, expositions, and discourses on the ways for the moral perfection necessary to realize "one family under heaven, with morality." Chŏngsan's ideal image of moral perfection is embodied in the person who, upon awakening to the truth of Irwŏnsang, knows, fosters, and uses his or her own prajñā-wisdom while requiting the Fourfold Beneficence in daily life. In this formulation is synthesized the essence of the teachings of both Buddhism and Confucianism. At a time when Buddhism was condemned for being negative, pessimistic, and otherworldly by the Confucianists, and Confucianism was blamed for being obsolete and anachronistic, Chŏngsan found moral truths in both systems of belief, like jewels hidden in the mire, and combined them into a single, more perfect one.

While enlightenment or seeing the self-nature (*svabhāva*) has been the central and the most important issue in the Zen Buddhist traditions and the subject of much contention within it, Chŏngsan has demystified the issue by saying, simply, that one must be enlightened to the truth of Irwŏnsang. The target of enlightenment is the inherent nature of all things in the universe, the original nature of all buddhas and patriarchs, and the Buddha-nature of all sentient beings.

Chŏngsan's aspiration and plan as the chief codifier of the new order included his concern for the destiny of Korea upon liberation from Japanese occupation and for world peace. In his *Treatise on National Foundation* (*Kŏngungnon* [1945]) his practical advice for the reconstruction of Korean nation contains suggestions that are still valid, not just for Korea but for the leaders of all countries. Chŏngsan proposed the ethics of triple identity as the moral principles that all religionists, races, and enterprises should observe for the universal harmony in the global village. His formulations were not simply wishes for the future: Chŏngsan believed that the world was slowly moving toward "realizing one family under heaven, with morality" and that the future was already upon us.

TRANSLATIONS

Part One

The Canon of the World (Sejŏn)

The Gāthā

With one truth within one fence,
As one family within one household,
As coworkers on the same worksite,
Let us realize the world of Irwŏn.

Chapter One

General Introduction

A human life can be perfect in both this and the eternal life only if there exist correct ways that one can learn and follow for each stage of life, from the moment when the numinous consciousness enters the mother's womb to the moments of being born, growing, living as an adult, and entering nirvāṇa.

Thus, there should be the way of care before birth, while one is still in the womb; after birth there should be the way of infant education during infancy; and during childhood there should be the way of integrated education in science and morality. In the family there should be the way for spouses to follow, the way for parents and children to follow, and the way for siblings and relatives to follow. In a religious order there should be the way of faith and the way for the laity to follow. In society there should be the way of men and women, the way of old and young, the way of strong and weak, and the way of the public well-being. In the state there should be the way of government and moral culture, and the way for the citizen to follow. In the world there should be the way for the human race to follow. In old age with one's lifetime work behind, there should be the way of rest and emancipation. Reaching the time of nirvāṇa, there should be the way of nirvāṇa and deliverance. Thus, the ways one ought to learn and follow throughout one's life can be limitless; however, an outline of those ways and principles is hereby drawn and entitled *Sejŏn* (*The Canon of the World*).

Chapter Two

Education

I. On Education

Education is the root of the evolution of the world and the foundation of human civilization. Hence, it can be said that the rise or fall and prosperity or decline of an individual, a family, a society, and a nation depend on whether or not people are educated well.

Although humans are said to be the most sagacious of all beings, supreme sagacity cannot be realized without education. A family, a society, a nation, or the world may be formed; however, they cannot be maintained or developed without the power of education. Therefore, one can be a useful person to one's family, society, nation, and the world only if correct ways are provided for care before birth, child rearing, and general education, that is, throughout the various stages of life—from the period in the womb that is the basis of one's life through that of birth and growth. Education can be divided broadly into two kinds: one is education in science, the other is moral education. Scientific education is the basis of material civilization, and is responsible for the external development of the world, while moral education is the basis of the spiritual culture, and is responsible for internal development of the world. These two kinds of education should be advanced equally, with moral education forming the basis for the application of the science education. Only then can human civilization be well rounded internally and externally and the happiness of human race can be perfect.

II. The Way of Education before Birth

Human education starts before birth with the influences that affect the unborn child. Prenatal education originated with King Wen's (1171–1122 BC) mother, Tairen, who started teaching her son while he was in her womb, and since then has spread through the world. A wholesome influence on the fetus in the womb can improve the temperament of the numinous consciousness that is originally good, and mitigate the temperament of the numinous consciousness that is not good. If a pregnant woman educates her unborn child poorly, by letting her body and mind run recklessly, the temperament of the numinous consciousness will get worse, regardless of its goodness or badness. Therefore, Grand Master Sot'aesan said, "Since the unborn child's numinous consciousness gathers while it is in the mother's womb, what the parents say, think, and do can easily influence its future character. Hence, the pregnant woman's self-restraint is of extreme importance."[1]

The way of prenatal influence includes the following threefold self-restraint. First is physical self-restraint. The pregnant woman should not lift any heavy object, climb or descend steep places, or go to places where cold, hot, damp, or dry conditions vary excessively. She should not eat any unripe fruit or spoiled food; she should be careful to avoid being too hungry or too full, overworked or indolent. Second is to keep the mind in purity: she should keep her mind from greed, anger, delusion, resentment, jealousy, and disrespect. She should not be disturbed by sorrow and pleasure, or love and hatred. She must be careful to subdue anxiety and agony and to keep her peace of mind in frightening and alarming situations; and she must learn the teachings of the Buddha and other wise and benevolent sages by attending dharma meetings regularly and maintain the standard of practice. Third is to have right conduct: the pregnant woman should abstain from killing, stealing, and sexual misconduct; she should not make silly remarks, use evil words, tell lies, or embellish words. She should deal with daily affairs fairly and right, treat all people with respect, and practice charity as much as possible. Wherever she goes, she should observe the laws and rules and the public morality of that place.

III. The Way of Childhood Guidance

Human nature is originally pure and devoid of good and evil; it can, however, become good or evil in accordance with mental spheres. Thus, it is easily influenced by good in a good environment and by evil in a bad environment.

Since consciousness during innocent childhood is not yet fully developed, whatever the child sees or hears can easily influence it. It is said that Mencius's mother changed her residence three times to find a right environment for her son to receive good influences, eventually helping him to become a sage. How could childhood guidance be neglected?

Grand Master Sot'aesan taught that there are four ways in the way of childhood guidance. The first is mental influence: one should keep one's mind upright, good, and peaceful, basing the practice on religious faith, so that the child is guided to follow the model of one's mind. The second is influence by deed: one must practice right and one's conduct should be in accordance with moral norms, so that the child could naturally model after such practice. The third is verbal teaching: the child should often be told the tales and anecdotes of the Buddha, bodhisattvas, and other great persons so that it can remember and model after their good deeds. The parents should teach the child by reasoning with it on facts and principles. The fourth is stern teaching, which is done only when necessary, and with dignity; this is not a method to be used often, since it is done to a mere child.[2]

IV. The Way of General Education

Even if one has had adequate prenatal influences and proper childhood guidance, one's life could still be worthless if one does not get both an adequate education in the scientific knowledge necessary for the age and the moral training necessary for the growth of one's fundamental personality during one's youth. One should thus receive timely education in school and moral training from youth to adulthood, which we call "general education."

The education one receives throughout one's lifetime has four parts. The first is education in science, the purpose of which is to help attain scientific knowledge and skills. The second is spiritual education, which is to help one be trained in moral culture and the practice of morality, mainly through moral education. The third is education in propriety, which lets one learn and practice all the ceremonies and rituals appropriate to the family, society, the nation, and the world. The fourth is work education, which is to cultivate diligence in ordinary times and to be trained to work productively.

Chapter Three

Family

I. On Family

Family is the foundation of human life. Where there are human beings, a family is formed, by the relationships of husband and wife, parents and children, siblings, and other relatives. Only if the right ways of those relationships are properly followed can there be a happy, peaceful, and improving family.

II. The Way of Husband and Wife

The origin of a family lies in husband and wife; there should be ways to be followed by them. In these lies the meaning of an ancient sage's saying, "The way of the prince (*junzi*) originates in the relationship of husband and wife."

The first way of husband and wife is harmony. Husband and wife should be earnest friends and companions to each other in mutual respect and love, a mutual understanding of each other's idiosyncrasies, encouragement of each other's good, generosity with each other's faults, and mutual help to each other's business. The second is fidelity: both should prize their chastity and should abstain from dissipation and other evils; both should share the suffering and happiness of life to the end; and both should forgive with generosity all the faults that are not egregious evils known to the world. The third way is diligence and sincerity. Husband and wife should, with a spirit of self-reliance, live diligently and sincerely, constructing a prosperous family and equally discharging their moral duties. The fourth way is service to the public interest: husband and wife should faithfully and in unison carry out their duties and obligations to the state and society, helping in the work of edification, education, and charity as much as they can.

III. The Way of Parents

There are ways that any parent should follow. First, parents should strive themselves to bring up their children and protect them by all good means until they become independent. Second, parents should exert themselves to educate their children in accord with their aptitudes and in a timely manner. Third, parents should let their children devote themselves to the public well-being, instead of fettering themselves to a family, so that they will unfailingly perform acts of justice and make efforts in the task of deliverance. Fourth, parents should not be concerned with their children's filial piety; they should render devotion and love to their children only as duty.

IV. The Way of Children

There are ways that any child should follow: one should be a truly and magnanimously filial child by practicing all of the "Articles for Requiting the Beneficence of Parents" detailed in the *Canon*.[3] If one obeys the unrighteous orders of parents only to keep their minds peaceful, one will be failing in the great filial piety by observing a petty one. If one is kept from serving the public in order to support one's parents, one is observing a petty filial piety, and failing the great one. If the parents are too old to judge right from wrong, the child should challenge them on their error with calmness and gentle words so that they can change their minds. If one cannot directly support one's parents owing to one's duty to the public, one should let one's brother or other relatives do the duty in place of oneself so that one can realize a truly great filial piety by fulfilling one's duty to the public. Even if one gets little parental love from one's parents, one ought only to follow the rightful way of children without complaints or resentment.

V. The Way of Siblings and Relatives

Siblings receive the same vital force from the parents, as they are born and raised; hence, it is the natural order of heavenly laws that the elder sibling ought to love the younger and the younger ought to respect the elder. Hence, siblings should share the pleasure of good things and worry together about bad things, but should not quarrel over gain and loss or envy a great fame of the other. The heaven-endowed affections should be kept by elder sibling by following the elder's way without minding the respect of the younger and by the younger by following the way of the young without minding the love of the elder. Relatives should move toward the way of blessings and happiness by taking special care of the members of their extended family while loving the public, correcting wrongs if there are any, helping one another to overcome any hardship, and encouraging one another to do the good.

It is not, however, the way of siblings and relatives to depend unjustly on others or to rely on the influence of others under the pretext of being siblings or relatives. Eternal harmony can only be enjoyed by siblings and relatives if one renders favors to siblings and relatives without seeking favors from them.

Chapter Four

Religious Faith

I. On Religious Faith

Religious faith is the fundamental requisite for the human spiritual life. For only if one keeps faith in truthful religion while living in the world can one maintain peace of mind in all the favorable and unfavorable or painful and pleasurable mental spheres. And thereby one can achieve great religious practice and public service with spiritual power based on a sound source, taking faith as the eternal guiding principle. Hence, there should be the correct way of faith, and one's faith can be a resourceful, effective, and eternal one only if one keeps the correct way of faith.

II. The Way of Faith

The first of the ways of faith is to choose and believe in truthful religion. One must choose the object of religious faith that is most perfect and truthful and the method of faith that is proper and realistic. For this one must understand that the object of religious worship can be perfect or partial, and truthful or untruthful, and the method of faith can be proper or improper, and realistic or superstitious. The second way of faith is to have faith in both other-power and self-power. Faith in other-power lies in believing in the object of faith with respect and reverence, while faith in self-power lies in one's inward faith and practice upon realizing that one's own nature is endowed with all principles and truth. The third is to keep one's faith and reverence in the source of one's religious faith, namely, sincerely to respect and revere the great teacher who elucidated the religious tenets, the doctrine, and the lineage of the dharma. One must also have faith in and reverence for all buddhas and sages of the three periods by realizing that doctrines of all religions are originated in the unitary fundamental truth. The fourth is to keep constancy of one's faith; one's faith and devotion should be constant throughout the eternal life without regressing or terminating in adverse conditions of any kind.

III. The Way of the Believer

Once one becomes a believer in a religion, one should follow the way of the believer, which the believer is required to observe. First, the believer should make every effort in the faith and practice in the religious doctrine. Second, the believer should make every effort to understand the order's functions and rites. Third, the believer should observe the rules and laws of the order and have proper faith in the leaders of the order. Fourth, the believer should help spread and proselytize the doctrine as much as one can. Fifth, the believer should fulfill the duty to make spiritual, physical, and material contributions for the maintenance and development of the order.

Chapter Five

Society

I. On Society

When people get together, a society is formed: a group of a few people, the nation, and the world all constitute societies, small or large. In any society there are differences: of men and women, the old and the young, the strong and the weak, and the wise and the foolish. Only by depending on various relations among its members can organizations of all sorts and ranks be formed. If people follow the right way in these complex relations, there will be peace and prosperity in the society; if not, the society will suffer from constant enmity and conflicts.

II. The Way of Men and Women

In a society there should first be the way that men and women ought to follow. The first is respect: men and women should respect each other's personality without neglecting the etiquette of mutual respect. The second is restraint: men and women should keep public morals sound by maintaining fairness and justice while associating with each other. The third is concession and cooperation: men and women should endeavor together to construct a vibrant society by showing the magnanimity of concession and the virtue of cooperation.

III. The Way of the Old and the Young

As an old saying goes, "Treat someone else's elders with deference, as you treat your own elder, and love someone else's child, as you love your own"; so it will be a beautiful social custom to treat elders with deference and to love the young.

Wherever adults interact with the young, there should be a way to be followed. First, the adult should thoroughly understand the new ethos that develops daily and should elevate the morals of the young with hope for a promising future. Second, the elder should treat the young in accord with their wisdom and their virtuous deeds without considering age difference.

There should also be the way to be followed when the young interact with their elders. First, the young should respect their elders for their rich experience and deep thought, treating them with faith and deference. Second, the young should give sympathy and comfort to helpless elderly people, protecting and supporting them as much as possible.

IV. The Way of the Strong and the Weak

In a society there are differences of rich and poor, noble and mean, high and low, first and last, learned and ignorant, and wise and deluded. All these differences can be summed up as differences between the strong and the weak. If the strong are disposed to oppress the weak and the weak are prone to rebel against the strong without following the way to be followed by the two, both will meet with calamity. And if the two follow the way of cooperation and mutual advancement in accordance with the way, the society will enjoy peace and prosperity. Hence, both the strong and the weak should constantly work together until both evolve into the strong in eternity by practicing the articles of "The Way of Progress for the Strong and the Weak" expounded in the *Canon*.[4]

V. The Way of the Public

When one lives in a society, one can be both a member of the society and in the position of facing the public outside that society. Therefore, a society cannot do without the way of the public.

The first of the ways to be followed with regard to the public is that one ought to honor public opinion that is generally regarded as right by the society. Hence, an individual should observe public law and honor public opinion. The second is for one to observe decorum: leaders and followers, men and women, the old and the young, the wise and the fool, and the strong and the weak should all observe the rules of propriety. The third way to be followed with regard to the public is for one to give primacy to the public interest: where self-interest conflicts with the public interest, the conflict should be resolved in favor of the public interest. One should work for the public interest as much as possible. One should also hold public properties dear and venerate those who devote themselves to the public's well-being. The fourth way is for one to be thoroughly awakened to, and put into practice, the principle of the way of the public: to value and benefit the public is to value and benefit oneself, and to serve the public interest is to carry out the fundamental duty of beneficence requital.[5]

Chapter Six

The Nation

I. On the Nation

In a nation it is inevitable that there be the ruler and the ruled, and the edifier and the edified. The rise and fall of the nation depends on whether the rulers and the ruled each fulfill or fail to fulfill their duties well, and the nation's prosperity and decline depends on whether the edifiers and the edified each fulfill or fail to fulfill their duties well.

Therefore, the leaders of the state should follow "the essentials of good leadership"[6] elucidated in the *Canon,* lest the nation's destiny and the future of the people become mired in difficulty. The nation will prosper and the citizens will all enjoy happiness only if leaders fulfill their duties.

II. Principles of Governing and Edification

There can be various ways of governing and edifying people, but their essential principles are as follows. The first is to govern and edify with the Way, which consists in letting people receive natural and spontaneous edification based on the principle of accomplishing all things without external interference. This can be done by letting all people be enlightened to their own nature which is the ultimate truth of the universe, and thereby letting them be naturally edified by the great way of neither birth nor death and the cause-effect responses. The second way of governing and edifying people is to bring to bear on them the moral influence of the leader's moral excellence. The leader should demonstrate virtuous influence by following the right Way ahead of the people, so that the people may be influenced by the virtue of the leader. The third way of governing and edifying people is to rule by means of laws. The people should be led by the enforcement of laws and the fair treatment of human affairs. In the past, one of these three ways was sufficient to govern and influence the people according to the times; in the future, people will be effectively governed or edified only if all three ways are applied together.

III. The Way of the People

The people are the sovereign of the nation. The nation will be prosperous and the people will be happy if the citizens of the nation fulfill their duties; if they do not, the nation will decline and the people will be unable to avoid misery.

The first way of the people is to obey national law; national law should be strictly protected and duly obeyed by the rulers and the ruled. The second way is for the people to fulfill their duties to the nation, and the duties of education, national revenue, and national defense. Diligent work should be done by the people. The third way is to do service to the nation within one's own occupation. One should contribute to national productivity and culture by making one's own living sound, applying the moral principle of mutual benefit and the spirit of public service. The fourth way is the way of unison and unity. The whole people should, for the sake of national development and interest, unite against greed and unfair profit on the part of any individual.

Chapter Seven

The World

I. On the World

The world is a grand household that takes all human beings as a unit; hence, while one fulfills one's duty to oneself, one's family, the society, and the nation, one should follow the way that a member of the household of fellow creatures of the world ought to follow.

While handling myriad affairs of the world, one should thoroughly understand that all the affairs of oneself, one's family, the society, the nation, and the world are but one affair, so one should handle what is small without losing sight of what is great. Accordingly, all human beings of the world should wish for, understand, and cooperate for world peace and the common benefit of the human race.

II. The Way of the Human Race

We human beings should cooperate in unison for the common well-being and prosperity. The essentials of the way of the human race are as follows. First, all the religionists of the world should come out from behind the walls of sects and cooperate to build one world, understanding that the fundamental principles of all religions are identical within one unitary household, propagating that fact and acting in accordance with it. Second, all races and all nations should, going beyond the boundaries of races and nations, cooperate to build one world with the understanding that all races and nations are of one family and one people, propagating that fact and acting in accordance with it. Third, all enterprises of the world should, breaking the prejudice of their own enterprise, cooperate to build one world with the understanding that all enterprises of the world are but one enterprise within one work place, propagating that fact and acting in accordance with it.

Chapter Eight

Rest

I. On Rest

There is the order of four seasons in heaven and earth; there are proper times in the human life span. Just as myriad things bud, grow, bear fruit, and are harvested when heaven and earth do not violate their orders, humanity can achieve perfection in life and the cycle of birth and death only if the proper times are not missed.

Therefore, Grand Master Sot'aesan said, "Except for special circumstances, one shall learn letters during childhood; learn principles of morality and exert oneself in the work of deliverance during the prime of life; then one shall enter a scenic and quiet place to train oneself in the great task of birth and death, severing attachments to the worldly things of love and desire during one's old age."[7] One should cultivate the foundation of personality with studies during one's youth, demonstrate the value of human life by engaging in an undertaking during the prime of life, and grow the sound spiritual seed of eternal life by spiritual cultivation during one's old age.

Hence, one needs adequate rest at the right time while doing business during one's youth; during one's old age one needs more concentrated rest. The spiritual and physical life in the eternal world will be without defect only if one follows the proper ways of rest and emancipation.

II. The Way of Rest

As one reaches the time for rest, one should realize the urgency and importance of the great task of birth and death and spiritual concentration, thus devoting oneself to the cultivation of spiritual concentration (samādhi) in daily life. The ways of rest are as follows. (1) Do not obstinately try to look at what is not in your line of vision. (2) Do not try to listen to what you do not hear. (3) Do not interfere with what is none of your concern even if you see or hear it. (4) Entrust your son, daughter, or other person in charge of matters of livelihood (food, clothes, and expenditure) and do not mind their treatment of you, whether it is generous or stingy. (5) Do not deplore the condition of old age, remembering the days of your youth. (6) Do not attach yourself to your property, your children, or other matters of your concern. (7) Free your mind from thoughts of resentment and regret of the past or present. (8) Do not be dragged by the right and the wrong of your past. (9) Practice seated meditation and the recitation of the name of Buddha (*Amitābha*) more diligently. (10) Continue the practice of timeless Zen.

III. The Way of Emancipation

There is no limit to worldly affairs and attachments to them. If one tries to handle worldly affairs with attachment, one will find no limit to attachment; if, however, one tries to handle them with an emancipated state of mind, one will experience neither suffering nor hindrance in all situations, whether favorable or unfavorable.

Therefore, in order to emancipate oneself from troublesome worldly affairs, one should first reflect on the origin of all truths and next apply the truth in all mental spheres. The ways of emancipation are as follows. The first is to emancipate oneself from the cycle of birth and death by reflecting thoroughly on the fundamental truth of no birth and no death and applying that truth to the situations of birth and death. The second is to emancipate oneself from the situations of suffering and pleasure by reflecting thoroughly on the principle of one's original nature, which is utterly devoid of suffering and pleasure, and applying that truth to the situations of suffering and pleasure. The third is to emancipate oneself from discriminations and gain or loss. For this, one must reflect thoroughly on the truth that the causal law of karmic retribution occurs in the realm that is originally devoid of discrimination and gain or loss. One must then apply this truth to situations of discriminations and gain or loss. Thus the statement in the Heart Sutra "by seeing clearly that the five aggregates (*skandha*) are all empty, thus securing his deliverance from all suffering and distress,"[8] is the general principle of emancipation.

Chapter Nine

Nirvāṇa

I. On Nirvāṇa

By nirvāṇa is meant clarity and calmness. By clarity is meant that our own nature is originally perfect, wanting nothing, strictly impartial, and unselfish; by calmness is meant that our own nature is originally undisturbed and devoid of afflictions and distress. Nirvāṇa thus means that one becomes enlightened to the principles of one's own nature and recovers original nature. If one masters the principle of original nature and enjoys blissful life without losing the light of original nature, one is said to have attained the bliss of nirvāṇa.

However, very few people attain to the true bliss of nirvāṇa and enjoy the perfect calmness of nirvāṇa; hence, in the Buddhist order the death of man is formally called nirvāṇa. Thus some people may attain true nirvāṇa by realizing fundamental truth, whereas many people may only attain a physical nirvāṇa, not entering into the true nirvāṇa and leaving the erroneous conditions to continue. Hence, practitioners of the Way should train themselves well in the way of nirvāṇa in daily life so that they may enjoy the bliss of nirvāṇa while in life and attain true nirvāṇa at the time of physical nirvāṇa.

II. The Way of Nirvāṇa

Concerning the way of nirvāṇa, Grand Master Sot'aesan has detailed the methods for close relatives to help send off the spirit of the one about to enter nirvāṇa and the ways to be taken by the one entering nirvāṇa. Hence, those ways should be followed.[9] At the last moment of one's life, one should leave with one clear thought and the strong aspiration to attain to buddhahood and to deliver sentient beings. The fundamental principle of nirvāṇa is well expressed by the statement "I aspire to become a buddha and deliver all sentient beings; and I take refuge in one pure thought."

III. The Way of Deliverance

To deliver is to guide and save by turning a wicked person into a good person and by lifting someone from a low to a high position. One can deliver oneself or one can be delivered by other-power. The first of the ways of deliverance is to establish an affinity with the Buddha. One should form ties with the Buddha since one cannot be delivered without having an affinity with the order of the correct religious doctrine. The second is to have a firm faith in truthful religion. One should have an integrated faith in other-power and self-power so that the two powers can function together. The third way is to attain enlightenment. One should be guided to make strong progress in the practice, with an integrated faith in other-power and self-power until one attains enlightenment, by the light of which one can ably follow the right course. The fourth way is to accumulate the merit of charitable work; ordinarily, one should render spiritual, physical, and material service to all sentient beings. If one gives generously to the work of deliverance, one will be admired and praised by many people for such beneficial virtue, so that one can attain deliverance without obstacles or hindrances wherever one goes. The fifth way is to keep the one mind pure. If one understands the merit and virtue of keeping the one mind pure and keeps it from being defiled by the five worldly desires, that merit and virtue will remain as beneficial enrichment, which will help one come and go freely through the going and coming of birth and death. In this way one can attain eternal deliverance.

Chapter Ten

An Outline

When we examine all things and events, we find that an effect has its cause and a cause leads to its effect. Past, present, and future are related in terms of causes, conditions, and effects, turning endlessly to form the limitless world. A thriving plant proves that it had a good seed, soil, and adequate applications of fertilizer. We can learn from this that, if we sow a good seed in good soil and apply fertilizer adequately, the plant will be healthy and vigorous. All beings sentient and insentient come to be, grow, and change following this principle. Therefore, if one lives a good life with the numinous consciousness as the seed, good affinities as the soil, and training in truth as the fertilizer, various merits and virtues will accrue accordingly. If the seed of the next life is nourished with the ways of rest and nirvāṇa, then eternal life will be ensured. Thus, all these principles work for the beginning, the middle, and the end of one's life, deciding one's destinies through numberless lives.

The most fundamental of all the principles underlying these various ways can be summarized by saying that to nourish and apply the pure, harmonious, benevolent, impartial, and just mind from before birth to nirvāṇa is the greatest law and treasure in the eternal world. That is why an ancient sage said, "One thought of pure mind is the enlightenment site (*bodhimaṇḍala*), and is superior to building seven-jeweled stupas as numerous as the sands of the Ganges. Those jeweled stupas will eventually be reduced to dust, but the one thought of pure mind produces right enlightenment."[10]

Part Two

The Dharma Words (Pŏbŏ)

I

Aspiration and Planning

1. Master Chŏngsan said, "At the ages of seven and eight I was troubled by a yearning to leave the ordinary way of humanity so that I could attain omniscience. For that purpose I sometimes left home in search of a prodigy; at some other times I prayed to the heaven. I wandered here and there for nine years in that way, but I have had no such troubles since I met Grand Master Sot'aesan. My only concern since that time was whether my mind was not like the empty sky, being attracted by selfish interests; whether the three great powers were deficient in me; or whether my heart for the public was limited. I was never attracted to or envious of scholarly achievements, skill, fame, or wealth." (CP 1:9)

2. The Master said, "While I was searching for truth in Kyŏngsang province during my youth, there appeared in my vision at times when I closed my eyes a great teacher with a perfect face and the scene of calm seashore. When I met Grand Master Sot'aesan at Yŏngsan, the perfect face I had had in my vision was none other than that of Grand Master Sot'aesan and the scene of the calm seashore with mountains and rivers was none other than Yŏngsan." (CP 1:6)

3. The Master said, "There are two things I rejoiced in my life. The first is that I was born in Korea; the second is that I met Grand Master Sot'aesan." He said further, "Everyone will undoubtedly feel gratitude toward Grand Master Sot'aesan; I have received one additional favor from him: that the Grand Master searched for me and then guided me." (CP 1:8)

4. While Master Chŏngsan was wandering in North Chŏlla province with the sole aim of searching for truth, he was met with great pleasure by Kim Haeun, who invited him to stay at her house in Hwahae-ri, Chŏngŭp county. While Kim Haeun was attending him with great respect, Grand Master Sot'aesan came to meet him there. Later, one of his disciples asked Master Chŏngsan, "We have heard that you performed various miracles before you met Grand Master Sot'aesan in Hwahae-ri. What kind of spiritual cultivation did you follow for that?" The Master answered, "It was because I did not know the right way at that time that such idle things happened; sometimes nothing but some strange traces occurred though I was not aware of them." (*CP* 1:7)

5. In July 1917 (WE 2), Grand Master Sot'aesan formed the first ten-member unit and filled eight positions with eight members, ordering the center position to be held temporarily by a proxy, saying, "For this position we shall invite a right person." He waited eagerly for the person and eventually welcomed Master Chŏngsan and appointed him to the center position. (*CP* 1:1)

6. At the last prayer meeting on August 21, 1919 (WE 4), Grand Master Sot'aesan asked his nine disciples whether they had any last words to leave behind before sacrificing their lives. Master Chŏngsan said, "We are going to sacrifice our lives with pleasure like this; however, we pray that you should not be troubled a bit by this matter of ours."[1] (*CP* 1:3)

7. The following month, Grand Master Sot'aesan sent Master Chŏngsan to Wŏlmyŏngam, on Mount Pyŏn, in Puan county, saying that the latter should not read any Buddhist scriptures, and Master Chŏngsan did not even look at the scripture stand. Again, after that, Grand Master Sot'aesan sent Master Chŏngsan to Mount Mandŏk, in Chinan county, saying that he should not stop off at Chŏnju, and he passed by Chŏnju without even looking at it. Later, Master Chŏngsan said to his disciples, "I have never given anything material to the Grand Master, however, I have nothing to regret as far as affection and righteousness are concerned. He was always in my mind and I have never been against his will on any matter." (*CP* 1:4)

8. The Master composed a verse at Wŏlmyŏngam, as follows: "The vital force of Earth floods the clouds of the high heavens; and the mind of Heaven penetrates to the whole moon." (*CP* 1:5)

9. A disciple asked, "Why did Grand Master Sot'aesan link his dharma affinity to the Buddha Śākyamuni? Ch'oe Suun and Kang Chŭngsan had no ancestral dharma affinity."[2] The Master answered, "Sot'aesan did so

because it was necessary for him to open a new religious order to edify the world with Buddha-dharma as its central doctrine." (*HH* 5:7)

10. The Master said, "Ever since I met Grand Master Sot'aesan I have never had any objection to his will; I have always followed his guidance. Though I was not sure about other things, I was quite sure of attaining buddhahood by this doctrine. If your wish is to attain buddhahood, practice only Grand Master Sot'aesan's teachings and follow my guidance. Before one knows the correct doctrine, one does ascetic and eccentric practices; you should follow only the correct doctrine once you find and know the right teacher." (*CP* 1:10)

11. Master Chŏngsan once took an oath, together with other followers, to Grand Master Sot'aesan: "It is fortunate that we have met this great order of the supreme Way and aimed to realize the great task of attaining buddhahood and delivering sentient beings. In order to accomplish this goal we, with a firm resolution and an unsurpassed aspiration, take an oath of the following articles. (1) Since we have consecrated our faith in Grand Master Sot'aesan's correct doctrine, we shall not have this one mind regress in any adverse and difficult situation. (2) Since we have found the correct way of the Threefold Practice, we shall never cease this practice in any temptation and hindrance. (3) Since we have learned the fundamental principle of the Fourfold Beneficence, we shall maintain the life of gratitude in any adverse condition and occasion for resentment. (4) Since we have learned the great cause of the selfless service to the public, we will devote ourselves to the public cause in any sort of hardship and privation." (*CP* 1:12)

12. At the funeral service for Grand Master Sot'aesan on June 1, 1943 (WE 28), Master Chŏngsan eulogized the holy spirit of Grand Master Sot'aesan. "When you taught and guided fools like us, you devoted yourself to the teaching with endless love, without minding all those troubles; thus you led our way out of the darkness with myriad expediencies and boundless doctrine. But for you, how could this ephemeral life have attained eternal life? But for you, how could this fool who could not distinguish primary from secondary know the causes of blessing and sin? But for you, how could I have awakened to the right way of humanity in this world full of temptations? But for you, how could I have aspired to find the way for realizing buddhahood in this endlessly confusing world? I have been indebted to you for your beneficence that was as endless as the limitless heaven and for your friendliness and kindness that were as deep as the sea." (*CP* 1:13)

13. At the inaugural ceremony of the head dharma master the next day, Master Chŏngsan told Grand Master Sot'aesan's holy spirit of his inauguration as follows: "Ever since I, your dharma son, embarked in this course of practice and public service under your guidance, I have always relied on you for all matters with utmost confidence in you, my dharma father. As you have suddenly passed away leaving me behind in the deepest sorrow, I am entirely lost, like a lamb that has lost its shepherd. However, I solemnly swear that the spirit you have breathed into me will remain as clear as ever in my mind, without ever changing through eternity. Though I feel greatly obliged in taking this office of head dharma master despite my being dull and ungifted, I shall do my best to learn and practice the spirit of the dharma father, in a very diffident manner, in accordance with the doctrine you have taught daily. Hence, I sincerely hope that I shall receive much help from fellow members of the order and the influence and protection of your holy spirit." (CP 1:14)

14. In June every year, Master Chŏngsan spoke to the holy spirit of Grand Master Sot'aesan as follows: "In general, the human spirit is cultivated by sound morality, and sound morality is elucidated by the enlightened sage, and the enlightened sage can radiate his light widely only if there is a religious order. Now the light of the enlightened sage is the lantern for the world and the spiritual life of all sentient beings. Alas! It had been almost three thousand years since the order of Śākyamuni Buddha dissolved, and it had been a long time since the traces of all the sages of the East and the West were obliterated. The world had consequently entered a critical situation, where true religious teachings had little influence and correct religious doctrine could hardly stand. At that critical moment Grand Master Sot'aesan came to rekindle the fading Buddha-sun and to set the dharma wheel turning again. We expect that this order will prosper greatly through eternity and that this doctrine will spread widely, helping the whole world transform into the paradise of Irwŏn and all the sentient beings into true sages." (CP 1:15)

15. In April every year, Master Chŏngsan solemnly celebrated the date of Grand Master Sot'aesan's enlightenment and the opening of the order with the following words: "This 28th day of April is the festive day on which Grand Master Sot'aesan of this order attained great enlightenment and opened a new religious order. Grand Master Sot'aesan, the new Buddha, came to this world with his great aspiration, which had consolidated over numberless eons, at a critical moment for this world, when the influence of the great morality was fading away. From when he

was a child, Grand Master Sot'aesan had had an extraordinary idea, to try to become awakened to the great truth of the universe, raising the great doubt by himself, practicing asceticism by himself, and attaining great enlightenment. Upon his great enlightenment he beat the great dharma drum and rolled the great dharma wheel in order to deliver sentient beings and to cure the world of ills. In order to open all those ways that were blocked in the past and unify all those laws (dharma) that were divided, Grand Master Sot'aesan revealed the great truth of Dharmakāya Buddha: Irwŏnsang, the origin of all beings of the universe and the unified body of myriad facts and principles. He showed the perfect ways of spiritual cultivation, inquiry into facts and principles, and heedful choice in karmic action; and he established the well-rounded moral principles for all sentient beings of the universe by elucidating the principles of the Fourfold Beneficence and the Four Essentials."[3] (CP 1:16)

16. In April 1953 (WE 38), Master Chŏngsan, setting up a monument to the memory of Grand Master Sot'aesan at Yŏngmowŏn, inscribed an epitaph on it, with the title "The Monument of Grand Master Sot'aesan, the Sacred Sage Who Was Enlightened to Irwŏn" as follows: "As the four seasons keep turning and the sun and the moon alternate in illuminating in the universe, myriad things attain the way of coming into being. As buddhas succeed one after another and sages transmit the laws from one to the other, sentient beings receive the beneficence of deliverance. This is the natural law of the universe. Ever since the Buddha Śākyamuni opened his order at Gṛdrakuta, his teachings passed the period of orthodoxy and vigor, and the period of semblance, finally reaching the period of decline and termination. The correct way was not followed in this last period, while the world was full of false doctrines; the spirit lost its power to the material, which was ruling the world. In consequence the bitter seas of misery where sentient beings were tormented got deeper and deeper; this was the occasion for Grand Master Sot'aesan, our savior, to come to this world again." Describing briefly Grand Master's career, Master Chŏngsan continued, "Sorely missed, Grand Master Sot'aesan, the model of all sages for eons, grew up in a remote and poor village. He comprehended the fundamental principle without any formal learning, and was enlightened to the great Way, the truth of Irwŏn, without a teacher's guidance. Though he lived in a world of great disorder and confusion, he did not hesitate to establish a religious order. When he met obstinate people, his ability to deliver them was unlimited. His appearance was like a high and steep mountain, yet his compassion was like the balmy spring breeze. He was

broadminded in handling daily affairs; yet he would solve the minutest problems of his disciples with genuine understanding and care. He reformed the doctrines of the past sages; yet the central tenets thereof were renovated for the better. He was curing the world of ills, yet he directed the world against obstinacy and intolerance. He unified all religions and moral doctrines into one; yet differences were made clearer. He applied the one truth to myriad things; yet the essence of the one truth was always manifested. Internally his spiritual life was based on a wondrous, supreme principle; externally he had a masterful comprehension of the details of matters and affairs. He opened the gate of a new religious order with the correct doctrine of the truth of Irwŏn for the entire world and eternity; he was the *tathāgata* that transforms into billions of *nirmāṇakāya,* and a complete concert composed of all sages." (*CP* 1:17)

17. A guest said, "Since your religious order is named Wŏnbulgyo (Won Buddhism), I would like to know the meaning of 'Wŏn.'" Master Chŏngsan said, "The metaphysical aspect of Wŏn (circle) is the realm that cannot be described in words or forms; however, the physical aspects of Wŏn are expressed in all beings of the universe. Thus, Wŏn is the origin of all Dharmas and the reality of all dharmas. Therefore, all religious doctrines, though they are expressed in various ways, are nothing but the truth of Wŏn and there is no other dharma." The guest asked, "If Wŏn has such a great and perfect meaning, wouldn't it be better to call your order Wŏndo[4] or Wŏn'gyo[5] for the purpose of including all religious doctrines in it? Although Buddhism is an old and great religion, the world still suspects that it has only a partial truth. Why do you not think this matter over?" The Master said, "The term *buddha* means enlightenment and mind. The truth of Wŏn may be so perfect as to include all dharmas; however, it will be just an empty principle if there is no mind that is enlightened to it. Thus, the two terms 'Wŏn' and 'pul' (buddha) are inseparably related to each other, referring to an identical truth. The fundamental doctrine of the Buddha's teaching was not originally partial; however, because of the different systems of propagation it has been misunderstood as partial. Hence, a renovation of the propagation system will clearly reveal the true face of Buddha-dharma in the world." (*CP* 4:1)

18. The guest asked, "What do you think of the development plan of your religious order?" The Master said, "As a sage in the past said,[6] things have roots and branches, and human affairs should be handled in the right order. If we prepare for the future with insight into what is first and what is last, we expect that this religious order will naturally grow." The guest

asked, "What do you think should be done first and what next?" The Master said, "The first thing to do is to prepare correct materials for religious edification. The second is to educate many men and women of ability. The third is to attain the economic power necessary for various enterprises; however, things are not going as I wish because of the troubled times of the country." The guest asked, "The leaders of a certain religion are so eager to spread their gospel that they proselytize in the street. Do you not do anything like that in your order?" The Master said, "We may need some adequate propagation, but we haven't gone as far as proselytizing in the street." The guest asked, "If you are going to propagate your religion, wouldn't it be better to do it more positively?" The Master said, "Just as a shop grows and develops naturally if the shopkeeper provides good merchandise and benefits customers, a religious teaching will spread if the religion, with the adequate preparation of edification materials, does not harm but benefits the public. Until now formal propagation has been the central force of development; I believe, however, that, from now on, real religious activities will be the central force of development." (*CP* 4:2)

19. At the inaugural meeting of the Diamond Association (*Kŭmgangdan*)[7] in 1946 (WE 31), the Master delivered the following address: "Your association is named Diamond Association, the meaning of which is profound. I hope that you do not forget the two characters *kŭm-kang* (diamond), so that you bring about good results of diamond (*kŭmgang*). Internally you should discover your original diamond nature. Once you have discovered your diamond nature, you should establish the clear and pure mind by removing delusive thoughts, just as a goldsmith tempers gold to remove impure elements from it. Just as the goldsmith makes good use of the pure gold, you should use your mind well in relevant situations to be a sage of perfect conduct. Externally this association should be based on fidelity and be united as firmly as diamond. Any member who tends to violate the precepts should be warned and admonished by the power of the association so that all members should develop figures like pure gold. As the power of the association expands, the power of its public service should be expanded, so that Grand Master Sot'aesan's true doctrine can be propagated widely and that the tasks we inherited from our forebears' unfinished work can be taken over forever. In this way the light of the association will shine clearly in the world like that of diamond." (*CP* 4:3)

20. At the first graduation ceremony of Yuil Institute in April 1949 (WE 34), the Master delivered the following address: "I am sorry that

you haven't received a satisfactory and sufficient education but have gone through hardships for the past three years. However, you should reflect on what this order has been doing in the course of its establishment. You may recall the hardships your forebears went through. None of them could get a three-month Zen retreat, let alone three-year education, as they had to work on the first embankment at Yŏngsan,[8] on such chores as running a charcoal business, a confectionery business, farming, stock raising, and managing orchards and pharmacies. Some of them had to work at a silk mill, others at a rubber factory. It seems inevitable for a religious order to follow a difficult course like this at its founding stage; and it is because of this that our forebears are revered. The life of a religion is faith; and the motivating power of an enterprise is altruistic spirit for the public. If you are equipped with these two, your future will be bright even if your learning is short. Hence, you should feel yourselves insufficient in these two more than anything else, and do your best to attain these two things more than anything else. Now you have finished the school courses and truly started a great learning. The great learning lies in learning while working and working while learning. Do not forget even for one moment that every word you utter and every move you make will have great consequence for Yuil Institute and the enterprises of this order. I hope that you will exert yourselves in your practice, through work based on faith and public spirit so that you may carry out Buddha's practice and Buddha's enterprise perfectly." (CP 4:6)

21. Publishing the *Wŏn'gwang* in May 1949 (WE 34), the Master wrote an aphorism: "The light of Irwŏn illumines the ten directions." He then set forth an essential point: "Whatever is truthful revives eventually, no matter how hard one tries to destroy it; and whatever is untrue perishes eventually, no matter how hard it tries to survive." (CP 4:7)

22. A disciple asked, "The organ and schools of our order carry the name Wŏn'gwang. What is its meaning?" The Master answered, "Though we generally use the name Wŏn'gwang so that the great truth of Irwŏn can be illumined, there are profound principles contained in the two words *wŏn* and *kwang*. *Wŏn*, being the ultimate essence of Irwŏn, refers to the noumenal nature of all beings and all dharmas, and *kwang* means the emanation of all beings and all dharmas from *wŏn*. *Wŏn* is the substance and *kwang* is the function, in which all dharmas are included. Do not forget this meaning and polish it up so that you can think, speak, and act in accordance with Wŏn'gwang. The development of our order will lie therein." (CP 4:8)

23. At the prize-awarding ceremony for those who carried out conversion duty in 1954 (WE 39), the Master delivered the following congratulatory address: "It is one of the sacred duties of the Won Buddhist to convert at least nine people to this order so that they can be blessed in the beneficence of Grand Master Sot'aesan's teaching. When Grand Master Sot'aesan first opened the gate of this order, he prepared its ground by organizing a unit of nine disciples and said, 'If you propagate the doctrine by converting more than nine people to this order, then the doctrine will spread throughout the world in the near future.' Since this method of propagation is like a stream of water originating from a spring that flows in all directions through branch streams, benefiting all living beings, Grand Master Sot'aesan called conversion duty 'the duty of origin' and encouraged his disciples to practice it. Hence, every one of us should have at least nine people find the way of faith in this teaching and, with a sense of duty as the origin, encourage them to have the merit of their practice and public service reach wide. This amounts to a great meritorious establishment in the creation of a supreme religious order; and if a great sage or a great benefactor comes out of them, the merit of being the origin will be great. Performing a ceremony and awarding prizes is nothing but a means to promote the practice. You should know that real and greater merits accumulate without being revealed." (*CP* 4:11)

24. At the opening ceremony of the Zen retreat for ministers (*kyomu*), the Master delivered the following instruction: "Those who edify and regulate people must do so knowing that there are three ways of edifying individuals, families, societies, the nation, or the world. The first is to regulate by morality and religious doctrine; the second is to regulate by the influence of virtue; and the third is to regulate by laws. I intend to explicate these three ways of edifying in the *Canon of the World* (*Sejŏn*). If this threefold edification is integrated, a perfect world can be built; if it is not, the world will be defective. Hence, you should understand these three ways clearly, and base the application of the teaching to individuals, families, societies, the nation, and the world on the integration of the three ways. If you do so, you will be good leaders of our immeasurable deliverance work." (*CP* 4:16)

25. A minister (*kyomu*) asked, "Tell us in detail how these three ways can be applied for the task of edification at local temples. The Master said, "To edify by moral and religious principles is to edify people by helping them understand the fundamental principles of the doctrine and to have faith in it. In order to do so, teachers should have a deep faith and

a clear awakening in the principle of the Dharmakāya Buddha and Grand Master Sot'aesan's doctrine before they can lead the laity's faith and practice or direct people's devotion and public service to what is fundamental. To edify by the influence of virtue is to edify people by kindheartedness and moral influence; the teacher must understand public sentiment and be attentive to each individual, down to the minute details, bringing the public around oneself for edification. To edify by governing is to edify people by laws and expedience. The teacher should be well versed in the general trends of the world and examine the general tendency of the laity so that the teaching is consistent with rules and regulations. Thus, a good teacher of the dharma (doctrine), having a well-rounded mind, should be able to edify people by various means." (CP 4:17)

26. At the inauguration ceremony for his third term as head dharma master (chongbŏpsa) in April 1959 (WE 44), the Master gave this speech: "It has been seventeen years since I took on the heavy responsibility to represent this order in the greatest grief at Grand Master Sot'aesan's nirvāṇa. There has been no major fault in my leading the order, which I attribute to the unceasing protection of the Dharmakāya Buddha, the Fourfold Beneficence, the hidden guidance, and protection of the sacred spirits of Grand Master Sot'aesan and our forebears. I am also heavily indebted to the wholehearted devotion of all members of the headquarters, branch temples, and various business sectors, and to the cooperation and help of men and women members of the laity. The growth of the order has been notable so that the society and the nation have become aware of who we are; and the ground for overseas missions is gradually consolidating. At this point of the history of the order, I am unable to decline your request and hence am much obliged to assume this new term. I believe that there will be guidance and protection from the Dharmakāya Buddha and the sacred spirit of Grand Master Sot'aesan and that the wholehearted cooperation and help of fellow members of the order will continue. Thus, I solemnly swear that I will do my very best to carry out this great responsibility. I would like to commemorate this day with a few words: 'Let us become great cosmopolitans,' and I would like to renew our original vow once again together with you." (CP 4:22)

27. The Master sent an admonitory note to a staff meeting: "The headquarters, like the human heart, controls all the branch temples, like limbs. Hence it is your dutiful function in the headquarters to take good care of them all impartially, regardless of closeness or remoteness and friendliness or estrangement, as if they were your limbs." (CP 4:32)

28. The Master wrote four lines for Kim Taegŏ:[9] "If the name is great but the reality is small, then there will be nothing to show in the end. Only real ability wins the final victory." He said, "An individual's real ability is threefold: to cultivate the power of spiritual concentration (samādhi); to inquire into and drill the truth (prajñā); and to keep the precepts (śīla). The ability of the order is also threefold: to put the canonical texts in good order; to cultivate clergy; and to manage the order's finances. If the order and its leaders have these abilities ready, and there is internal harmony and an increase of outside laity, the order will grow accordingly." (CP 4:33)

29. A disciple asked, "What is the meaning of the saying that the era of Maitreya Buddha is approaching?" The Master answered, "By 'Maitreya' is meant 'diligence and true heartedness.' Being diligent, people will live on self-power instead of depending on others. In the past people tried to receive awesome power by praying to the Buddha, God, or divine spirits and did not know about self-power in religious faith. In the secular world, too, people had a tendency to live depending on other-power without making efforts of their own, but in the future people will upon enlightenment have faith in self-power and try to live with the spirit of benefiting others in spirit, body, and matter. By 'true-heartedness' is meant the attitude of life that insists on giving up empty formalities and advocating substance. In the past the essential doctrines and rituals of a religion contained too much of solemnity, and in the secular world, there were too much bluster and trickery in the conduct of life; however, in the future, people will live their lives with a truthful, trustworthy, and impartial spirit. Hence, you should be a person who can attain the new energy of Maitreya Buddha era by being diligent and true-hearted in all circumstances." (HH 5:9)

30. The Master said, "The era of the aristocratic class and the era of the rich are gone, and now is the era of external splendor. In the near future, a new era will arrive, in which people value the Way and regard virtue as wealth and the common weal as one's own glory." (HH 6:7)

31. The Master said, "Śākyamuni Buddha's life was described in 'The Eight Aspects of the Buddha's Life'; Grand Master Sot'aesan's life should be described in 'The Ten Aspects of Grand Master Sot'aesan's Life.' They are (1) the aspect of raising questions while looking at the sky, (2) the aspect of praying on the Sambat hill, (3) the aspect of ascetic practice in search of a right teacher, (4) the aspect of deep meditation by a river, (5) the aspect of great enlightenment at Norumok, (6) the aspect of constructing an embankment at Yŏngsan, (7) the aspect of receiving dharma

authentication from heaven and earth through the 'bloody prints left by clean thumbs,' (8) the aspect of the formulation of the doctrine at Mount Pongnae, (9) the aspect of spreading of the doctrine at Sinyong, and (10) the aspect of entering nirvāṇa in 1943." (*CP* 1:18)

32. The Master made an admonitory speech to the devotees and wrote, "Make your aspiration and planning penetrate the whole universe, and keep your truthfulness consistently through all ages." He explained his advice thus, "Success cannot be great unless the aspiration and planning are great. A great task cannot be accomplished unless one keeps one's devotion and effort consistent until the aspiration is realized." (*CP* 12:1)

33. The Master said, "A harsh history of the afflictions that people have suffered for righteous cause is illustrious for all ages; a history of indulgence in unrighteous pleasure, on the other hand, leaves only shame for all ages. Jesus Christ suffered the punishment of crucifixion for all people, and I Ch'adon (d. 528) sacrificed his own life in order to spread the gospel of the Buddha and delivered sentient beings of evil karma with miracles. When we reflect that these sages did not spare even their lives for the public cause, what need is there to mention other examples of ascetic practice and austerity? These can indeed be the exemplars of public spirit for all ages." (*CP* 12:4)

34. The Master said, "The spirit of the following three people are examples of public spirit: the spirit of Admiral Yi Sunsin (1545–1598), who was content with his lot and kept a peaceful state of mind, had no resentment when he was ignored by his superiors, and was concerned only with the national affairs without minding about his status; the spirit of the prime minister Lin Xiangru of Zhao, who avoided his political rival for the sake of his state though people regarded him as a coward for it; and the spirit of the prime minister Hwang Hŭi (1363–1452), who assumed a government position for the sake of the masses though he was falsely accused of being a man of no principle." (*CP* 12:5)

35. The Master said, "To collect the mind divided into thousands of branches and tens of thousands of leaves into one mind by reflecting them on one's original nature is to attain the unity of mind. To help one's family live happily and peacefully by uniting their mind is the unity of the family. To work in concert, talking without reservation and sharing the fate of life and death with one's dharma comrades, is the unity of dharma comrades. To create a financial foundation for the public inter- est by preventing waste on such commodities as clothing and food and encouraging thrift and diligence is the unity of votive offering. To real- ize the unity of the world by edifying the human race with the correct

dharma of supreme truth is the unity of the world. Personality will be improved by the unity of mind, and a family will prosper by the unity of family. An organization will develop by the unity of comrades, and an organization for the public interest will be created by the unity of votive offering. And the world will make a great improvement by the unity of the human race." (*CP* 12:34)

36. The Master said, "When you make silent confessions, always pray for the whole world, for your comrades, and for all people under heaven. Only if you proceed in your practice by regarding the suffering and happiness of all people and comrades as your own, will you be connected through moral energy to them, all thus being continuously interpenetrated, one with the other, so that you will achieve great success." (*CP* 12:40)

37. The Master said, "You should not, if you are pulled by selfish desires, forget your great original vow. Concerning your practice, if you aspire to become a particular figure by following a particular practice, your practice is infected with selfishness; hence, it will not be a great practice. If you calculate the merit of public service from the point of view of your own reward, you will never achieve true public service. Great practice can only be done if your practice is based on the ground of no-self and no-desire from the very beginning of the aspiration, and great public service can only be accomplished if your public service is rendered on the ground of extreme fairness and unselfishness." (*CP* 12:44)

38. The Master said, "It has been said since ancient times that the wielding of power is followed by grudges and danger. A religion, too, starts being infected with ills if it relies on power or wields power by misapplying its doctrine. Hence, you, the leaders of this order, strive to maintain this order eternally free of ills by not wielding power or being arrogant as the order's influence grows more and more prominent, by being humble as you become increasingly knowledgeable, and by being modest as you ascend to a higher position. In the original nature there are no differences of high and low, or noble and humble." (*CP* 12:58)

39. The Master said, "The leader's conduct should contain the following four essentials. First, to manage all affairs fairly and honestly without violating any rules and regulations or being partial out of friendliness and estrangement. Second, to manage all affairs based on the wider view, by examining the whole instead of the small self, and the far without being bound by what is near. Third, to manage all affairs harmoniously and generously, based on humanity and justice. And, fourth, to manage all affairs with clear and constant accounting." (*CP* 12:62)

II

Taking Care of the Fundamentals

1. Master Chŏngsan said, "Only if you take a good care of the fundamentals of whatever you do, will its branches come out right. The fundamental of the six roots is the mind, and the fundamental of the mind is self-nature. The foundation of the conduct of life is trust, while power, fame, and avarice are branches." (*CP* 9:1)

2. The Master said, "The most fundamental part of wisdom is to know the root and branches of the mind, to know how to cultivate the mind, and to know how to use the mind well. Thus it is said in a sūtra, 'If one wishes to know all the facts of the three periods, one should know that all the facts of the universe (*dharmadhātu*) are made of the mind.'"[10] (*CP* 9:2)

3. The Master said, "You should make adequate preparation in advance for any task by figuring out its root and branches and first and last. Focus your energies on what is fundamental from the viewpoint of eternity, without being fettered by concerns of immediate gain or loss. Common people live their lives such that they end up taking care of their bodies without knowing how to take care of their mind, which is fundamental. How hidebound that is!" (*CP* 9:3)

4. A student asked, "Wouldn't a bowl of rice be more important than dharma to a person starving to death?" The Master said, "If we consider the primary and the secondary importance of this matter, dharma is primary and a bowl of rice secondary. For the maintenance of the body, a bowl of rice is primary and dharma secondary. Hence, the starving person should be given a bowl of rice first. However, you must take the

spirit as the root of your daily living and earn clothing, food, and shelter with cultivation, inquiry, and heedful choice."[11] (*CP* 9:4)

5. The Master said, "Take the fundamental dharma as the standard, and make good use of material things, distinguishing what should be done first and what last, according to the occasion. What is great is not the possession of material things but the creative transformation of the mind." (*CP* 9:5)

6. A student asked, "What kind of practice is the most fundamental practice in the world?" The Master answered, "Mind cultivation is the most fundamental, because mind cultivation includes all other practices. For without mind cultivation, all other practices will not make right applications." The student asked again, "What kind of skill is the most fundamental skill in the world?" The Master answered, "The skill to maintain harmony among people is the most fundamental. For the skill to be in harmony with others controls all other skills and all other skills cannot be applied without it." (*CP* 9:6)

7. The Master said, "The ground of progress is education, and the fundamental of all education is the moral education. All other learning and skills are useful for progress, but they should be based on truth and public spirit if they are to benefit the world." (*CP* 9:7)

8. A student asked, "What is the foundation of moral education?" The Master answered, "The cultivation of the spirit to return the fundamental beneficence and the requital of beneficence are the foundation of moral education. The great fortune of the New World will be endowed only on a society where moral education is well done." (*CP* 9:8)

9. The Master said, "Just as a fruit tree grows well and bears good fruit only if its roots are well fertilized, a person, whose roots are the mind, can form a good personality only if one strives in cultivation of the mind. How can one hope for the fruit of wisdom and blessing without mind cultivation?" (*CP* 9:9)

10. The Master said, "What we seek in the world is simply blessings and wisdom. The world is the field of blessings, the universe is the mass of truth, and we are endowed with the elements for receiving blessings and wisdom like the Buddha. Since we do not receive blessings and wisdom if we do not make the effort to attain them, who would bar us from receiving them if we did make the effort to receive them? However, if you do not receive blessings and wisdom no matter how hard you try, it is because you do so against truth. If we want to receive them, we must seek after them, and we must do so in accord with truth." (*CP* 9:10)

11. The Master said, "A well does not dry up because it is fed by a spring, and a tree does not wither because of its root. Likewise, the present enjoyment of blessings and happiness will not dry up only if the seeds for the reward of virtue are hidden in the nature of mind. Hence, you must check to see what kinds of buds are sprouting in your mind, and you must then strive to grow the good buds. The seeds for the reward of virtue are faith, public spirit, and compassion." (CP 9:11)

12. The Master said, "If you wish to be blessed, grow the buds of blessing in the formless mind; if you do not like to suffer punishment, eradicate the roots of sin from the formless mind. Taking good care of someone only in the mind makes seeds for the reward of virtue." (CP 9:12)

13. The Master said, "Just as it is important for a surveyor to ascertain the cardinal point first, it is important for us practitioners to ascertain the cardinal point of practice and public service. Find the cardinal point of practice in mind cultivation, and that of deliverance in the deliverance of oneself. However, this does not mean that you deliver others only after you have finished your own deliverance. Rather, it means that you study all learning on the basis of mind cultivation and work on the deliverance mission while working on the deliverance of your own self." (CP 9:13)

14. While ordering the relief campaign for war victims after the liberation of Korea, the Master said, "The relief campaign has the dual significance of relief and deliverance. For the war victims among our compatriots the relief task is urgent, however, our mission should not end with it; we should do it together with the task of deliverance. How could we bring about true happiness and peace with material prosperity and armed forces alone? True happiness and peace can be brought about only if the mind-ground is well cultivated. Since the greatest of all enterprises of the world is the religious mission, we must carry out the dual task of relief and deliverance together." (CP 9:14)

15. The Master said, "There are many ways to benefit others, but none will surpass what helps one develop a right aspiration; and there are many ways to harm others, but none will surpass what causes one to develop an evil aspiration. For aspiration is the seed of good or evil for the person's eternal life." (CP 9:15)

16. The Master said, "The establishment of a local temple may seem easy, but it cannot be done unless there are many blessed people in that district. The merit of establishing a temple is much greater than that of any material donation. It is good to give to starving people in a year of famine; it will be a greater merit to establish an industry for many people

to depend on for living. It will be a great merit to give material help to them once. But wouldn't it be a greater merit to establish a school for many talented youths to learn, or to provide myriad people with convenience by the result of an eminent research? Better still! What could be a greater merit than establishing a religious temple where many people are edified on morality so as to be good human beings?" (CP 9:16)

17. The Master said, "Buddhas and bodhisattvas take the empty dharma realm of heaven and earth as their own household and sow the seeds of blessings and stipends endlessly in the eternal life. You may designate many things as great. But what could be greater than the Buddha's boundless aspiration? You may name many things as vast, but what could be vaster than the Buddha's limitless storeroom?" (CP 9:17)

18. The Master said, "There are three ways to practice charity. The first is spiritual charity. That is, to do things for the good of others, to aspire to save the world, to pray for the benefit of others, and to treat others with sincerity. The second is charitable work by action, that is, to practice charity by the function of one's six sense organs, by giving one's property, and by benefiting others. The third is the charity of dharma, that is, to practice charity by inheriting the wisdom-life of the true law and rolling its dharma wheel throughout the universe for the three time-periods, and to help a religious order develop greatly by making spiritual, physical, and material contributions. This last charitable deed is the most fundamental merits and virtue." (CP 9:18)

19. The Master said, "It is mainly for one thing, namely, mind cultivation, that we live in this precinct of the enlightenment site (bodhimaṇḍala). While we try to do mind cultivation, we must also provide for clothing and food, and for this purpose, we have to work together, do public service, and establish various organizations. However, there are some practitioners that forget the fundamental task, losing their mind to worldly desires and worldly vanities. How can I not worry about those who mistake the means for the end?" (CP 9:19)

20. The Master said to the students, "Although practitioners live together in the precinct of the enlightenment site, the degree to which one's mind is pulled varies from one to another. There are some whose thought and aspirations are concentrated on this practice and public service. Some practitioners' minds are pulled by some other things but return upon reflection on their original vows. Some practitioners have their minds pulled considerably but take care of their duty after listening to their mentor or comrades. There are some whose conduct reveals that

their minds are being pulled, but who do not reflect on their minds even when they are admonished by their mentor and comrades, ruining their way ahead. Reflect on your mind to see which level you are on, so that you may not have regrets in the eternal world." (*CP* 9:20)

21. The Master said, "When I see someone who, residing in this precinct, loses the aspiration for mind cultivation altogether, I feel sorry for that person, seeing how thick the past karma layers must have been. If one considers the principle of birth and death and that of transgression and blessings, one should be overtaken by awe. When I see someone living with no reflection on these principles, I only feel pity for that person." (*CP* 9:21)

22. The Master said, "When a thought occurs to your mind, check it to see whether it is a public or private affair and whether it is right or wrong, so that you can develop your thought to be fair and just from the very beginning. There is a saying 'Through a needle's hole enters an ox's wind.'[12] As soon as an evil thought takes place in the innermost recesses of the heart, you should reflect on your original vow in order to correct your mind, so that you may have nothing to regret. If you idle away your time in the precinct of Buddhist practice without earnest practice for fear of losing face, you will inevitably become corrupted and turn your back on the Buddha's order in your next life, although you may make it through this life. Transgression committed in the public order is repaid much more severely than that committed in one's private household. Hence, you ought to awaken from any misapprehension, so that you may have nothing to regret in eternity. One mind with which to reflect on your original vows is the mind that comes close to the Buddha; the practitioner should only think of the Way and be envious only of the Buddha." (*CP* 9:22)

23. The Master said, "While residing in the precinct of the enlightenment site, you must distinguish the host mind from the guest mind. Now, what is our host mind? Do we reside here to gain money, power, fame, or any other pleasures? No: we live in common in this precinct of the enlightenment site, with the sole end to attain to buddhahood and deliver sentient beings. Hence, the aspiration to attain to buddhahood is the host mind, and the aspiration to deliver sentient beings is the host mind. If we lose our host mind, and are gripped by the guest mind, putting first what should be last, what will become of our future? Thus, the foundation of our goal will be solid only if we always keep our host mind firm, making good use of the guest mind but not letting the guest mind rule the host mind." (*CP* 9:23)

24. The Master said, "The vow to attain to buddhahood and deliver sentient beings is the highest and greatest of all wishes of humankind, and the place where people reside in common in order to attain to buddhahood and deliver sentient beings is the most sacred and precious place of the world. How heavy our duty is, and how noble our living here is! However, human mind is such that it easily relaxes as time passes, or it is easily disturbed in adverse mental spheres. At this time, when human mind changes easily due to the public unrest and the complications of daily living, you are in danger of finding your duty buried and forgotten, even in this precinct of the order, if you are off guard even for a moment. Hence, always be heedful to reflect on your original goal as you pass the time and whenever you meet with any adverse mental spheres. As your practice becomes mature, after a long time, your goal will eventually be achieved of itself with no trouble, reflecting on your original aspiration. When our practice matures, the whole world will transform into the buddha land." (CP 9:24)

25. The Master said, "The dawn and night prayers are the ritual in which we celebrate our own roots, and the time in which we take care of our mind. Hence, you ought to perform the ritual with your spirit refreshed, reflecting on your original vow if you become negligent because of mental and physical fatigue. Seated meditation at dawn is a good time to see our authentic nature; hence, practice seated meditation even if only for a short while, reflecting on your original goal if you feel negligent because of languor, unless you suffer from illness. The regular dharma meeting and evening dharma meeting are the special opportunities to provide our spirit with dharma food. Hence, you ought to attend them with endless devotion, reflecting on your original goal if you feel negligent because you are enslaved by a complicated life. Precepts are the life of a practitioner and the ladder for attaining to buddhahood. Hence, you ought to observe all the precepts without fail, reflecting on your original vow if you feel negligent due to the foolish demands of mind and body. Scriptures are the bright lanterns leading us to our goal; hence, exert yourselves by studying them, reflecting on your original goal if you feel negligent because you have lost time to other things."[13] (CP 9:25)

26. The Master continued, "The articles of the order's constitution are the lifeline that guides the people. Hence, you ought to protect the order's laws as you do your own life, reflecting on your original goal if you feel like violating any of them because of a personal opinion or bias. Since we are gathered here not for individual fame and right but for the order's fame and right as our common glory, you ought to promote also

the public fame and right, reflecting on your original goal if any wicked thought rises in you for personal fame and right. We are gathered here not to provide for our personal ease and satisfy our greed but to sacrifice ourselves for the whole community. Hence, you should not compromise your vow of selfless service, reflecting on the original goal if the stupid thought occurs to you to provide for your personal ease and satisfy your greed, neglecting the safety and interest of the general public. We are gathered here not to pursue the common learning but to learn and teach morality, the root of all other learning. Hence, you ought to reflect on your original goal not to lose sight of the order of primary and secondary if you are inclined to the arcane scriptures from outside the order, slighting the fundamental canon of morality. We are gathered here not to pursue a splendid worldly life with its momentary human pleasures but to obtain serene and eternal spiritual bliss. Hence, you, reflecting on your original goal, should keep your great plan from falling into oblivion if you are attracted to the swirling seas of greed and thereby idle thoughts arise in your mind, which are useless to the life of a true practitioner." (*CP* 9:26)

27. The Master continued, saying, "Together with the practice of reflection on our goal, we must also practice reflection on our self-nature (*svabhāva*). Although the true practice of reflection on self-nature can only be done by seeing into self-nature, a truly faithful one, even if one has not yet seen into self-nature, can practice reflection on self-nature by relying on the Buddha's teaching. The main principle is to search for the precepts (*śīla*), concentration (*samādhi*), and wisdom (*prajñā*) of self-nature in myriad mental spheres, taking the Essentials of Daily Practice as the standard, as spelled out in the *Canon*.[14] I will illustrate the main point with some examples. If you occasionally experience an unfair thought on a matter because you are making a biased discrimination between yourself and others, reflect on your self-nature and think of the realm of Irwŏn that is by origin devoid of any discrimination between self and others. If you, at times, have a mind to look down upon your junior with thoughts of discrimination, think of the realm of equality that is devoid of discrimination by reflecting on your self-nature. If you, at times, cannot maintain spiritual stability because of burning evil passions, think of the pure realm devoid of evil passions by reflecting on your self-nature. If you, at times, experience an excessive attachment because you have yielded to the attachment of hatred and love, think of the realm of highest good devoid of hatred and love by reflecting on the self-nature. If you, at times, find it difficult to cut off the desire for gain because you

are attached to existence, think of the realm of true emptiness (*chin'gong*) by reflecting on your self-nature. If you, at times, give rise to a nihilistic thought, being attached to nonexistence, think of the realm of wondrous existence (*myoyu*) by reflecting on your self-nature. If you, at times, feel attached to life and fear of death confronting an occasion of life and death, think of the realm of Dharmakāya that is devoid of arising and ceasing, by reflecting on your self-nature. If you, at times, cannot adapt yourself to ordinary society because a false notion of dharma has arisen in your mind, think of the realm of no false notion by reflecting on your self-nature. If you practice like this, your mental function will gradually be unified with original self-nature regardless of whether you have seen into self-nature. And if you keep this practice up for a long time, you will always be unified with self-nature at any place, and eventually you will be brightly enlightened to the truth of self-nature, and the light of self-nature will naturally appear. This is the realm of the Buddha and the functioning of the sage." (*CP* 9:27)

28. The Master said, "In the physical life, there are four kinds of occupation, namely, scholar-official, farmer, artisan, and tradesman. Analogously, there are four kinds of occupation in the spiritual life. Of all the scholar-officials, the one who learns and teaches the Way and its virtue (*todŏk*) is the best scholar-official. Of all kinds of farming, the farming of humans that raises talented men and women is the best farming. Of all factories, the mental factory that remodels the mind is the best factory. Of all trades, the trade of dharma that manufactures correct dharma and spreads it into the world is the best trade." (*CP* 9:28)

29. The Master said, "Material things are no more than auxiliaries to our daily living. What cannot be done without to the end is our mind. Hence, we should keep accumulating the three great powers (cultivation, inquiry, and heedful choice) in our mind and prepare for the eternal world always ahead of time." (*CP* 9:29)

30. The Master said, "Instead of exerting yourselves to fill up your store of material things, exert yourselves to fill up your store of immaterial things in the realm of truth. If a practitioner is avaricious in the secular world and attached to it, that desire for the secular world may, with avarice as the seed, be fulfilled in the next life, but one's practice will be dimmed and one will be easily led astray by a slight error." (*CP* 9:30)

31. The Master said, "People in the secular world regard gold, silver, and ornaments as the most precious treasures; however, all those things with forms are devoid of reality. There are two kinds of true treasure for

human beings. One is our true mind which, being eternally immortal through innumerable lives in the eternal world, becomes the true self. The other is the correct dharma, which helps us find our true mind and thereby attain blessings and wisdom. Our eternal true treasures are the true mind and the correct dharma." (*CP* 9:31)

32. The Master wrote to a student, "There is a great treasure that can be compared neither with jade nor with gold. What sort of a treasure is it? It is the virtue that one has cultivated through one's whole life and the pure mind at one's last moment." (*CP* 9:32)

33. The Master said, "Buddha-bodhisattvas do without ado, manifest their perfect character without harboring any false notions in their mind, reveal their true selves by forgetting their egos completely, and perfect themselves by dedicating themselves to the public interest." (*CP* 9:33)

34. The Master said, "Grand Master Sot'aesan made clear the essential way to attain wisdom and blessing by quoting an ancient scripture, which reads, 'Not to be apart from one's own nature is the greatest practice; to harbor no false thought after rendering favor is the greatest of all virtues.'"[15] He further said, "If you harbor the false notion of rendering charity, charity itself can be the cause of transgression and harm. When humans bring up their offspring, they have in mind no false notion of bringing it up, and that is why bringing a child up remains a great beneficence. Thus, rendering favors to others becomes a great charity only if one has no notion of rendering favors in mind." (*CP* 9:34)

35 The Master said, "The inexhaustible treasure house is none other than the internal three great powers and external charitable deeds performed with no false notion of them. These two are the original source of boundless blessings and happiness." (*CP* 9:35)

36. The Master said, "The enlightened person enjoys endless blessings because he or she cultivates the cause of blessings while enjoying it. Deluded beings, while enjoying the small blessings they have earned, attach themselves to them; or they become arrogant and often corrupted. If abused, blessings can be the capital of calamity; if put to a good use, calamity can be the capital for blessing." (*CP* 9:36)

37. The Master said, "Do not complain that your charitable deed is not recognized while practicing charity. If you get all the praise for the charitable deed, you will have received half of the blessings for it. Think of the deficiency of your charitable deed, and do not regret that you do not receive blessing right away." He said further, "If you spare the blessings returned to you, you will be blessed for a long time." (*CP* 9:37)

38. The Master said, "It is not just in games of chess or the game of *Go* that possess the secret of moves. Deluded beings can only see the immediate move; sages can see tens and hundreds moves ahead. Thus, deluded beings, being preoccupied with the immediate gains and comfort of this life, accumulate countless offenses and suffering. Sages, preparing for eternal wisdom and blessing, exert themselves in cultivation of the mind and in impartial public service, disregarding present small blessings and pleasures, being content amid poverty and taking delight in the Way." (*CP* 9:38)

39. The Master said, "Sages receive infinite true benefit by not taking present small gains and even by suffering loss, but deluded beings suffer losses by committing evil while seeking small gains. True benefit can only be attained if it stands on the ground of justice and in accord with a great cause." (*CP* 9:39)

40. The Master said, "If you seek after fame, position, and power in accord with the Way, you can practice more charity therewith without committing transgressions. If you do not accept them or decline one position in favor of another, even though you deserve them, then this will be accumulated as hidden fortune. To receive the whole blessing is to waste it; to bestow blessings on another without enjoying it oneself is to accrue interests." He said further, "Even an enlightened sage cannot realize his plan and aspiration unless he gets a position; thus, the position is something that is not bad but necessary. However, the enlightened sage must get it only in accord with the great cause after a careful consideration of the situation. And the position can only be kept safely for a long time if the power granted to the position is not monopolized after it is held." (*CP* 9:40)

41. The Master said, "Buddha-bodhisattvas and deluded beings are alike in liking what is good and disliking what is bad. But they are unlike in that Buddha-bodhisattvas do not take what is good no matter how good it is if it is not right, while deluded beings take it although it is not right. Buddha-bodhisattvas are different from deluded beings in that the former have no attachment to love and hate when they are confronted with the mental spheres of joy, anger, sorrow, and pleasure, while the latter are attached to what they like or dislike. They are alike in that they cannot realize their aspiration without attaining a position. But they are different in that deluded beings are more likely to use position, power, and property as the means to commit transgression, while Buddha-bodhisattvas use them as the means of benefiting the people in the world. And the

more they enjoy position, power, and wealth, the more reward of virtue they render to people. Hence, buddha-bodhisattvas are always endowed with abundant rewards of virtue and, hence, all the articles for daily use offered to them turn out to be sacred items to benefit the world." (*CP* 9:41)

42. The Master said, "You cannot honor yourself; to treat others well amounts to doing yourself due honor. You cannot raise your merit for yourself; to raise someone else's merit amounts to raising your merit." (*CP* 9:42)

43. The Master said, "You get a day's wage right away, but you harvest a year's farming only in the fall. Likewise, a great benefit is obtained late and a great practice takes long time. Do not be impatient if the reward of virtue does not return quickly after doing a small charitable deed, but keep practicing charity. Do not be complacent if there is no immediate retribution after you have committed a transgression, but repent and correct your ways. Whatever is to return will return when it reaches the limit; hence strive to accumulate merit without dropping your guard." (*CP* 9:43)

44. The Master said, "An ephemeral creature can see only one day, and a mantis can see only one month, hence, an ephemeral creature does not know a month, and a mantis does not know a year. Deluded beings can see only one life without knowing eternal life, but Buddha-bodhisattvas can see the eternal life, and hence, they make the longest-term plan and exert themselves in the most fundamental matters." (*CP* 9:44)

45. The Master said, "As deluded beings attach themselves to the worldly joy that is impermanent and ever changing, they are ruined when their fortune ends. However, Buddha-bodhisattvas train their minds in the formless and immutable bliss of a hermit's life and enjoy paradise. You should enjoy the immutable and simple bliss and glory of eternal morality without being attached to ephemeral pleasures and prosperity." (*CP* 9:45)

46. The Master said, "A propitious and lucky day is not in the lucky day but in one's way of mind and action. A particular lucky day is the day when one meets a true mentor and the day when one has a firm resolution in the true dharma, and the day when one is enlightened to the principle of one's own nature. An ordinary lucky day is the day when one observes the precepts well, prevents wicked thought, keeps peace of mind and forbearance, repents prior faults without committing new transgressions, practices charity and altruism, and pays off old debt patiently by overcoming incidental suffering." (*CP* 9:46)

47. The Master said, "To a practitioner, the birthday of the mind is more important than that of the body. Our birthday of the mind is the

day when our mind takes a vow toward the great way of neither arising nor ceasing, the day when the new mind arises by refreshing the dejected mind, and the day when, responding to the mental spheres, one mind of bright thought arises, and one mind of good thought arises. As an ancient sage said, 'Every day is a good day,'[16] so we must live every day as a birthday. I hope that you will live a splendid life in the infinite world by reflecting on your original vow and developing new good thought, so that you become a great figure that benefits the vast world eternally." (CP 9:47)

48. The Master said, "The five worldly blessings and five blessings of the practitioner have different standards. In the section 'The Great Plan' of the Book of History (Shujing), longevity, wealth, health, love of virtue, and peaceful death are regarded as the five blessings.[17] In the secular world, however, the five blessings are longevity, wealth, honor, health, and numerous sons. Common people regard a long physical life as longevity, but practitioners regard as longevity awakening into the realm of neither arising nor ceasing. Common people regard their private property as wealth, but religious practitioners regard as wealth the knowledge that the whole universe is one's own possession. Common people regard obtaining fame and a post in the government as honor, but religious practitioners regard as honor the realization, by acting in accord with moral laws, of the value of the supreme creature. Common people regard a physical state without illness as health, but religious practitioners regard as health a mind devoid of evil passions and attachment. Common people count only their own offspring when they wish for many offspring, but religious practitioners regard all sentient beings in the universe as their own offspring. Now, if you possess the practitioner's five blessings, then there is a principle that the secular five blessings can return to you. Hence, you must find the spring of these five fundamental blessings so that you can enjoy secular as well as hermit's five blessings." (CP 9:48)

49. The Master said, "With regard to budgeting and the settlement of accounts, there are different standards for balancing income and expenditure in the secular life and in the monastic life. Secular life will be rich and complete only if the actual income is abundant, but, from the aspect of truth, one's reward of virtue will be abundant only if there are enough savings in the realm of truth, even in the event of actual loss. Deluded people, however, do not know the true meaning of income and expenditure, and hence, take the immediate income by all means, even by deceiving others. This is like a debtor who makes his debt heavier. When will he see the reward of virtue returning to him? Therefore, you, under-

standing the correct way of income and expenditure, should cultivate the infinite field of blessings daily and monthly, balancing true income and expenditure by benefiting others with words and deeds, while balancing your actual income and expenditure in accord with the spirit of mutual benefit." (*CP* 9:49)

50. The Master said, "There are two kinds of official rank: the official rank conferred by Heaven and that conferred by humans. A governmental office can be taken away because it is conferred by humans, but the official rank conferred by Heaven cannot be taken away because it is given by the Truth. Regarding this official rank conferred by Heaven as precious, Buddha-bodhisattvas hold the attainment of the three great powers internally as the true glory, and the deliverance of the world externally as the true occupation, being praised by all the people under Heaven. Now, this is the official rank conferred by Heaven. If you attain the official rank conferred by Heaven, then the official position conferred by humans will naturally come to you, so that you can enjoy eternally the official rank conferred by Heaven and the official position conferred by humans." (*CP* 9:50)

51. Greeting the New Year, the Master gave a sermon on the topic "Exorcism by Reading Scriptures": "An old custom in this country (Korea) is a ceremony of exorcism done with the reading of scriptures by a Buddhist monk or a blind person invited by a household. However, it is not certain whether this ceremony can exorcise, or bring about good fortune. If the exorcist reads the scriptures only word for word without understanding their original intention, the whole ceremony will turn out to be nothing but a kind of superstition. We dissolve any unhappiness, at the beginning of a new year, not by asking someone else to read the scriptures once overnight, but by reading them ourselves daily. We get rid of evil, not by reading them aloud, but by reading them silently in mind, not by reading them at a desk at a set time, but by reading them in our minds all the time, in all circumstances of movement and quiescence. If we, reading our scriptures thoroughly and putting them into practice, read and make good use of the real scriptures displayed throughout the world, we can drive away our own woes and calamities and bring blessings to our families, societies, and the nation." (*CP* 9:51)

52. The Master said, "The Buddha gave out three kinds of scriptures, in accord with the intellectual capacity. The first is the scripture that was later written in ink on paper. The second is the actual scripture manifested in all things in the world. The third is the formless scripture that is originally complete in our own nature. The actual scripture is greater

than the scripture written in ink on paper, and the formless scripture is more fundamental than the actual scripture manifested in the myriad things in the world." He said further, "It is said that before the birth of the sage the Way subsisted in Heaven and earth; after the birth it resides in the sage; and after his death, it remains in scriptures. The greatest scripture is the Way of Heaven and earth, which appears to be accidental or natural." (CP 9:52)

53. The Master said, "There are three kinds of mentors to a Buddhist practitioner: a human mentor, who teaches one by talking, writing, or acting; the universal mentor, who awakens one to the silent reality displayed in front of one; and the conscience mentor, who awakens the self. If you aspire to attain to the great Way, you must receive the guidance of these three mentors." (CP 9:53)

54. The Master said, "The Fourfold Beneficence is a field of blessings for us all. Buddha-bodhisattvas sow the seeds of edification in a boundless impartial field throughout their eternal lives, and thereby become loving parents and spiritual guides of the three worlds. Deluded beings sow the seeds of greed in the limited ground of selfishness and are absorbed in work their whole lives; nonetheless, eventually there remains not much of benefit. Buddha-bodhisattvas work hard farming on the formless mind-field for many worlds and thereby harvest pure (anāsrava) blessings and infinite wisdom in infinite future worlds. Deluded beings work hard on such phenomenal things as wealth, sex, fame, and gain, yet everything turns out to be in vain when they leave the world, even though there seemed to be some benefit while they were working hard on them." (CP 9:54)

55. The Master said, "The most important conditions of our practice, for eons, are our vow and dharma affinity. The vow helps us choose our directions, and the dharma affinity guides and fosters the vow." (CP 9:55)

56. The Master said to Cho Chŏng'wŏn, "We can expect good fruit of a fruit tree only if its seed was of a good species, if it meets fertile ground, if it meets favorable rain and dew, and if it gets long-term human care. Likewise, to perfect one's personality, these four conditions must be present. For a human being, the habit force becomes the seed. Human beings are each born with different minds and modes of action because the seeds of habits are all different from one another. Therefore, you should exert yourself in the preparation of good seeds by good habits. The ground of a human being is his or her affinity with parents, brothers

and sisters, and mentors and comrades. One can be a good person only if one enjoys good affinity with these conditions. One's seed will not produce right if one has unfavorable affinities and fails to receive correct guidance, or if one's intention to do the right thing is opposed, or if one does not sow the seed in the correct religious order. Therefore, you must strive to develop many, good affinities. The rain and dew of the human being are those of dharma. The seed of the mind will grow well and make progress and improvement only if one comprehends the scriptures and the canons of wisdom and listens to the teachings of mentors and comrades. Thus, you must receive the rain and dew of dharma. The long-term human effort for the perfection of a personality is the power of one's own effort. Even if one has good habit force, a good dharma affinity, and hears good dharma sermons, one cannot realize a good personality without one's own long-term effort and ability. Therefore, one can realize the great personality who can attain to buddhahood and deliver sentient beings only if one accumulates actual merits one after another until one's deluded being transforms into a buddha." (CP 9:56)

57. The Master said, "A story has it that a man gave his three daughters away in marriage, each with one *mal* (18 liters) of unhulled rice. In a few years, he looked into their lives and found out that one was living poorly, because she had used the rice for food. The second one was living with the rice hung to the ceiling as a souvenir. And the third one had used the rice as seed for farming; she was living well, with a productive farm. Likewise, everyone has come to this world with the seeds of blessing and wisdom. There are those who are ignorant and poor, who have no blessings and wisdom because they have wasted all of them. There are those who are not debauched, because they are prudent, but they live as usual without knowing how to cultivate blessings and wisdom. And there are those who grow the three great powers, endlessly preparing for blessings and wisdom, and have blessings grow constantly accumulating because they enjoy only part of their blessings and use the greater part of them for rightful public causes. If one abuses or wastes blessings, even if one is born with them, there will be little to expect on the road of one's own future, as one will be harming those blessings. If one uses blessings correctly in the practice and in public service and does not spare effort or property, then one's wisdom and blessings will always be abundant." (CP 9:57)

58. The Master said, "Supernatural power is like branches and leaves, whereas seeing into one's self-nature and thereby becoming a

buddha is the root. If you take good care of the root, branches and leaves grow vigorously, but if you take care only of the branches the root will naturally wither away. As supernatural power is a minor concern for the sage,[18] Grand Master Sot'aesan, too, stringently prohibited his disciples from attaining it, after founding the order. Taking the essential ways of humanity as the main principle, he delivered deluded beings with daily rules of propriety and commonplace laws. This is the unexcelled path." (*CP* 9:58)

59. The Master said, "Cultivate your minds, so that you can become masters to the New World.[19] One becomes a master naturally if one realizes that the affairs of the whole world are one family business within one clan. If one is not a master, one stops doing good when one is tired, and becomes disaffected when one is displeased. The master works without wishing for rewards and works without being asked to." (*HH* 1:1–3)

III

Fundamental Principles

1. During the pioneer days of Won Buddhism, Grand Master Sot'aesan instructed some of his disciples to compose verses and asked Master Chŏngsan to compose one with the title "Irwŏn" (one circle). Master Chŏngsan wrote, "All things harmonize to become one; heaven and earth are one great circle." (*CP* 1:2)

2. Master Chŏngsan delivered a sermon at the ceremony enshrining the Dharmakāya Buddha–Irwŏnsang in a branch temple: "The original nature of Dharmakāya Buddha cannot be described in words or symbols; however, in its reality, all beings of the universe are nothing but Dharmakāya Buddha. Thus, the truth of Dharmakāya Buddha is eternal and independent of the enshrining of Irwŏnsang. It is difficult, however, for the public to know what they can take as the object of refuge of their mind, unless an object of faith is shown, or what they can take as the standard for practice. Even if they know, they can easily lose sight of the standard for the examination of their mind. Grand Master Sot'aesan had Irwŏnsang enshrined as the symbol of Dharmakāya Buddha in temples and homes so that Irwŏnsang could be taken as the object of religious worship and the standard of practice whether one walks, runs, sits, reclines, talks, keeps quiet, moves, or rests. By enshrining and worshiping Irwŏnsang, we should discover the real Irwŏn, maintain the true nature of Irwŏn, and use the perfect mind of Irwŏn. By unifying perfectly the truth of Irwŏnsang and our life, we will be the owners of limitless blessings and immeasurable wisdom." (*CP* 5:1)

113

3. The attendant asked, "In our order, the Dharmakāya Buddha, Irwŏnsang, is the object of worship and hence we pray to it but do not pray to either Śākyamuni Buddha or Grand Master Sot'aesan at all rites. How is Dharmakāya Buddha different from Śākyamuni Buddha, and how is the worship of the one different from that of the other?" The Master answered, "Grand Master Sot'aesan has established the way of Dharmakāya Buddha worship in order to unify all the objects of worship. Dharmakāya Buddha is the noumenal nature of all beings in the universe and the original nature of all buddhas and sages. They are always one with their own original nature; hence to pray to the Dharmakāya Buddha is to pray to all buddhas and sages. Without a personal buddha, the truth of Dharmakāya Buddha cannot be known; and without the truth of Dharmakāya Buddha the personal buddha has nothing to explicate. Thus, the way of worship is not two; however, if we were to make a distinction, we can say that the worship of Dharmakāya Buddha is the worship of Truth and to worship a personal buddha is to believe in the Buddha for his teachings." (*CP* 2:11)

4. The Master said, "As the principle of Irwŏnsang is beyond relativity, it cannot be expressed in words, or thought, or described in any name or form. Such is the empty substance of Irwŏn. In the empty substance is numinous awareness, the light of which includes the universe and the providence of which is ubiquitous through all beings of the universe. This is the wondrous existence of Irwŏn. In between the true emptiness and the wondrous existence of Irwŏn, myriad dharmas are in motion, making the differences of arising and ceasing, and going and coming, and the differences of good and evil karma. In accordance with these differences, sentient beings ascend or descend through the six paths and the four forms of birth. This is Irwŏn's law of causality. True emptiness, wondrous existence, and causality are three aspects of the same truth of Irwŏn. Thus, Grand Master Sot'aesan took this Irwŏnsang as the fundamental source of the doctrine. He then let all practitioners of the Way have faith in it, inquire into its truth, and practice it in order to help them enter the great Way easily, transcending each step, and to disclose the profound principle for practical application. Hence, the seeker of the truth will find no other truth than this; the seeker of the Way will find no other way than this; and myriad dharmas are nothing but this dharma." (*CP* 5:2)

5. The Master said, "Why do we worship Irwŏnsang? We worship Irwŏnsang (1) to see that our mind is none other than the Buddha and our original nature is none other than dharma; (2) to believe that the

profound principle of causality is extremely fair and bright, so it cannot be deceived or violated; (3) to know the details of the Fourfold Beneficence that rule over the karmic retribution of blessings and punishments actually, so that the object of worship can be relevant and realistic to our worship; and (4) to practice a limitless worship such that, since the Buddha is manifested everywhere, everything should be done as an offering to the Buddha. Since this is the way of worshiping the Truth actually, Grand Master Sot'aesan made it the mainspring to practice the correct doctrine by cultivating self-power and accepting other-power." (*CP* 5:3)

6. The attendant asked, "All the rites are performed with Irwŏnsang as the object of religious worship; how should a rite be performed where Irwŏnsang is not enshrined?" The Master answered, "If the performer of the rite carries it out with Irwŏnsang in mind, then all beings with form and no form are none other than the truth of Irwŏnsang and the ten directions become the whole body of the Dharmakāya Buddha. Hence there is no place where the Dharmakāya Buddha does not respond in accord with the mind." (*CP* 2:3)

7. The Master said, "From ancient times, buddhas, sages, philosophers, and other eminent figures have expressed the fundamental reality of the universe differently. In Buddhism it is expressed as Dharmakāya or the Buddha-nature; in Confucianism as sincerity, principle, or *taiji;* in Taoism as *Dao* or the mother under heaven; in Christianity as God; in philosophy as principle and rule, energy, or will; and in science as energy. All these different terms are used to refer to the ultimate reality of the universe. Grand Master Sot'aesan used the 'Irwŏnsang' to refer to it. Because the different theories expressed the ultimate reality in abstract terms, they did not render great help to our daily life, and even when they did, they were deficient. Irwŏnsang, however, is perfect and has no deficiency, as Irwŏnsang signifies in such a way that we can realize the aim of religion by taking it as the object of religious faith and as the final goal of morality by taking it as the standard of practice. By nourishing, knowing, and practicing the truth of Irwŏn, we attain the great power of Irwŏn and unify ourselves with the inherent nature of Irwŏn. In this way, we humans become one with Irwŏn and can make endless application of it. These are the salient characteristics of Irwŏnsang." (*HH* 3:4)

8. The Master said, "Dharmakāya Buddha is the Truth Buddha which is the origin of all dharmas; Sambhogakāya Buddha and Nirmāṇakāya Buddha are the manifestations of the Truth Buddha. Some nirmāṇakāya buddhas are complete manifestation of the Truth Buddha as such;

and some nirmāṇakāya buddhas are partial manifestation of the Truth Buddha. All buddhas and sages are the former; and all remaining sentient beings are the latter. The sentient beings are called partial nirmāṇakāya buddhas because they are all endowed with the Buddha-nature. Hence, you should know that you are a complete nirmāṇakāya buddha when your mind is clear, pure, and right; and a partial nirmāṇakāya buddha when vicious and dark." (*CP* 5:5)

9. The attendant asked, "In traditional Buddhism Śākyamuni Buddha is the principal teacher and hence all his followers devote their worship and faith to him. In our order, our devotion and attention to Grand Master Sot'aesan is much deeper than to Śākyamuni Buddha. What is the relationship between the two sages and how should the ways of faith and devotion be distinguished?" The Master answered, "Upon his great enlightenment Grand Master Sot'aesan realized that Buddhism is the most fundamental of all religions and Śākyamuni Buddha is the holiest of all sages. Grand Master Sot'aesan himself found the origin of his enlightenment in Śākyamuni Buddha and we received the truthful law from Grand Master Sot'aesan in his order. Hence, Śākyamuni Buddha is like our grandfather and Grand Master Sot'aesan our father, both of whom should be respected and attended in accordance with due proprieties. However it cannot be helped that one's affection to the father is stronger than to the grandfather." (*CP* 2:12)

10. The attendant asked again, "Grand Master Sot'aesan's memorial tablet in the Yŏngmowŏn carries the title *tathāgata*, which in traditional Buddhism was used only for Śākyamuni Buddha. Wouldn't some people think it presumptuous to give the title to Grand Master Sot'aesan?" The Master replied, "It is true that *tathāgata*, one of the ten epithets given to Śākyamuni Buddha, is one of high respect. If, however, there should be only one person to whom the title *tathāgata* can be given and no other person like him should rise, then such Buddhism will be destined to decline. It will be an unnecessary spiritual oppression if the title is prohibited even if there is someone who deserves the title. It is imaginable that Śākyamuni Buddha must have come to the world many times in order to deliver sentient beings during the past 2,500 years. If so, it will be unreasonable for the identical Buddha with the same power of Buddha truth not to have the title *tathāgata*. Therefore, in our order, we have set the highest dharma stage as *tathāgata* of the six dharma stages.[20] The title shall be conferred, not only on Grand Master Sot'aesan, but also on anyone in any generation in accordance with their dharma power if

a qualified dharma master gives sanction to that person or the mass of people reveres the person. This is not to abuse the holy title, nor is this to corrupt Buddhist religious tradition. When one is promoted to the position of *tathāgata*, the rules of propriety for ascent should be followed; and the lineage of the tradition should not obliterate the generational differences of ancestor and descendant. If you call this presumptuous, I do not have to defend myself against the charge; however, to be reasonable, I think that this practice will amount to keeping the gate of Buddhism wide open rather than being presumptuous." (*CP* 2:13)

11. The Master said, "If you are given only the name of someone you do not know, it is difficult to believe that anyone by the name really exists. Just as the picture of someone you do not know can help you see what that person looks like, the picture of the Truth, if any, can help you see what it could be like. Grand Master Sot'aesan has shown us the picture of the Truth itself by Irwŏnsang, making it much easier for us to see the realm of Truth. Irwŏnsang is the picture of the totality of Truth; hence, anyone who takes this picture as the object of sincere inquiry will attain the realm of Truth easily. Thus, Grand Master Sot'aesan said, 'Śākyamuni Buddha's order in the past was that of one buddha with one thousand bodhisattvas; in the future one thousand buddhas and ten thousand bodhisattvas will arise in this order.'" (*CP* 5:6)

12. The Master said, "The nature of true emptiness is the absolute realm that is beyond relativity, which is the ultimate emptiness of the truth of Irwŏn. The mind of wondrous existence is the numinous calmness. The substantial energy is the Fourfold Beneficence. The principle of cause and effect is that of circulation. These four principles can be applied to a human being. The nature is the realm where not an iota of thought has yet arisen, and where no dream can be found. Mind, though empty of joy, anger, sorrow, or pleasure, has the essential element to differentiate, to achieve the standard of balance, and become numinous. Energy is what contains nature and mind. Principle is what gives rise to acting, seeing, breathing, and the emotions of joy, anger, sorrow, and pleasure." (*HH* 3:42)

13. The Master said, "When a huge circle (*wŏnsang*) turns, thousands and tens of thousands of smaller circles (*wŏnsang*) turn accordingly, just as small wheels of a machine turn as its motor turns." (*CP* 5:7)

14. The Master said, "Just as the truth of no birth and no death subsists in the universe, the life of dharma is eternal. If one leaves the world after merely raising one's offspring, then one's life is not much different from that of a beast or a bird. What makes human life precious lies

in leaving the trace of dharma behind. Though no trace can be found of Shennong (2737 BC), who lived thousands of years ago, his art of farming will remain eternally valid. The utility of electricity, invented by Edison, will also endure as long as humankind exists. The light of the laws explicated by the sages will shine more broadly than any other inventions. An old saying has it that 'the Tao is in heaven before the birth of the sage; it is in the sage during the sage's life time; and it remains in the scriptures when the sage is gone.' This means that a sage's law propagates eternally." (*HH* 1:30)

15. The Master said, "To be enlightened to the realm of the universe that has no differentiation is to attain the knowledge of the Buddha; to know the realm of the universe which has differentiation, and to act in myriad situations accordingly, is to do the act of the Buddha." (*CP* 5:8)

16. The Master said, "Though our original nature is pure in its substance, its unimpeded functioning becomes good and its obstructed functioning becomes evil in response to activity in the mental sphere; this is the dividing point of good and evil. Its straight functioning becomes rightness and its crooked functioning becomes wrongness. This is the dividing point between right and wrong. Its obscured functioning becomes ignorance and its true functioning becomes enlightenment; this is the dividing point between wisdom and delusion." (*CP* 5:10)

17. The Master said, "Our original nature is neither good nor evil, neither pure nor impure. However, it is because of numinous awareness in our original nature that there are differences between ordinary sentient beings and sages or good and evil. The numinous awareness of ordinary sentient beings is swayed by habit forces and karma, in response to mental spheres to produce various delusions. The Buddha illuminates situations with numinous awareness, reflecting light inward on the original nature without being drawn to external conditions, so that the light of pure wisdom shines forth. This is the difference between the Buddha and ordinary sentient beings." (*CP* 5:11)

18. The Master said, "The original nature is the realm where not a single thought has yet arisen, and nature is what heaven has mandated.[21] There is nothing displayed in the universe that is not nature. All sentient and insentient beings are none other than the Buddha-nature. When a thought is pure and sound, it is called spirit, which is the state of mind devoid of differentiation and attachment. (*HH* 3:39)

19. The Master said, "All beings of the universe consist of spirit, vital force, and matter. Spirit is the original substance of all beings of the

universe and it is their immortal nature. Vital force is that which, as the vital energy of all beings, makes them animated. Matter, as the material of all beings, forms their bodies." (*CP* 5:13)

20. The Master said, "Vital force contains numinous awareness, and numinous awareness contains vital force; hence, vital force is numinous awareness and numinous awareness is vital force. All those things with or without forms, animals, plants, all those that run, and all those that fly are caused by the vital force and are the manifestation of numinous awareness. The great nature (the prime mover) is the nondual unity of numinous awareness and vital force." (*CP* 5:14)

21. The Master said, "Myriad things in heaven and earth, including human beings, are composed of soul (*ryŏng*), energy (*ki*), and matter (*chil*). Soul, though invisible, controls things with form or without form. Heaven and earth are the unitary, grand soul while human beings are individual souls, which, when united with the former, become one. Energy is the power to manifest creative transformation, which gives rise to the cycle of the four seasons and the changes of wind, clouds, rain, and frost. In human beings it causes breathing and action. Matter is the basis of principle. The matter of heaven and earth is the earth; the matter of human beings is bone and flesh. If the three are in harmonious balance, heaven and earth as well as human beings will be normal; if the three lose the harmonious balance, unusual happenings occur in heaven and earth, and illness befalls human beings." (*HH* 3:84)

22. A disciple asked, "You said that vital force and numinous awareness are not two but one. Why don't we see numinous awareness in plants?" The Master replied, "There are differences in the transformations of things. If numinous awareness leads a thing and contains vital force secondarily, that thing becomes an animal; if vital force leads a thing and contains numinous awareness secondarily, that thing becomes a plant. Animals have individual spirits, but plants share one universal spirit." The disciple asked again, "What is the relationship between individual spirits and the one universal spirit?" The Master answered, "In the state of tranquility (samādhi) the mind unites itself with the one universal spirit; its motion makes individual spirit. Mind in its tranquility unites itself with the great virtue; when it functions, it creates its karma. Man does not join the universal spirit only at death; birth and death are one." (*CP* 5:15)

23. A disciple said, "I want to know how ignorance arises in our original nature." The Master replied, "An analogy may help. Although the empty sky is originally clear, winds arise as energy moves, and clouds

arise accordingly, causing darkness under heaven. Although our nature is originally pure, ignorance arises in accordance with the motion and quietude of the mind. When the mind calms down, its purity and brightness are restored; when the mind is agitated, ignorance arises. However, if the mind functions without disturbance, it keeps calmness in motion, maintaining its brightness; and if the mind moves in disturbance, ignorance comes into existence, causing darkness in the mind." (*CP* 5:16)

24. Hearing the theories of Mencius that human nature is good and of Sunzi that it is evil, Master Chŏngsan said, "Human nature is devoid of good and evil in its calm state, but it can be good or evil when it functions. Since good nature is manifested when one acts by modeling after nature's substance, it will be better to call it a 'continuity of good' theory." (*HH* 3:90)

25. The Master said, "The sun and the moon shine bright through the empty sky; the law of cause and effect is ubiquitous through the truth of emptiness. The emptier it is, the brighter it is. Because it is extremely bright, it becomes ubiquitously numinous." (*CP* 5:17)

26. The Master said, "It is because of the providence of a shapeless and unknowable energy that trees are bare of leaves in the fall and they become thick with leaves again in the spring. It is also because of a formless energy that we cannot escape from birth, old age, illness, and death. It is also because of a formless energy that the universe goes through the cycle of formation, abiding, decay, and extinction. It is the formless energy that governs what has forms." (*CP* 5:18)

27. The Master said, "The body with a form is ruled by the formless mind. Material things are localized and limited and hence are either deficient or excessive; however, the realm of emptiness is complete and hence it is the origin of everything." (*CP* 5:19)

28. The Master said, "Emptiness is the master of all beings of the universe; heaven and earth manifest their virtue through emptiness. The empty mind is the master of myriad things; hence, you will make good use of material things only if you know how to use the empty mind well. Zen lets you know of emptiness; it is the great learning that teaches you how to use the mind's emptiness. If you know and use the emptiness of the mind well, you will be the master of the world." (*CP* 5:20)

29. The Master said, "The quintessence of the Buddhist scriptures is emptiness (*śūnyatā*), and Grand Master Sot'aesan also said that the truth of Irwŏn can be summarized in terms of emptiness, perfection, and rightness.[22] Cultivate and nourish purity of mind by learning the principle of

emptiness and modeling yourself on it, and cultivate impartiality of mind and put it into practice in daily life." (*CP* 5:21)

30. The Master said, "What does not exist is greater than what exists; no-thought (*munyŏm*) is greater than a thought (*yunyŏm*). It is because existence has its form while nonexistence does not. Merits accumulated with false thought are followed by blessings mixed with afflictions. Merits accumulated without any false thought are followed by blessings, which lead to nirvāṇa. Someone in the ancient times said, 'Heavenly virtue does not have any sound or smell.'" The Master said again, "The one who possesses hidden virtue has heavenly virtue, ruling the ten directions. Do not try to receive only human blessings: accumulate heavenly merits, and receive heavenly blessings. Do not try to be the teacher of humans only; try to be the teacher of the three worlds." (*CP* 5:27)

31. The Master said, "If we ponder on the principles of heaven and earth, we can see that beings with forms and shapes come from what has no form or shape and what exists returns to what does not exist. People work hard for what has form and shape and do not know how to work for what has no form. It is vain to do so. If people work for what has no form and shape with only half the effort for what does have form and shape, they will attain a magnificent moral perfection, and what has form and shape will accompany it. If you win an argument to your satisfaction, there remains nothing to hope for. If you harbor a false notion after doing a favor for someone or take the full reward for that instantly, there will be no merit remaining for future blessings. When you do things, do so with magnanimity. When you do the good for others, do so in private, so that it may be a hidden virtue. Accumulate hidden merits. The longer you keep a deposit in the bank, the more interest it accrues. Likewise, merits for blessings grow larger while they are not duly recognized. Do not be discouraged when you are in a low or a troubled situation, since such a situation is a necessary condition for a bright day in the future. It is said that Arisaema Japonica (*Chŏngangsŏng*) is a star located in a poor position; but what it governs is a good position. This teaches the lesson that to be in a disadvantaged position is necessary for a prosperous future." (*CP* 5:28)

32. The Master said, "If you devote yourself to a rightful task, it will be accomplished sooner or later without fail, though it may depend on the degree of your sincerity and the nature of the matter. Certain goals can be reached gradually, in accordance with your devotion; sometimes the goal is achieved suddenly by the influence of a miraculous power.

When Grand Master Sot'aesan's nine disciples proved their devotion and sincerity by the blood seals,[23] this order was authenticated by the dharma realm. No great event can happen in the phenomenal world unless there is an authentication in the noumenal world (*ŭmbu*)." (*CP* 5:30)

33. The Master said, "Do you have firm faith that you will obtain the potent influence of the union of yourself and the Truth of the universe by offering silent prayers at dawn and night? It may seem unlikely that a moment of silent prayer could bring about any potent influence, but whatever we think penetrates the empty dharma realm. Hence, you should be heedful over the movement of your mind, not only at the moment of offering silent prayers but always. Do not forget that if you sincerely offer silent prayers at dawn and night, you will thereby get great help for your practice and attain an influence of great power. That we could go through the war[24] safely is due greatly to the wholehearted silent prayers of our congregation. If we unselfishly take care of others and cultivate our mind without grasping at false notions (*sang*), our order, the country, and the world will be greatly influenced thereby." (*CP* 5:31)

34. The Master said, "If you always let others keep their joyous and peaceful mind, you also will have a peaceful countenance yourself; if you make others feel ill at ease, you also will keep a gloomy countenance. You should treat a person with sincerity and a truthful mind that is internally and externally uniform. If you help others by concealing their faults and letting their good be recognized, they also will render you help. Hence, even if you dislike a person, you should speak of the person with the feeling of reciprocal help and thereby remove the barrier between you and that person. If you do so, you will feel a great power of influence responding to you." (*CP* 5:32)

35. The Master said, "Although water is very soft in its nature, the gathering of water drops makes great rivers and seas. Likewise, although the mind is extremely minute and feeble, it attains a great power if you keep gathering it into one mind; the light of wisdom can be far-reaching only if you have nourished the mind after gathering it." (*CP* 5:33)

36. The Master said, "The universe is based on the principles of change and immutability. To the principle of change belong the cycle of formation, abiding, decay, and extinction of the universe; the cycle of the four seasons; the birth, old age, illness, and death of humans; and the vicissitudes of fortunes and misfortunes and calamity and happiness of life. To the principle of immutability belongs the original substance of true thusness (*bhūtatathatā*) that neither arises nor ceases, being permanent

with no beginning or end. In comprehending the principle of change, we correct our old habits, renew our mind, reform an obsolete system, and develop all these into new ones. Awakening to the principle that what changes is based on what does not change, you will be enlightened to and establish your original true character, and myriad changes will follow. With that understanding, you should fulfill your original vow until your virtue forms a unity with that of heaven. The point here is that we should change well where we should, by comprehending heaven and earth's principle of change, and we should not change where we should not, by comprehending the principle of immutability of heaven and earth. These principles are, however, two aspects of the truth of nonduality. Be awakened to this principle of nonduality, and cultivate your own way of practice thereby." (*CP* 5:34)

37. The Master said, "If you do not know the principle that being and nonbeing are not two, then you are troubled by sufferings when you encounter them and you are attached to pleasures when you encounter them. In this way you do not escape from suffering. When you are hit by poverty and lowliness, you are troubled by them; and, when you become rich, you are attached to wealth, inviting an unending poverty and lowliness. Unless you can keep the mind of nonbeing in the situation of being, and the mind of being in the situation of nonbeing, you cannot be a sage who transcends being and nonbeing and manages freely suffering and happiness and misery and blessings." (*CP* 5:35)

38. The Master said, "When yang reaches its acme, it produces the three ten-day periods of the hottest weather that are called triple yielding (*san fu*). It means that yin attempts to rise but yields three times to yang, being suppressed by the dominant power of the latter. After the last yielding, however, yang gradually weakens and yin gradually gains power. This is the universal principle of nature, namely, that a change takes place in whatever reaches its highest point and that whatever is minute can become enormous. Difficulties of political power and prosperity and the decay of an individual or an organization follow this principle. Hence those who understand this principle always behave with modesty, defer to others, and help them." (*CP* 5:36)

39. The Master said, "The way in which yin and yang alternate in dominance is governed by the principle of cause and effect. Actions in accordance with this principle produce the karmic reciprocity of mutual benefaction; actions against this principle produce the karmic retribution of mutual destruction. Sages understand this principle of causality

and live in accordance with the way of mutual benefaction. But ordinary sentient beings, being ignorant of this principle, are attracted by greed, fame, and power and accumulate evil karma in accordance with the way of mutual destruction; hence, there is no end to their transgression and suffering." (*CP* 5:40)

40. The Master said, "The relations of karmic causality can be broadly classified as the causality of mutual benefaction, mutual destruction, favorable consequence, and reverse consequence. The causality of mutual benefaction, being the causality of good effects from good causes, is where the causal law is favorably applied for mutual benefaction. This is the causal relation of mutual help and reliance, whereby all affairs are perfectly accomplished. The causality of mutual opposition, being the causality of evil effects from evil causes, is where the law of causality is inverted. This is a bad causal relation, in which the causal affinity is based on opposition characterized by mutual hatred and interference. The causality of favorable consequence is where one makes an effort in one's practice, setting up a good aspiration, good hope, and vows. The causality of reverse consequence is where one receives the reverse consequence of one's wishes on account of arrogance despising others or being cruel to humble people, thus incurring lowly karmic retribution." (*CP* 5:41)

41. The Master said, "Truth inspires tremendous awe; for the eye of the Truth affixes a seal (of confirmation) of a person's good and evil in empty space unseen by human eyes. A wrongdoing committed in the world may escape the net of penal laws; the retribution of Truth, however, is done spontaneously with no-thought on it, hence, it cannot be cheated or evaded." (*CP* 5:42)

42. The Master said, "Just as there are three trials on a case in a court of law, there are three trials in the judgment of the dharma realm. The first is the trial by conscience; the second is the trial by the public; and the third is the trial by Truth. Through these three trials, one receives the verdict of what one has done. This is the strictly impartial judgment of the laws of karmic retribution, which cannot be effected by worldly judgment alone." (*CP* 5:43)

43. The Master said, "It sometimes happens that a good man lives a wretched life and a villain lives a prosperous life. It is because a man, though good in this life, cannot escape any evil karma from his previous life; and a man, though bad in this life, receives good karma from his previous life. Hence, do not judge a man on the basis of what you see now." (*CP* 5:44)

44. The Master said, "The essence of Buddhism lies in showing the way of seeing into nature and awakening to the Way, believing in the law of cause-effect karmic retribution, and fostering great compassion and great pity. If the Buddha had not attained great wisdom, all sentient beings, ignorant of the roots of transgressions and merits, would have suffered in the sea of birth and death and lived in the dark clouds of greed, anger, and delusions. The Buddha, upon attaining the great wisdom, taught the principle of no birth and death so that sentient beings could transcend the cycle of birth and death or could learn the principle even if they might not transcend it. As he taught the principle of karmic causality, sentient beings came to know the causes of transgression and merits, and suffering and happiness. As he taught that one's original nature is pure and undefiled, they could recover pure self-nature by ridding themselves of the three poisons of greed, anger, and delusion. This is like the appearance of a bright New World when the sun has risen in the mid-sky. However, it is inevitable that the dharma, as it ages, gives rise to corruption, and sentient beings are sure to suffer in the bitter seas of misery. It was at this juncture that Grand Master Sot'aesan was enlightened to the great Way of Irwŏn and rekindled the Buddha sun to our limitless blessings. Therefore, you ought to attain the light of wisdom by diligent practice so that you can be apostles to turn the dharma wheel anew." (*HH* 4:11)

45. The Master said, "We receive the effects of our karma sometimes not long after what we do and sometimes in the remote future. Sometimes the effects last long and sometimes a short while. If you lament that blessings do not accrue to your meritorious deeds right away, you are like someone who, upon finishing a seed bed, laments that there is no rice crop right away." (*CP* 5:45)

46. The Master said, "One may be anxious to know about one's former life as well as one's next life. This is a matter both easy and difficult. It is a wise saying of the Buddha, 'If you want to know about your former life, it is what you receive in this life; if you want to know about your next life, it is what you are doing now.' If the karma from your former life is good, you will receive what is good; and if the karma from your former life is bad, you will receive what is bad. The one who knows this principle tries to do more good; the one who does not know this principle does nothing but lament." (*CP* 5:46)

47. Kim Hongch'ŏl asked, "What is the karmic retribution if one incurs the karma of mutual opposition for the sake of a public cause?"

The Master answered, "One cannot escape the effect of personal karma; however, the effect of the karma will be mitigated because one will be promoted by the merit and virtue rendered to the public. If you are afraid of doing what is right for fear of the law of karma, you are worse than someone who does not know it." (CP 5:51)

48. Yi Chŏngŭn asked, "What is the seed of goodness?" The Master said, "The habit of loving goodness becomes the seed of goodness. The habit of the past becomes the seed of the present and the habit of the present becomes the seed of the future." (CP 5:53)

49. A disciple asked, "Does the Buddha get incarnated in accordance with the twelvefold dependent co-arising?" The Master answered, "The Buddha is incarnated freely without following the twelve links." The disciple asked again, "Wasn't the Buddha deluded before his attainment of buddhahood?" The Master answered, "He could be deluded temporarily during an incarnation, however he is enlightened quickly to his original nature. What is cultivated in one's previous life is manifested before long as it is; hence, raising one's cultivation to the level of what was done in one's former life is easy." (CP 5:54)

50. The Master said, "There are two kinds of causal affinity, good and bad. What opens the bright future for oneself, helps one have aspirations, and obtain spiritual awakening is a good affinity. What closes someone's future, what encourages laziness and depravity, and what splits up good affinities are all unwholesome affinities." (CP 5:55)

51. The Master said to Ko Hyŏnjong, "The blessing of good affinity is the best of all blessings; and the Buddhist affinity is the best of all causal affinities. The root of the five blessings[25] lies in the fortune of good affinities. Be diligent in making friends with those of good seeds." (CP 5:56)

52. The Master said, "There are two kinds of precious affinity: one is in blood ties and the other is the affinity of dharma. The family of blood relatives consists of blood ties; the dharma family consists of dharma affinities. Both affinities are precious; however, from the point of eternal life, the dharma affinity is more precious than the blood tie. Only those who devote themselves to religious practice to attain to buddhahood can be eternal friends; the friendship and affinity tied by temporary business or interests dissolve easily." (CP 5:58)

53. The Master said, "If you have a thorough mastery of the fundamental principles and delusive thoughts have gone from your mind, an unequalled paradise is realized. If you know how to be peaceful in your lot, you will be free from trouble. If you know the fundamental principle

in advance, your mind will always be at leisure. When delusions rest, simplicity emerges in the concentrated one mind, and a limitless paradise is realized." (*CP* 5:59)

54. "The Master said, "What is the strongest thing in the world? The softest thing is the strongest.[26] Water, being the softest of all things, is the strongest. However, air is softer than water, and morality is softer than air. Therefore, morality is the strongest thing under heaven. The soft conquers the hard—this is truth." (*HH* 1:17)

55. "There are two kinds of power that conquer a person: awesome power and spiritual influence. To overcome with coercive power is temporary; to overcome with spiritual influence is eternal. Therefore, the influencing force that truly overcomes people eternally lies not in oppressing people with temporary coercion, political or military, but in influencing people with fair and righteous action, morally clean and pure action, and warm compassion." (*HH* 1:18)

56. The Master said, "Just as dead wood does not bloom when spring arrives, one cannot receive the vital force of the age of spring if one's mind is not ready to receive it. The wind from the east and the south is that of sages and princely men; the wind from the west and the north is that of an intrepid hero. King Shun wrote an ode to the south wind: 'How comfortably warm the south wind is! It resolves the grudges of us people. How timely the wind of south is! It helps increase the living of us people."[27] (*HH* 1:20)

57. The Master said, "The upright mind is the root of myriad goodness; learning based on the upright mind is like jewels wrapped in silk; learning based on the evil mind is like a sword held in a robber's hand. Any thought or opinion should be based on the upright mind. Democracy is said to be the best ideology, but it can bring unhappiness to people if applied wrongly. Communism is said to be good, but it can make people unhappier if misapplied." (*HH* 1:21)

58. On the New Year's Day morning of 1946 (WE 31), the Master said, "People in the world say that today is auspicious because it is today when they pray for blessings and ask that calamities will be driven away. However, there is no particular day that is lucky; the lucky day is in the mind. An anecdote has it that a subject of King Wu (1169–1116 BC) is said to have remarked that because the day that King Wu of Zhou (d. 1154 BC) attacked the last king Zhou of Yin (1766–1154 BC), was the day, month, and year of *jiawu*, it was a good day. Hearing this, someone is said to have commented that it was a good day for King Wu but a bad

day for the last king Zhou of Yin. Therefore, an auspicious day is the day that one spends with a mind of purity, wisdom, and compassion free from greed, anger, and delusions. And an unlucky day is the day one spends with the poisonous mind that causes loss to others." (*HH* 1:22)

59. The Master said, "Human fortune and misfortune, rising and falling are like the clearing after rain. Hence, you have only to follow the right way without paying them any mind." (*HH* 1:23)

60. The Master said, "A goblin has, it is said, a magic wand; however, it is nothing but your own mind. If you only make a good use of your mind, it is better than possessing a magic wand. The sages are all said to have obtained the talismanic pearl because they found this mind and used it well. Let us therefore discover this mind and make good use of it; it will be the same as having obtained a magic wand." (*HH* 1:24)

61. The Master said, "Eyes are the most important of all the sense organs because without them a person, unable to see, will have difficulties and be apt to fall into ditches. If the formless mind's eye is not open, one will be ignorant of the human affairs of right and wrong and gain and loss, as well as the principle of noumenon and phenomenon, and existence and nonexistence. Beneficence turns, then, into the cause of resentment, and whatever one does with hands and feet, will turn into transgression and suffering. Thus, it is of utmost importance that you have the mind's eye open, to master myriad facts and myriad principles. (*HH* 1:25)

62. The Master said, "A renowned painter said that the mysterious merit of a masterpiece (portrait) lies in the eyes. It does so because the eyes are the most important part of person's appearance. What then is the most important part of a person? The mind decides the value of life, depending on how it is used. It depends on the mind of the leader whether a family, society, state, or the world will go forward or backward. Therefore one should always have one's mind in order." (*HH* 1:26)

63. The Master said, "Mencius said that only if you look down upon yourself, will someone else despise you.[28] One should make one's own self honorable and respectable without despising one's own person. Personality has two aspects. One is knowledge and skill externally revealed, and the other is pure conscience and virtue internally concealed. The former is secondary and the latter primary. Comparing personality to a plant, the external aspect is like branches and leaves; and the internal aspect is like the root. A plant with healthy roots but poor branches and leaves may look poor for the moment but will have new buds and will live long. A plant that has poor roots but vigorous branches and leaves may have a

good appearance for the moment but cannot live long. Just as a plant with good roots as well as good branches and leaves is truly a good plant, the person with both external and internal virtues is like satin embroidered with flowers." (*HH* 1:29)

64. The Master said, "There are four things that can be construed as life. First, some people take property, fame, or power as life; second, some take the breath of life as life; third, some take justice as life; and fourth, some take moral integrity as life. A man went to Grand Master Sot'aesan and said, 'I married to a woman with a son from her first husband. Now I am troubled by her greed for my property.' Sot'aesan said, 'Instead of being troubled thereby, why do you not distribute the property?' At first he seemed to take the words seriously; but upon returning, his greed for his property grew like blazing fire, so he kept the property to himself for quite a long time. The family discord lasted so long that he got ill and died. Thus, the one who has high regard for property, fame, or power is foolish. In the second case, the one who regards his or her breath of life as more important than property, fame, or power is higher than the first one. In the third case, the one who regards justice as more important than the breath of life is higher than the second one. The life that is ignorant of justice is like that of an insect. Loyal subjects, filial sons, and patriots live the eternal life leaving names rendered honorable by the sacrifice they made of their own lives. An Chunggŭn,[29] only five feet tall, left his name throughout the country after death, and his life shines forever, though human life does not last one hundred years. In the final case, the person who regards the Way as life is the one who lives the true life; the life that does not know the Way is the life of an empty shell. I hope that you attain the life that is as eternal as heaven and earth through diligent cultivation of the Way." (*HH* 1:31)

65. The Master said, "Some people live with a dead mind and some with a live mind. When spring comes to the earth, myriad things grow from its energy, but no new buds come out of dead wood, which has no ability to receive its vital force. The order of a grand religion is filled with the beneficence of a sage, and those who purify their old habit force with unwavering faith and tireless practice can attain buddhahood and deliver sentient beings. Those who lack faith and practice and who therefore cannot cast off old habits are on the path of demotion; it is because their mind is dead. Ordinary people know only the bodily life and death; however, the life and death of the mind is more important. Those who are always aware of the imperfection of their practice and who exert themselves in

the practice are alive; those who are conceited and complacent in their practice and who therefore make no progress are spiritually dead." (*HH* 1:32)

66. Kim Chungmuk (1920–1998), being fascinated with materialism, pedagogy, and psychology while studying at Yuil Institute, denied the principle of karmic retribution of the three time-periods, advocating that the law of karmic retribution be taught as a means to regulate people to do the good. Hearing this, the Master said, "The truth of karmic retribution cannot be a piece of knowledge; it is the realm that can only be intuited by someone whose mind is open. How can it be known to someone whose mind is covered with impurities? Was your mind a tranquil suchness while sitting in meditation? The truth of karmic retribution can be intuited by the mind of a practitioner who has reflected on the causal law of karmic retribution only after three months in a continued state of samādhi. How can you deny the causal law of karmic retribution with dry knowledge gained from a few books?" (*HH* 2:1)

67. The Master said, "In the future people will be enlightened to the causal law of karmic retribution early in their youth. Some will be enlightened while listening to a lecture; some will talk about their former lives as if they are what happened yesterday or the day before yesterday." (*HH* 2:2)

68. "There are two kinds of karmic retribution: discord and attraction. The former is produced by the force of mutual opposition and the latter by the attachment force of love and greed. A practitioner can attain great spiritual power only by transcending the causal law of karmic retribution." (*HH* 2:6)

69. "People are apt to regard all good things as due to their own merits and all bad things as the faults of others. However, one receives the fruit of the seed one planted in the past. Therefore, one must examine oneself when one faces calamities and misfortune, renew one's vow to improve one's lot, and put it into practice." (*HH* 2:35)

70. The Master said, "Selling and buying goods should be done on the principle of mutual benefit. The buyer's getting goods too cheaply, or the seller's charging too much, incurs debts. One should not enjoy buying things cheaply from a pawnshop. Some of the things from the pawnshop are the items that caused pains in the heart of the loser. Inadvertently, the buyer may have to pay for the painful loss." (*HH* 2:39)

71. The Master said, "If someone with whom you have no negative affinity slanders or disgraces you, it is because an evil spirit that bears a

grudge against you is attached to that person. Hence, you should not hate or antagonize that person. A long-smoldering grudge against that person will make him or her your enemy." (*HH* 2:41)

72. The Master said, "From the human perspective, the idea of ego varies greatly. Some regard their own body as self, some their own family, some their own town, some one's own country, and some the whole world. However, the Buddha regards the whole universe to be his own self. From the minimalist perspective, a fish can be viewed as an individual life; from a maximalist perspective, the whole body of seawater is a life. Thus, a human being is an individual life from a minimalist perspective; from a maximalist perspective, he is the Dharmakāya itself. Therefore, the great material energy containing the universe's earth, water, fire, and air is none other than Dharmakāya, and the great 'I,' and the individual that breathes the air is the body and the small self. The great self is Dharmakāya, and the small self is Nirmāṇakāya. The common run of humans exert themselves to maintain the small self day and night, but the Buddha exerts himself as the great self. Here lies the difference between common run of humans and the Buddha." (*HH* 3:5)

73. The Master said, "The blessing and suffering that come from heaven and earth are of two kinds: external and internal. An example of external blessing and suffering is found in farming. If a farmer conforms himself to the four seasons, he will be benefited; if he does not, he will embrace loss. Internal blessing and suffering can be found in one's moral realm. If one hurts someone in secret, suffering will surely be on one's way; and hidden virtue incurs blessedness." (*HH* 3:9)

74. In September 1951 (WE 36), Master Chŏngsan finished the new compilation of the *Canon of Rites* (*Yejŏn*)[30] at the Won Buddhist Temple in Sugye and said to his attendant, Yi Kongjŏn, "The forms and rules of propriety are not uniform in different countries and times. Yet this is the critical time for constructing a New World out of the Old World. It follows that this cannot be the complete and final system of the rules of propriety; let us therefore enforce this temporarily, in mimeograph, for the next ten years and try to establish it gradually as the new rules of propriety for the New World." Master Chŏngsan then said, "The essence of propriety is respect; and the essence of our *Canon of Rites* (*Yejŏn*) is to respect widely and to hold the public in esteem. While explicating the rules of propriety, we should remember that propriety has its essence, which should never be changed throughout eternity, and its applications, which should be flexible according to the times. If the essence is altered,

the rules of propriety cannot stand; if the application is not renovated in accordance with the times, the rules of propriety are useless." (*CP* 2:1)

75. The Master said, "Human beings are related to one another by heavenly moral principles; hence, if one cuts off such relations with words of injustice, one commits the serious evil of destroying the moral system mandated by heaven. If you turn one person against another with evil words intentionally or unintentionally, thus making them enemies, it will be a grave offense with bad karma. You should speak to one another using good words, either truthful or expedient, which can dissolve existing resentments and grudges. You should use words that can inspire your listeners to do good things and help push them forward, thus improving the spirits of those persons. To do so will set a good example of truthful decorum and merit and virtue." (*CP* 2:17)

76. The Master said, "If you harm others, the harm returns to yourself. Thus, by harming others you harm yourself. If you respect others, the respect returns to yourself. Thus, by respecting others you respect yourself." (*CP* 5:49)

77. The Master said, "Many people know that it is a sheer stupidity to borrow money at two hundred percent interest rate and open a business that yields only ten percent profit; but few know that it is stupider to take part of the public fund to help one's family. Many know that to harvest bushels from a measure of seed is the principle of agriculture; but few know the principle of karmic retribution that, if one does a small charitable deed for a public cause, tens of thousands of blessings return to one. Thus, few understand the principle of gain and loss." (*CP* 5:50)

78. The Master said to the students in a class on discourses on scriptures, "Imagine you are the ten kings of the Hades, and answer my questions in heavenly words. Heavenly words are those spoken fairly and unselfishly without partiality or deficiency. What would happen to those who do as they please without knowing their duties, who have no sense of shame or rules of propriety?" Pak Ŭn'guk replied, "Since they have not followed the proper way of humanity, they will become beings unworthy of the name of humanity; and at the end of this life, they will be born in the evil realm." The Master asked, "What would happen to someone whose body is in the religious order but whose mind is in the secular world?" Sŏ Sein answered, "One's affinity with the Buddha gets more tenuous and eventually one will fall into the secular world." The Master asked, "What would happen to the one who, being a devotee,[31] has rendered no merit to the public but rather caused spiritual, physical, and material damage

thereto, or caused worries to the leader through dishonest private gain under the pretext of public cause?" Yi Ŭnsŏk answered, "Since a debt to the public is said to be much greater than that to an individual, it would be harder to pay it back. The one who caused a loss to the public intentionally will have to pay it back as a cow or a horse incarnation. As the result of having caused worries to the leader, one will be born in a hellish realm of dark world." The Master asked, "What would happen to the one who steals from the Buddhist order and the one who unrighteously takes things from others though they may be trivial?" Kim Chŏngyong answered, "Grand Master Sot'aesan said, 'Do not pick up a thing left on the road. When you pick it up, you bring together the thing and the calamity of pain which the loser suffered.' From this, we can see that the person should have to pay back the debt with the karma of a cow or a horse incarnation. If incarnated in the human world, the person will be poor and distressed, and will lose his or her property often." The Master asked, "What would happen to the person who causes calamity to the Buddha's order by saying what he or she pleases without knowing the facts, or to the person who blocks a person's future by revealing that person's secret and hurts the faith and altruistic mind of the assembly?" Kim Yunjung answered, "Because of the evil karma of misusing one's tongue, one will be subjected to the malicious gossip. Since one has disrupted the Buddha's task, one's own future will be blocked or one will be incarnated a deaf-mute." The Master said, "Your words are all heavenly words." (CP 5:52)

79. The Master said, "If you keep a sense of respect and reverence for friends with a bright future, for the mentor with high virtue, and for the past sages you are not familiar with, then your affinity with them will be closer and you will be helped by them." (CP 5:57)

IV

Exposition of Scriptures

1. Master Chŏngsan said, "The *Canon* is the principal scripture, in which the fundamental principles of the doctrine are elucidated; the *Scripture of Sot'aesan* is the penetrating scripture, which helps one attain a thorough comprehension of myriad dharmas through the doctrine. These two will be the main scriptures of this order for ages to come." Yi Kongjŏn, his attendant, asked, "What is the core teaching of the other scriptures such as the *Canon of Rites?*" The Master said, "The core teaching of the *Canon of Rites* (*Yejŏn*) is reverence; that of the *Hymns*, harmony; and that of the *Canon of the World* (*Sejŏn*), right." (*CP* 6:1)

2. The Master said, "The founding motive of this order[32] lies not in opposing civilization based on science, but in strengthening and correcting the spirit of humans who seek and make use of it, so that they may make good use of it." (*CP* 6:2)

3. The Master said, "Irwŏnsang[33] is the master plan of all beings of the universe, the empty dharma realm, and the Truth Buddha (Dharmakāya). It is a *hwadu* for seeing into self-nature and realizing buddhahood. It is the object through which Truth is worshiped and is the standard of daily practice." (*CP* 6:3)

4. The Master said, "There are three levels of religious worship. People of low intellectual capacity, since they lack intelligence, can have faith only in an object of specific shape. People of high capacity, opposing idol worship, rely on the name of a specific higher being for religious faith. People with still higher capacity, being enlightened, believe in the essence

of Truth itself, which is devoid of name and form. These levels are like the following intellectual capacities. A child can be soothed with a candy. When the child grows, it can be persuaded to do things by invoking the name of an adult. An adult can be awakened only by an explanation of the whole situation. The intellectual level of the contemporary world is generally no higher than the second level. The intellectual level of humankind is gradually reaching adulthood; hence the popular sentiment will turn toward the great way of Irwŏn in the near future." (CP 6:4)

5. Master Chŏngsan explained the way of fairness,[34] one of the ways of the beneficence of heaven and earth as follows. "Fairness has two aspects. One is the aspect of common mind, in the sense that heaven and earth do not favor any one particular thing but is the common property of all things. The other aspect is impartiality, in the sense that without being swayed by remoteness and closeness or friendliness and estrangement, heaven and earth respond to each and everything for whatever they do." Explaining what is reasonable and what is unreasonable, he said, "What is reasonable is that which can be done and what is unreasonable is that which cannot be done." (CP 6:5)

6. Kwŏn Tonghwa asked, "Do heaven and earth have wishes, and are they pleased if their beneficence is returned?" The Master answered, "It is the way of heaven and earth that they do not harbor any false idea after bestowing favor to all things. However we can discern their wish if we see what they do and we can guess what they may like if we reflect on what we like. All sentient and insentient beings are none other than heaven and earth." (CP 6:6)

7. A disciple said, "I would like to know in detail why the beneficence of parents can be requited if I follow the essential way of humanity and the essential way of practice."[35] The Master replied, "The honorable names of your parents will be known to the world forever. Heavenly blessings will return to them for donating such buddhas and bodhisattvas to the world. It is easy for them to be influenced by their wise children in this life and the next." (CP 6:7)

8. The Master said, "Grand Master Sot'aesan has revealed mainly the way of reciprocal benefaction among the various truths of the universe and thereby elucidated the fact that we owe our lives to the Fourfold Beneficence.[36] Hence, you should realize that the tenet of the Fourfold Beneficence, Grand Master Sot'aesan's way of reciprocal benefaction, is the greatest way to deliver all sentient beings, and that the principle of

requital of the Fourfold Beneficence is the greatest fundamental power by which the world may be kept in peace." (*CP* 6:8)

9. Explaining the meaning of the Four Essentials,[37]the Master said, "The core of the principle of cultivation of self-power lies in taking self-power as the main source of life, even though both self-power and other-power may be relied on. The core of the principle of the wise one as the standard lies in letting the wise lead, though there is no fundamental discrimination between the wise and the deluded. The core of the principle of the education of the others' children lies in making education available to everyone, either one's own child or someone else's. The core of the principle of respect for those who serve selflessly for the public lies in putting the public interests prior to one's self-interest though the two should both be promoted." (*CP* 6:9)

10. The Master explained the meaning of self-power[38] as follows. "While living, one has duties and obligations which one has to fulfill. One should make it one's basic principle to carry them out by one's own effort and ability. In the spiritual realm, too, one should base one's religious faith on the faith in self-power, making oneself the master of one's religious faith. In the area of practice, one's practice should not be passive; one should be the master of one's own practice. While working in a specific public service one should exert oneself as if one were the owner. Thus, in affairs of all sorts, one should conduct those affairs mainly with one's self-power and ability, though one should utilize both self-power and other-power." (*CP* 6:10)

11. The Master said, concerning the mind of deluded people who would depend on others for their living, "First, they try to live an easy life, shifting to someone else what they can do for themselves. Second, they are deluded to have faith only in an illusory other-power, without understanding that both transgression and merits originate in one's own self and grow on the balance of self-power and other-power." (*CP* 6:11)

12. Explaining the statement "Education in general in the past did not increase in self-power; it did not get beyond other-power,"[39] the Master said, "Because of harsh governmental oppression, the people could not generate, or express, the public spirit needed to explore and develop any public enterprise. Religious orders were attached to many obsolete traditions so that their teachings were not for the public and their faith was based on the principle of other-power. People in their family lives were shackled to superstitious practices or geomantic predictions, so that they

abandoned themselves to fate, waiting for whatever the fate might bring. Thus, the public enterprise was deficient." (*CP* 6:12)

13. Explaining the statement "People enter the gate of suffering instead of happiness because they are ignorant of the cause of suffering and happiness,"[40] the Master said, "If one does not know the cause of suffering and happiness, one may bring about happiness by chance but will eventually enter the gate of suffering. This is like the case of a man who cannot distinguish sugar from arsenic and who may take sugar by chance but eventually ends up taking arsenic after serving himself several times." (*CP* 6:35)

14. Explaining a section of the description of dharma stages "formulates the standards of right and wrong, and gain and loss in accordance with the principles of the absolute and the phenomenal, and existence and nonexistence,"[41] the Master said, "A sage necessarily establishes moral laws for humankind reflecting on the truth of the universe. In the doctrine of our order, the fundamental tenet of Irwŏnsang is established to reflect the realm of the absolute. The details of the Fourfold Beneficence are established on the principle of the phenomenal. The tenets of cause and effect, the precepts, and other tenets are established to reflect the principle of existence and nonexistence. Thus, a sage establishes religious and moral laws in accordance with true principles so that the doctrine is formulated with clear distinctions of right and wrong, and gain and loss. This principle can be applied to personal practice. To cultivate one mind using Zen, by modeling oneself after the noumenal nature of Irwŏn, is to realize the realm of the absolute. To requite beneficence everywhere and to do all things as offerings to Buddha is to realize the phenomenal nature of Irwŏn. To use one's mind in accordance with the principle of existence and nonexistence without attachment thereto and to prepare for success in human affairs in accordance with the principle of change is to adapt the principle of existence and nonexistence." (*CP* 6:36)

15 A disciple asked, "The last three of the six dharma ranks[42] provide the criteria for being a sage. Do all those who have risen to one of those ranks have the same dharma power?" The Master answered, "Among the noted calligraphers some are experts in cursive and some others are experts in script. Likewise, those dharma masters who have ascended to the position of "subjugation of *māra* by the power of dharma and beyond" can be experts in different areas; and masters of the same rank do not necessarily have the same capacity of the dharma power." (*CP* 6:37)

16. A disciple asked whether anyone in the position of "subjugation of *māra* by the power of dharma" could freely transmigrate through the six paths. The disciple asked this question because one of the definitions of the position of "subjugation of *māra*" is "the position of the one who has attained emancipation from the sufferings of birth, old age, illness, and death." The Master answered, "The spiritual capacity of the position of 'subjugation of *māra* by the power of dharma' is marked only by the ability not to be pulled by the force of birth, old age, illness, and death. One must ascend to the position of 'transcendence' (*ch'ulga*) in order to be free from the six paths." (*CP* 6:38)

17. The attendant said, "There are some people who regard our order as a sect of traditional Buddhism." The Master said, "Śākyamuni Buddha preserved some tenets of Brahmanism, and Jesus Christ used the Old Testament as the origin of his teaching; however neither Buddhism nor Christianity is regarded as a sect of the older religions." The attendant asked again, "What is the relationship between the old doctrine and our doctrine?" The Master said, "Grand Master Sot'aesan has mainly created the doctrine, sometimes renovated the old doctrine, and sometimes adopted specific points from the old doctrine." (*CP* 6:39)

18. A guest asked, "Is the doctrine of your religion theism or atheism?" The Master replied, "We do not hold the view that there is a transcendent anthropomorphic deity. However, we hold the view that the numinous truth is ubiquitous throughout the universe. It is our aim to discipline and train our mind so that we could receive the great power of the truth and make use of it." The guest asked further, "Is your religion materialism or idealism?" The Master replied, "We hold that matter and mind are not two. The fundamental substance of all beings of the universe is that in which matter and mind are not two but identical. In its operation, however, mind becomes the substance and matter becomes its function." (*CP* 6:40)

19. While the Master was discoursing on the *Diamond Sūtra*, he explained the statement "The Tathāgata cannot be seen in his bodily shape or his voice"[43] as follows. "You cannot say you know what kind of a person someone is by simply looking at the external appearance of that person. You can say you truly know that person only after you have seen the dignified mien, words, knowledge, and mental functioning of that person. Likewise, the Tathāgata is in a realm that no ordinary man can see. One cannot say to have seen the whole of the Tathāgata unless one has seen the

whole of the Buddha's three bodies, namely, Dharmakāya, Sambhogakāya, and Nirmāṇakāya, by being enlightened to the realm which, transcending existence and nonexistence, is devoid of any phenomenal characteristics and discriminations of self and others." (*CP* 6:41)

20. The Master said, "In a Buddhist sūtra there occurs the term 'purity of three wheels.'[44] It means that giving can only be a true giving if giver, receiver, and gift are all empty. Therefore, one can be a true ancestor in the true dharma realm only if one gives material things, children, and oneself to the Buddha's business with empty mind." (*CP* 12:46)

21. Upon listening to a student's explanation of the Four Noble Truths, the Master said, "Of the eight characteristics of the truth of suffering, the first four, namely, birth, old age, sickness, and death are inevitable, natural forms of suffering. The second four, namely, parting with what we love, meeting with what we hate, failing to attain our goals, and suffering of all the ills of the five aggregates (*skandhas*), are forms of suffering that we create ourselves. Regarding the truth of the cause, form (*rūpa*) (which is the aggregate of earth, water, fire, and air), is an inevitable, natural aggregate; and consciousness (*vijñāna*) (which is the basis of perception, conception, and mental function), is a functional aggregate, which is continuously created anew. To submit peacefully to the natural forms of suffering and to the aggregates is the right course of practice; to bring about good karma out of the functional forms of suffering and the aggregates is the right course of practice." (*CP* 6:44)

22. Upon listening to a student's explanation of the twelvefold dependent co-arising the Master said, "The course of the twelvefold dependent co-arising is the course that the Buddha and all sentient beings follow to transmigrate. However, the Buddha is not deluded, because he knows the principle and the path, but sentient beings are deluded. The Buddha has a different practice in the present three causes of the twelve links, namely, craving, grasping, and being. While going about myriad kinds of business, the Buddha neither craves with greed, nor grasps with craving, nor attaches himself to whatever he does. His karma is thus perfectly pure and hence he is never deluded in the cycle of transmigration, which he ably transcends." (*CP* 6:45)

23. A student asked about the triple Buddha body (*trikāya*). The Master answered, "Dharmakāya (law body) is the true essence of the Buddha's own nature, which is originally pure and clean and devoid of any phenomenal reality. Sambhogakāya (reward body) is the perfect numinous awareness, namely, the prajñā-wisdom that reflects on the Bud-

dha's own nature. Nirmāṇakāya (transformation body) is the Buddha's discriminating mind and body, with which he delivered sentient beings by innumerable skilful means." (CP 6:46)

24. A disciple asked about "the formulas of refuge in the three precious ones." The Master answered, "The formula 'I take refuge in the Buddha, the precious one replete with wisdom and blessings' refers to a person who lives relying on the enlightened one who is replete with blessings and wisdom. Just as the seed of a plant needs the earth in order to send out a root and grow, a person must have the root of the mind in the Buddha and live with a firm faith, immovable in any favorable or adverse condition. The formula 'I take refuge in the Dharma, the precious law free from greed' refers to a person who cuts off greed by Buddha-dharma. Just as a spider relies on its webs, we must live relying on the laws and rules of the Buddha-nature and follow the practice of tracing back to the light and looking back on the radiance of the mind. The formula 'I take refuge in the sangha, the order of priests high among the sentient beings' refers to the person who disciplines himself or herself, relying on a teacher of high morals. We are to learn truth and morality from monks, priests, laity with good faith, and sages, and discipline ourselves taking our conscience as teacher." (CP 6:49)

25. A disciple asked whether worship of the Buddha image was nothing but an empty formality. The Master answered, "Even the worship of the Buddha image can be efficacious, depending on one's state of mind. When one holds a service sincerely in front of the Buddha image, one's mind will be purified; and if one makes good seeds with such a mind, one will reap a good crop. Thus, the image worship can be an expedient means." The disciple asked whether a service with a food offering would not be useless formality. The Master replied, "It could be a way of expressing your mind; however, you can make your mind sincere more effectively by performing your purification and by working for the public." (CP 6:50)

26. A disciple asked about the three worlds. The Master answered, "The three worlds of sentient beings are revealed as three realms, corresponding to the mental world of attachment. The world of desire is the mental realm of sentient beings that are attached to such corporeal desires as appetite for food, carnal desires, and desires for wealth. In order to satisfy those desires they commit various evil deeds and rush about madly with no sense of morality and shame. The world of form is the mental realm of those who are disturbed by too much thinking, measuring, and scheming because they are moved to do good things for

others by the desire for fame. Such people are jealous of their superiors and despise their inferiors while they do good things for the public. The formless world is the mental realm of those who cling to the illusory sign of dharma, namely, the thought that they are not attached to fame or thinking, measuring, and scheming, disliking such people who are so attached. You can transcend the three worlds only if you annihilate the clinging to the illusory sign of dharma." (CP 6:51)

27. A disciple asked about the six paths and four forms of birth. The Master answered, "The world divided into the six paths and four forms of birth is created and revealed by our differentiating mental states. The level of *devas* is the realm where one transcends all situations of suffering and pleasure and hence finds and enjoys happiness in suffering without being dragged into suffering. The level of humans is the realm where one can do good or evil, and find good and evil, standing at the crossroad of progression or retrogression, so that one can become better or fall into the evil realms. The level of animals is the realm where one has no sense of propriety and shame. The level of *asuras* is the realm where one has fallen into dead emptiness because one lives doing nothing, believing that it makes no difference after death. The level of hungry ghost is the realm where one expects blessedness without working for it and struggles for one's own fame, property, and so on without sharing with others. The level of hell is the realm where one's mind is always dark with boiling anger, where one sticks to one's own view and agrees with no one else. Thus, you should be able to enjoy the realm of *devas* by knowing that the six paths are built of your mind. You can be free from the six paths only if you can transcend even the realm of *deva*." (CP 6:52)

28. A disciple asked whether the Pure Land is really in the west. The Master answered, "The west belongs to metal, of the five primary elements,[45] and metal is said to belong to the energy of autumn. Autumn is clear and cool, and hence mental energy that is calm and clear is represented as of the west. Therefore, anywhere in the universe is the Pure Land if our mind is unimpaired, clear, and cool." (CP 6:54)

29. A disciple asked, "It is said that there are ten kings, daily messengers, and monthly messengers in the hall for 'the region of the dead' in Buddhist temples. Is it true?" The Master said, "The ten kings of Hades are the ten directions of the Truth realm. It means that numinous Truth, which is ubiquitous throughout the universe, is checking our good and evil actions, our transgressions and merits. Daily messengers and monthly

messengers are the sun and the moon, demanding death and judgment constantly." (*CP* 6:55)

30. The Master said about benevolence (*ren*) and righteousness (*yi*), "Benevolence refers to the Buddha's compassion and Christ's love. Righteousness lies in doing all things without violating heavenly principle and in the ways man ought to follow. Benevolence and righteousness can be minor or major. When one practices benevolence and righteousness, one must practice both minor and major. By practicing benevolence and righteousness in balance, one should demonstrate a public spirit of dignified calmness, even after subjugating hundreds of thousands of evils as a result of the grand influence of virtuous edification." (*CP* 6:57)

31. The Master said concerning loyalty (*zhong*), filial piety (*xiao*), and chastity (*lie*), "The Chinese character for 'loyalty' is composed of two characters standing for 'central mind,' which means the true mind that does not differentiate inside and outside. If people render services to society, contribute to the nation, and make efforts with this true mind in their position and everywhere, this is the application of loyalty. This is different from the narrow interpretation of loyalty of the past, according to which loyalty lay only in serving a single sovereign. This loyalty is also different from foolish loyalty, by which one had even to sacrifice oneself for a wicked king, regardless of national interests. The meaning of loyalty is vast and truthful, so that it is the fundamental moral principle of the world and the fair and equitable characteristic of humankind of all time. If you examine the mentality of the public today, you will see that its loyalty has been weak for a long time. Internally, people deceive their own consciences, showing no sign of repentance, and cheat on society with no sense of shame. Thus, human life has become complicated and social disorder is rampant. If this disorder is to be turned to a holy and truthful world, the spirit of loyalty should be promoted, so that the world should recover loyalty. Otherwise it will be difficult to realize an ideal world." (*CP* 6:58)

32. He continued, saying, "What is called filial piety (*xiao*) lies in all actions of beneficence requital. Now, requital of the beneficence of parents is the most fundamental of all acts of beneficence requital, for no one can know all other beneficences without knowing the beneficence of parents, especially the fundamental beneficence of heaven and earth, brethren, and laws. Therefore, the practice of filial piety lies in discovering all the beneficences, starting with that of parents. If everyone always

discovers all the beneficences everywhere and changes adverse conditions into occasions for gratitude, this is none other than the application of filial piety. This is not the kind of filial piety practiced in ancient times, when it was thought unfilial to leave one's parents at any time in one's life, causing one to neglect one's duty to the society and all other beneficence requital. The principle of filial piety is therefore truly vast and perfect, such that it is the fundamental moral principle of the world and the root of humanity. The general moral sentiment of today reveals that the world has long been weak in filial piety. In the family, one resents one's parents; away from one's family, one resents heaven and earth, brethren, and laws. Consequently, the mood of the world is dark and human life becomes dangerous. For this critical situation to be changed so we have a peaceful and comfortable world, the spirit of filial piety should be promoted in the public by all good means, so that the general public will fulfill the moral duty of filial piety." (*CP* 6:59)

33. The Master continued, "Chastity (*lie*) lies in not compromising one's determined righteous purpose. One can be said to be chaste if one keeps to one's determined righteous purpose. This is so because one should value one's integrity as highly as a woman should value her chastity. A woman who does not value her chastity as important would certainly not be sincere about the rest of her moral character. One should therefore be true to one's principles in all situations, just as woman guards her chastity. Thus, the practice of chastity lies in doing justice and not doing injustice with utmost effort by having one's will firm and in keeping to one's social position. This is different from the narrow interpretation of chastity in the ancient world, where a woman would grow old at the home of dead man with whom she had only been engaged. Nor is this the foolish chastity of a woman who would immolate herself on the death of her husband, ignoring her other duties and obligations to humanity. Thus, the significance of chastity is truly broad and widely applicable as the eternal moral principle of the world and the standard of humanity under heaven. To judge from today's public sentiments, chastity has been compromised for a long time. People have confused primary and secondary, and the host with the guest. A resolution made in the morning is broken in the evening; the theory of yesterday is changed today. The order of the world is not bright, and the standard of humanity is incorrect. The teachings of sages have lost authority, and human life has become disordered. It will be difficult to change the disordered world into a good one unless the spirit of chastity is advanced by all good means and the mind of the people returns to chastity." (*CP* 6:60)

34. The Master continued, "A prophet said, 'The world lacks loyalty, filial piety, and chastity; thus, everything under heaven is sick. Dispense medicine that can remedy the ills of the world.' What the prophet meant is that in the future, loyalty, filial piety, and chastity would be affected by moral disease, and hence, loyalty, filial piety, and chastity ought to be revived. The sickness of loyalty, filial piety, and chastity is the sickness of the world, and the religious doctrine of Grand Master Sot'aesan is the very prescription to cure the sick world. The daily cultivation of our true nature is the practice to revive loyalty; our efforts to requite the Fourfold Beneficence is the practice to revive filial piety; and consolidation of our faith and observation of the precepts[46] is the practice to revive chastity. But for our practice, how can loyalty, filial piety, and chastity be revived? How can all the sentient beings suffering in the seas of misery be saved without reviving loyalty, filial piety, and chastity? Therefore, you should exert yourselves in the practice so that you can be persons with no moral illness; our whole order shall be free of moral illness, and with moral power advanced, you will be the king of medicine, curing the whole world of moral illness." (*CP* 6:61)

35. The Master commented on the five relationships, "The moral principles of the five relationships were the standard of the oriental ethics and morality, and all the rules of law pertaining to family, society, and state were based on them. However, in recent years, this law became lax, and the ability to practice it has weakened. Thus, this law should be reformed to fit the new times. The old norms are (1) there ought to be affection between father and son, (2) there ought to be justice between the sovereign and the subject, (3) there ought to be difference between husband and wife, (4) there ought to be orderliness between senior and junior, and (5) there ought to be trustworthiness between friends. This should be reformed as follows: (1) there ought to be affection between father and son, (2') there ought to be righteousness between senior and junior, (3') there ought to be harmony between husband and wife, (4') there ought to be orderliness between adult and child, and (5') there ought to be faithfulness between brethren. In this way, the original meaning of the teaching can be revived, and the original intention of the ancient sage can be fulfilled." (*CP* 6:62)

36. The Master expounded the moral virtues of sincerity (*sŏng*), respect (*kyŏng*), and faithfulness (*shin*)[47] as follows. "Sincerity lies in doing all things with a pure mind, without any trickery or calculation; respect lies in doing all things carefully, on a basis of sincerity and guarding against negligence; faithfulness lies in maintaining one's faith to the end,

based on sincerity and respect. Hence, sincerity, respect, and faithfulness are three when divided, but one when united. Of the three, sincerity is the most fundamental." (*CP* 6:63)

37. A student asked, "It is written in the *Tonghak*, 'Pray to God for blessing and stipend; pray to me for longevity.'[48] What does this mean?" The Master said, "Since the principle of cause-and-effect response is the heavenly path of justice, one receives the effect from heaven in accordance with your transgression or merits that are the cause. One should learn the principle of immeasurable longevity by being enlightened to the principle of neither birth nor death from a sage who is enlightened to the heavenly way. That's why the sage said that prayer should be offered to him." Later on, the Master commented on the aphorism, 'As the vital force of the Way (*togi*) is maintained for a long time, no wickedness can invade my mind; I do not take the same way as stupid people in the world.'[49] The aphorism would be better if the last part of it were replaced with 'if the one mind is clear and pure, everything will be contented.' Is that not so?" (*CP* 6:64)

38. The Master said, "When Grand Master Sot'aesan formulated the ethics of the Fourfold Beneficence,[50] he did so by identifying the truth of the universe with beneficence, not just for curing the ills of resentment of the world." (*HH* 3:7)

39. "There are two kinds of efficacy of the Fourfold Beneficence. The first is the blessings and happiness one receives by putting into practice the measures for the requital of the Fourfold Beneficence; for instance, a farmer can gather in a huge harvest by farming well. The second is the efficacy brought through the realm of formless truth by silent prayers offered in one's mind. It is like the miracle of the bare thumbs pressed on a sheet of white paper that changed into bloody finger-prints."[51] (*HH* 2:8)

40. A disciple asked, "In the *Canon*, the way of heaven and earth has eight characteristics: it is exceedingly bright; exceedingly sincere; exceedingly fair; reasonable, and natural; vast, and limitless; eternal and immortal; with no good or evil fortune; and harboring no idea of return upon bestowing favors.[52] Why have you made 'having no thought upon bestowing beneficence' as representative of the eight ways of heaven and earth?" The Master answered, "The way of heaven and earth is bright, sincere, and fair because it is based on the principle of harboring no idea of return upon bestowing beneficence." (*HH* 3:10)

41. The Master said, "One can change the life of resentment to that of gratitude: first by wisdom, second by truth, and third by practice." (*HH* 3:11)

42. A disciple asked, "Laozi said that an enemy should be revenged with virtue, while Confucius said that an enemy should be revenged by uprightness.[53] What do these statements mean?" The Master said, "Laozi suggested that one must treat even an enemy with benevolence by transcending enmity, while Confucius taught that one cannot escape revenge if one produces an enemy." (HH 3:12)

43. The Master said, "The principle of heaven and earth can be the matrix for the beneficence of laws,[54] but it is not the beneficence of laws itself. It is part of the beneficence of heaven and earth. The beneficence of laws consists in the moral system that sages formulated reflecting on the principle of heaven and earth, in constitutive laws drawn up by legislators, and in legislators who made moral and penal laws and government officials who govern in accordance with morality and laws." (HH 3:14)

44. The Master said, "An actual offering to Buddha is the making of an offering to the myriad things in the yang-realm of heaven and earth; a noumenal offering to Buddha is the making of an offering to the yin-realm of the empty dharma realm. In order to have a perfect faith in buddha images everywhere and to do all things as making an offering to Buddha, one must put into practice both kinds of Buddha offerings." (HH 3:15)

45. The Master said, "The method of offering prayers is as follows. First, prayer should be offered, not to a particular object such as a pagoda tree,[55] a rock, and so on, but to the truth of Dharmakāya Buddha, Irwŏnsang, the fundamental source of the myriad things in the universe. Second, one must do one's utmost as follows: (a) cleaning the place of religious offering, ablution, wearing clean clothes, and maintaining spiritual purity by observing precepts; (b) resolving any grudges by eradicating any resentment and maliciousness that block the spiritual force; (c) being impartial and keeping no selfish desires in the mind, because the universal energy, being extremely fair, and unselfish, does not respond to anyone harboring selfish desires; and (d) not deceiving one's conscience, but putting into practice the articles one confesses in front of Dharmakāya Buddha, because, otherwise, one will incur severe punishment. Third, if one does one's utmost to offer prayers with consistent faith for a long time, one will be endowed with the great power of Dharmakāya Buddha, so that what one wishes will all be realized sooner or later." (HH 3:18)

46. The Master said, "Silent confession and prayer [56] should, for efficacy, be based on the balance of self-power and other-power. If the content of silent confession and prayer consists only of appealing to and entreating the Dharmakāya Buddha, it is leaning to the other-power.

Hence, silent confession and prayer will help one accomplish what one wishes only if one first declares one's resolution to practice, appealing to the Dharmakāya Buddha to bestow on one great power so one may do so. Only then will silent confession and prayer be balanced with regard to self-power and other-power." (*HH* 3:19)

47. The Master said, "Confession and prayer have subjective and objective efficacy. First, their subjective efficacy, which lies in the attainment of the spiritual concentration with which one can correct vicious habits and the success one will have in whatever one does by better concentrating oneself on what one does. Second, their objective efficacy, which lies in achieving what one does by moving people and heavenly will with utmost sincerity. Normally, one's mind does not slacken while one lives with seniors, and the true senior is the Truth.[57] If one deceives one's mind, the Truth knows it first, the Buddha whose Truth eye is open knows it, and last, sentient beings know it. One's deceit is known equally by the Truth, the Buddha, and sentient beings; the difference is only a question of time." (*HH* 3:20)

48. A disciple asked, "Sentient beings get life in accordance with the twelvefold dependent origination. How does the Buddha get his life? Since the Buddha has no karmic consciousness, does he get birth skipping one of the links, unlike deluded beings? The Master answered, "Sentient beings get their birth as the result of being dragged by the wheel of the twelvefold dependent origination. Their birth follows the law of causation by action influence,[58] in the sense that they get birth with consciousness (*vijñāna*) of habit force that is formed upon the mental function (*saṁskāra*) of a deluded mind (*avidiyā*). A buddha's birth is in accord with the causality of true thusness (*bhūtatathatā*), since a buddha is conceived not with ignorance but with wisdom, and not with consciousness of habit force but with pure consciousness developed with wisdom. Therefore, a buddha's conception occurs when the causality of action influence becomes that of true thusness." (*HH* 5:17)

49. The Master said, "A person ought to be both humane and righteous; one who lacks humaneness and righteousness is not worthy of being human. If one's humaneness is excessive and righteousness is ignored, or vice versa, then one's personality is defective. Humaneness and righteousness should be balanced according to the principle of the Mean." (*HH* 1:58)

V

Exhortations for the Practice of the Way

1. Master Chŏngsan said, "Depending on the mental condition of the audience, commonplace words become truthful dharma words, or dharma words of great significance can become commonplaces. Therefore, one who listens to the dharma must pay sincere faith and utter devotion to the preacher, with determination not to miss a word. Only then will the dharma words deeply be engraved on one's heart so that one will not forget them for a long time but will apply them in actual mental spheres. Only then, one will attain the benefit of the dharma." (CP 7:1)

2. The Master said, "The saying that is interesting to listen to but that lacks any point that one can learn is a clever saying; the saying that sounds plain to listen to but that has a marvelous richness as one keeps considering the meaning is a good dharma sermon. The saying that is lengthy but that lacks a point is an invalid saying. The saying that is brief but rich in meaning and clearly applicable is a good dharma sermon. Wise people discover dharma sermons in noisy idle talk and gossip in the marketplace, and hence attain awakening and meaning from the awkward speech of a beginning student. However, unwise people do not know how to get benefit from the sermon of a Buddhist priest of high virtue because they only measure the sermon with their own oversharpened talent. This is certainly a significant loss. Though the preacher of the dharma must check his or her knowledge and conduct in order to make a sound speech,

the listener should not mind the conduct of the preacher but only make use of the sermon in order to be benefited." (*CP* 7:2)

3. The Master said, "An enlightened person regards myriad things in the universe as buddhas and hears a constant dharma sermon from them;[59] such a person is of high capacity. A sensible person who loves to learn often comes into close friendship with the Buddhist priest of high virtue and enjoys listening to words of wisdom; this person is next in capacity. A foolish person lives irresponsibly without set standards, and even on hearing a good dharma sermon, does not know how to make use of it as laws; this person is of low capacity." (*CP* 7:3)

4. The Master said, "A deep-rooted tree is not uprooted by the wind, and a well fed by a deep spring does not dry up in a drought. The root of human life is religious faith, and the spring of human life is practice. The life with deep faith will not bend under any hardship and adverse condition, and the living with deep practice will transcend any temptation and attain tranquility." (*CP* 7:4)

5. "In ancient times, the Buddha received a body the color of gold; his status was of prince in the royal court; his wealth and prosperity was the very country under his sovereignty. The beauty of his consorts, the privileges of his authority, and the luxury of his dwelling and food had no match. However, foreseeing that all these things were vain and not wanting to be detained for long, he climbed over the castle walls in the middle of the night and pursued a path of extreme self-mortification. Eventually, he discovered the true treasure of neither arising nor ceasing, and thus became the great teacher of humanity and heaven. This can be the model for searching for the Way through eternity." (*CP* 7:5)

6. The Master said, "The greatest of all aspirations in the world is the four great vows.[60] You take the vow to save innumerable sentient beings. In order to realize this vow, you eradicate all defilement from your mind without ceasing, learn the dharma teaching with utmost sincerity, and continue to cultivate the Way of the Buddha throughout your eternal life. Then you will accomplish the great vow to realize buddhahood and save sentient beings. The difference between Buddha-bodhisattvas and ordinary sentient beings is like that between a huge tree and a seedling. The little seedling will be a huge tree when it has grown; a sentient being becomes a Buddha-bodhisattva with continuous practice. Therefore, if you have an unwavering will to do something, then you can do it, no matter how difficult it is. However, if you are unwilling to do anything, nothing will be accomplished. If, understanding that the Buddha and you are not

two, you steadily cultivate the Way with the four great vows, there will be nothing that cannot be accomplished." (*CP* 7:6)

7. The Master said to Shin Chegŭn, "Reflect on yourself to see whether you have secured the great aspiration and the faith not to leave this order throughout your eternal life. Take the vow to be enlightened to the truth without fail and not to lose the dharma affinity of the enlightened master. Be consistent with your vow to attain to buddhahood and deliver sentient beings with diligent practice through eons." (*CP* 7:8)

8. The Master said, "Once Grand Master Sot'aesan said, 'Who will know my true self?' Only now I feel the extreme acuteness of what he said. You will regard even a single word as gold and jade and put it into use only if you have an unwavering true faith; and only the practitioner who practices with utmost sincerity will understand and believe in Grand Master Sot'aesan." (*CP* 7:9)

9. The Master said, "Grand Master Sot'aesan said, 'It is difficult to deliver an imbecile and also is it difficult to deliver a superficially clever person. But, if you should deliver either of them at all, the imbecile is better than the clever one.' You should be so truly clever as to gather the essence of the words and thereby establish a firm faith; otherwise, you should take the straight path, as if you are stupid. It is difficult to deliver a clever person because the root of his faith is feeble." (*CP* 7:10)

10. The Master said, "The roots of faith vary in depth. If you are drawn to various theories and assertions without a fixed view of your own, and are shaken hither and thither and ruin your life by acting as you please, the root of your faith is an unstable one like fallen leaves. If you have firm faith in the true dharma, such that your faith is not shaken by minor adverse conditions but is shaken by major ones, though you do not become depraved thereby, the root of your faith is like that of a tree. If your faith is deep, such that you are never shaken by any adverse circumstance or difficult situation, and such that you do not fall into the suffering of transgression, because your conscience leads you, the root of your faith is like that of a huge mountain." (*CP* 7:11)

11. The Master said, "Self-power and other-power are so closely related to each other that neither can be separated from the other. There are some who, making too much of other-power, stick to the view that one has only to have faith. And there are others who, making much of self-power, hold the view that since mind is none other than the Buddha, one need not heed either precepts or the laws of karmic retribution. Neither of these positions has escaped being excessive or deficient. In the

case of faith in the Buddha, to have faith in his personality of enlightenment and practice is faith in other-power; to know that one's mind is none
other than the Buddha and cultivate the Mind-Buddha that is unified with
the Buddha is faith in self-power. In the case of faith in the dharma, to
believe in the dharma that the Buddha expounded in the realm of his
enlightenment is faith in other-power, and to do every action in accordance with the dharma upon awakening to the mental dharma of one's
own mind is self-power. In the case of faith in sangha, to believe in one's
mentor of the Way is to have faith in other-power, and to find one's true
conscience and act in accordance with it is to have faith in self-power.
Thus, one will succeed only if one has faith and practice in both self-power
and other-power integrated, so that the two powers are united." (*CP* 7:12)

12. At the opening ceremony of a Zen retreat, the Master said,
"There is a saying that only if I take good care of the Buddha image in
my temple will other people also take care of it. You must discover Buddha in yourself and make sincere offerings to it. Making an offering can
be done to oneself or to an object; both of these two must be complete.
In terms of order, of what is primary and secondary, however, making
offerings to oneself is fundamental. To do one's own mind cultivation
first is to learn the formula for making offerings to Buddha." (*CP* 7:13)

13. The Master said, "As I always say, when you offer a silent prayer
at dawn and night, do not forget to do so not just for yourself; do so also
for the world and the order. The merit will be much greater." (*CP* 7:16)

14. The Master said, "I offer my daily silent prayer like this:
'Dharmakāya Buddha, the Source of the Fourfold Beneficence! Bestow
upon us sentient beings the light and power of great mercy and compassion so that we can turn to morality and take refuge in correct Dharma.
Help us attain the mind of wisdom by transforming the mind of delusions. Help us attain the mind of compassion by transforming the mind
of violence and evil. Help us attain the mind of righteousness and truth
by transforming the wicked and untrue mind. Help us transform the
mind of jealousy and resentment to that of love and gratitude, the mind
of covetousness and greed to that of integrity and fairness, and the mind
of quarrel and injury to that of harmony and protection. Help us purify
the root of evil karma and let the way of wisdom and blessings open.
Let the international situation change for the better so that this country's
blessing will be limitless. Let the peace of the world be everlasting, and let
all people enjoy a bright future, tranquility, and happiness, living in the
Holy Land of the Buddha. I pray this with my whole heart!'" (*CP* 7:17)

15. The Master said, "Use the following as the model for the prayers at all dharma meetings: 'Dharmakāya Buddha, the Source of the Fourfold Beneficence! We are gathered at this dharma meeting. Bestow upon us special light and power so that the root of our faith and devotion may get deeper and the gate of wisdom and blessings may open wider. Let the three great powers of cultivation, inquiry, and heedful choice strengthen daily to transcend the realm of deluded beings to the path of bodhisattvas. Let us cultivate the path of bodhisattvas to enter the buddha stage. Let us remove evil barriers from the path of practice and public service. Let there be no barriers throughout east, west, south, and north so that we can benefit the public and receive welcome and protection wherever we go. Let words and actions all be truthful, and let us receive hidden help and hidden virtue. Let friends and brethren be in harmony with each other and unite to make this order known to the whole world, so that the merit of the doctrine of this order can help deliver all sentient beings.' " (CP 7:18)

16. The Master said to the students at Yuil Institute who offered prayers, "If you fail to keep a promise with an individual, there cannot fail to be a punishment for deceiving your own mind. You have consecrated a great vow to save sentient beings and cure the world of moral ills, to increase the divine brightness of heaven and earth, and your vow and pledge are important and great. If you break your vow and pledge halfway through the task, bear in mind that you will not escape severe punishment." (CP 7:19)

17. Hearing that Song Hyŏnp'ung was inquiring into perpetual motion, the Master said, "Just as machinery needs the unlimited motive power, we religious practitioners need an unlimited power source, and the unlimited power source of the practitioner is faith and devotion. It is faith and devotion that creates a sage out of a common mortal." (CP 7:25)

18. At a New Year's Day ceremony, the Master said, "Greeting the New Year, we should become new persons and thereby construct a new country and a New World with our effort, rejoicing that we are in a new paradise together. The way for us to become new persons lies in forming good habits with a new mind, rendering new charity to the world by reforming public service, which is not functioning, and recovering our originally complete self-nature by cultivating our original nature." (CP 7:28)

19. The Master said, "If we exert ourselves to practice and public service with new mind, our whole life will be new, our order will be new,

and our world will be new. And the fundamental source of the new mind lies in applying great compassion with great public spirit, based on a firm and great faith." (*CP* 7:29)

20. The Master said, "As frost and snow reveal the merit of pine and bamboo, it is favorable and adverse conditions that reveal the merit of the practitioner. It is when one experiences an insurmountable barrier, or when there are insurmountable barriers in the order, that the value of faith and merit of practice are revealed. It is for use in emergency that the country trains the army; so it is for the application of the power of mind in adverse conditions that the followers of the Way do mind cultivation." (*CP* 7:31)

21. The Master said, "What is most important for practice is to hold a standard in mind. For instance, if you read a scripture inattentively without any standard, the scripture will continue to be remote from you even if you read several hundred volumes; thus you will gain nothing. Religious practice does not lie exclusively in reading scriptures or learning letters; you will gather the true harvest of practice if you check your movement against the standard." (*CP* 7:34)

22. The Master said to the students, "Only to the one who earnestly seeks obtains what is sought. When the Buddha in ancient times attained the Way, seeing the morning star, it was not because the star had any special meaning that he attained enlightenment, seeing it. It was because his utmost aspiration to resolve his query concerning human birth, old age, illness, and death had deepened, layer on layer, that he was finally awakened. It was also due to the deepening, from the age of seven onward, of his utmost aspiration to attain the Way that Grand Master Sot'aesan attained great enlightenment. Thus, when you hear a dharma talk, listening attentively will be quite different from listening inattentively, and learning facts and principles with inquiring mind will be different from seeing and hearing carelessly. If you study all the theories with the *Canon* in mind, you will be brighter on the doctrine. If you hear the theories otherwise, your mind will only be distracted. Therefore, Grand Master Sot'aesan said that you must clarify your mind through seated meditation in the morning and inquire into principles using the scriptures during the day." (*CP* 7:35)

23. The Master said, "There are three ways to read the sūtras. The first is to read the scriptures written by ancient sages as books, and thereby brighten your knowledge and wisdom. The second is to acquire teachers and examples by observing the good and evil in people. The third is to

discover the teaching of truth in affairs and things that you handle. An enlightened person reads in all three ways, making every step and everything a great holy scripture." (*CP* 7:36)

24. The Master wrote in the preface to *A History of Founding the Society for the Study of Buddha-dharma*,[61] "It is said that history is the mirror of the world; it is because the rise and fall, prosperity and decline of all things are reflected in history. However, one cannot be said to have seen the true face of history by simply memorizing the written names of places, people, and chronology. The observer of the history can be said to have seen the true face of the history only if he or she has comprehended the general trend of the times, the mental state of the leader, the system of law, and its course. Only then, can history be a mirror that reflects both internal and external. Hence, a good study of the history of this order must enquire into the nature of the mission of this order and the characteristics of the times, the sagehood of Grand Master Sot'aesan, the course of founding the order, and the future prospectus of this order." (*CP* 7:37)

25. The Master said, "An ancient Zen master said, 'The ordinary and constant mind is the Way.'[62] 'Ordinary' means making no distinction between high and low rank and not discriminating between others and oneself. 'Constant' means abiding in the realm where the distinctions between old and new, and between existence and nonexistence, are all annihilated. This saying refers to one's self-nature, which is the great moral principle of the universe. Therefore, if one clearly comprehends the truth of 'ordinary and constant,' one has seen into this nature and mastered the Way. In the practical application of the mind, however, one puts into practice the ordinary and constant mind depending on the occasion, even if one has not completely comprehended its truth. Hence, we must inquire into the truth of ordinariness and constancy and make good application of the ordinary and constant mind." (*CP* 7:45)

26. The Master continued saying, "The practical application of the ordinary and constant mind can be interpreted with some illustrations. (1) Once one stands on the ground of justice for whatever one does, the ordinary and constant mind lies in keeping faith in it constantly. As firm faith transcends circumstances, neither acceptance nor rejection can increase or decrease it; neither ignominy nor glory can easily change or remove it. Once a resolution is made, one will break through myriad difficulties and, being calm and unperturbed, show no shaking or apprehension, even when facing the barrier of life or death. This is the ordinary and constant mind manifested in faithfulness. (2) Once one has formed the beneficent

relationships with others, the ordinary and constant mind lies in a perfect and pure spirit of camaraderie. One insists on fairness when faced with any matter, in a spirit that is above factions and not distracted by hatred or love. One insists on no-thought when rendering favors to others, so that one is free from favoring one side while harming the other, or from loving at one time and hating at other times. Even if the beneficiary becomes ungrateful, one does not change the mind that one had at the time of rendering beneficence. This is the ordinary and constant mind manifested in friendship. (3) When one is faced with wealth and poverty in the world, the ordinary and constant mind resides in candidness of emotions facing them. The mental attitude is always tranquil; the attitude being calm, one is not mean when poor, or extravagant when rich. Even if one wears and eats luxuriously, one does not show signs of arrogance; nor of shame, when one wears and eats poorly. This is the ordinary and constant mind manifested in wealth and poverty. (4) In all the cases of safety and danger that one is confronted with, the ordinary and constant mind is manifested when one keeps one's spirit concentrated. When one is safe, one does not drop one's guard against danger. When one is in an emergency, one does not violate any moral norm or overstep the bounds of moderation, so that one's unshakable and composed spirit never alters, in safety or in the midst of turmoil. This is the ordinary and constant mind manifested in safety and danger." (*CP* 7:46)

27. The Master continued, saying, "This can be put in a general principle. In all places and at all times, not to lose the one mind is the motivating power for the application of the ordinary and constant mind. The practitioner who is awakened to the truth of the ordinariness and constancy will easily master the marvelous method of emancipation from suffering and happiness of birth and death, and demonstrate the practice of the sage by applying the ordinary and constant mind. Thus, the saying 'The ordinary and constant mind is the Way' is indeed a pertinent teaching." (*CP* 7:47)

28. The Master said, "If a thing has the force of attraction within, then it has the tendency to attract energy from outside itself. It is due to the attracting force of liquor that drunkards go to a tavern. It is due to the attracting power of virtue that people gather around a virtuous person. If a practitioner of the Way works hard to cultivate the formless mind, formless mind power will grow, making it possible for him or her to attract and apply the enormous power of the universe. This is called the supreme power of the three worlds." (*CP* 7:49)

29. The Master said, "True freedom comes from perfect emancipation, and the ultimate principle of freedom is based on the truth of the universe and self-nature." (*CP* 7:50)

30. The Master said, "Up to the dharma stage of subjugation of *māra* by dharma power,[63] you should make the effort to become more vigorous in your practice, with zealous resolution asking, 'Who is Buddha, and what am I?' After reaching the dharma stage of subjugation of *māra* by dharma power, your practice will advance continually only if you take it to be your practice to eradicate false notions and an air of ascent by the philosophic view that the Buddha and a deluded being are originally one." (*CP* 7:51)

31. The Master said, "Just as the great sea receives waters from hundreds of thousands of valleys but leaves no trace of receiving them, a great person leaves no trace of practice and public service. Though one has a mastery of all facts and principles, one leaves no trace of such mastery; though one delivers myriad sentient beings, one leaves no trace of such deliverance." (*CP* 7:54)

32. The Master said, "By the practice of Irwŏn is meant the practice of the truth of Irwŏn. The method is to inquire into facts and principles in order to prove the fundamental principle of our original nature and the totality of the truth of Irwŏn without getting lost in mere branches. The practice should not stop at knowing the principle; we should protect the perfect original nature by reflecting its light on itself. Further, the practice should not stop at calmness of original nature; we should make a good application of the way of Irwŏn when we deal with myriad things. In these three practices lies the way of cultivating the substance and function of Irwŏn." (*CP* 5:4)

33. The Master said, "While a gifted youth, upon obtaining a post in the government, was paying a courtesy visit to the village elders, he went humbly to see His Excellency Ryu Hujo, former prime minister. There was a stream to cross. An old man with a topknot was fishing on the other side of the stream. The youth asked the old man help him cross. While he was being carried on the old man's back, he saw that the old man had on the sides of his horsehair headband jade beads that could only be allowed to a former supreme official. Realizing only then that the old man was His Excellency Ryu Hujo, the youth, trembling all over, tried to get down into the water. The old man said, 'What's the matter with you?' The youth said, 'Your Excellency, I have committed a grave offense.' When he was laid down on the other side of the stream, the youth threw himself on

the knees and humbly begged for his pardon. Then His Excellency Ryu Hujo said, 'You will get in trouble if any one takes notice of this. Do as if nothing has happened. Since you've come to see me, make a bow and go.' Saying so, it is said, he forgave the young man. The human mind should be as magnanimous as this." (*HH* 1:84)

VI

Moral Culture

1. Master Chŏngsan said, "By 'correct enlightenment and right practice'[64] is meant the following: (a) acting perfectly upon enlightenment to the truth of Irwŏn; (b) acting fairly and unselfishly upon enlightenment to the utterly fair and unselfish realm; (c) attaining emancipation from birth and death upon enlightenment to the realm of no birth and no death; and (d) keeping oneself, with the knowledge of emptiness of all phenomenal things, from being drawn to the mental spheres." (*HH* 3:45)

2. The Master said, "We discipline ourselves through the Threefold Practice of cultivation, inquiry, and heedful choice. The final goal and standard of cultivation is emancipation, that of inquiry is great enlightenment, and that of heedful choice is the mean and right." (*CP* 6:18)

3. The Master continued, "The essence of cultivation lies in ridding oneself of delusive thoughts and nourishing the true nature. The essence of inquiry lies in polishing one's wisdom and exerting oneself to comprehend the ultimate source of all beings. The essence of heedful choice lies in following the mean and right and forsaking wickedness and wrong." (*CP* 6:19)

4. The Master said, "There are two sides to the three great powers. One is accumulation and the other is application. One accumulates the three great powers while one is at rest and applies the three great powers to various situations when one acts. The three great powers that are accumulated at rest, if not applied in daily life, will be powerless, like a plant grown in the shade. The three great powers applied in daily life, if

not based on those accumulated at rest, will be powerless, like a plant with weak roots. Hence, the two should be pursued together, so that substance and function can be integrated and motion and calmness can be based on each other. In this way the discipline of the three great powers can be perfected." (*CP* 6:20)

5. The Master said, "One can attain the power of spiritual concentration only if one can maintain the one mind without being drawn to anything. One will attain the power of perfect concentration only if one can ably take or forsake anything in accord with the nature of each matter that one handles." (*HH* 3:21)

6. The Master said concerning the Threefold Practice,[65] "The Threefold Practice in the traditional Buddhism includes precepts (śīla), concentration, (samādhi), and wisdom (prajñā). This is different in its scope from our Threefold Practice, namely, spiritual cultivation, inquiry into facts and principles, and heedful choice in karmic action. While śīla puts emphasis on the individual's keeping the precepts, the practice of heedful choice in karmic action specifies the essential ways to choose the right in the cultivation of personal life, regulating the household, governing the country, and keeping the world in peace. While prajñā focused on the wisdom that emanates from the self-nature, inquiry into facts and principles is the way of comprehending all human affairs and all principles. While samādhi aims at concentration of mind, spiritual cultivation is the way of the one mind that maintains the self-nature in motion and at rest. One will achieve great success in whatever one does through this Threefold Practice; there is no other way of practice superior to this." (*CP* 6:13)

7. The Master said further about the Threefold Practice, "Even those who are not following this practice may be living on the principle of the Threefold Practice. However, their Threefold Practice is accidental, purposeless, and temporary; while the follower of the Way does the Threefold Practice with a clear purpose to attain moral perfection in accordance with regulations, and with constancy." (*CP* 6:14)

8. The Master said, "Our practice of timeless Zen and placeless Zen includes Zen practice at a set time and a set place. Our practice of doing all things as an offering to Buddha because the Buddha image is everywhere includes the requirement that we should sincerely perform the making of offerings in front of the Buddha image at a set place." (*CP* 6:29)

9. The Master said, "Water freezes if the north wind keeps on blowing. Just as freezing water ends up thawing if the south wind blows back a weak north wind, the practitioner who wishes to attain the threefold

great power ought to live with the unwavering aspiration for practice; one will regress if one's aspiration to practice is lost." (*HH* 1:46)

10. The Master said, "There are three stages in following nature. In the first, the right mind commands one's six sense organs; hence, the meaning of 'commanding.' In the second, one follows the nature that is perfect, complete, utterly fair, and unselfish; hence, the meaning of 'following.' In the third, one is enlightened to self-nature and thereby uses joy, anger, sorrow, and pleasures in accord with the Mean; hence, the meaning of 'using.' The Chinese ideograph *shuai'* (K. *sol*) in 'The Essential Discourse on Following Original Nature'[66] is used with the sense of 'commanding.'" (*HH* 3:78)

11. The Master said, "The fact that the sixth patriarch Huineng[67] attained enlightenment on hearing the reading of the *Diamond Sūtra* on the street while selling firewood proves that an ignorant person can be enlightened. Learning is necessary for edification as a skillful means; but in the moral order, dharma power is regarded as more important than academic learning." (*HH* 1:57)

12. The Master said, "The main rubrics of spiritual cultivation are repetition of the name of Buddha, seated meditation, timeless Zen, and placeless Zen; however, inquiry into facts and principles and heedful choice in karmic action are also necessary. The method of inquiry into facts and principles lies mainly in the extension of knowledge, learning of principles, and thinking; however, its necessary bases are spiritual cultivation and heedful choice in karmic action. The practice of heedful choice in karmic action lies mainly in experience, cautiousness, and resolution; however, its necessary bases are spiritual cultivation and inquiry into facts and principles." (*CP* 6:15)

13. The Master said, "As a result of spiritual cultivation one eventually attains freedom from birth and death, perfect bliss, and success in everything one does. As a result of inquiry into facts and principles, one will attain a mastery of facts and principles, deliver sentient beings, and succeed in whatever one does. As a result of heedful choice in karmic action, one will attain perfection in whatever one does, perfect blessings, and success in whatever one does." (*CP* 6:16)

14. The Master, explaining the basic points of the *Correct Canon of Cultivating the Mind* (*Susim chŏnggyŏng*) and of the concepts of external cultivation (*oe suyang*) and internal cultivation (*nae suyang*), said that external cultivation is the practice of taking a stand against the mental sphere externally. "First, it is the practice of avoiding the external mental

sphere, that is, staying away from external temptations at the initial stage of practice. Second, it is the practice of forsaking, that is, to drop any matter that is not urgent or too complicated. Third, it is the practice of relying on the dharma, that is, to have faith in the dharma of emancipation, and to seek peace of mind in the Truth. Fourth, it is the extension of knowledge, that is, to listen to the true stories of many master minds to expand one's magnanimity. If you follow all these practices, the external mental spheres will become calm and your mind will be peaceful. Internal cultivation is the practice of cultivating one's mind internally. The first practice is to seize the mind (*chipsim*). That is, to get hold of the mind by sitting in meditation and reciting the name of Buddha, or at any time, lest the mind be distracted to the external mental spheres, just as the oxherd gets hold of the ox's rein and does not let go of it. The second is the practice to watch the mind (*kwansim*), that is, being satisfied upon completion of seizing the mind, to watch the way the mind moves, eliminating worldly thought just as the oxherd loosens the reins, taking sanctions only against the ox's misbehavior. The third is the practice of no mind (*musim*). When the practice of watching the mind is mature, one lets go of the idea of watching, so that you watch, but there is nothing to be watched, just as the oxherd enters the realm of no difference between man and ox so that movement and quiescence are uniform. If the one mind is clear and calm, then myriad external mental spheres are all clear and calm, so that the Pure Land will be realized with no gap between subject and object." (*CP* 6:65)

15. The Master continued expounding on external concentration-calmness (*oejŏngjŏng*) and internal concentration-calmness (*naejŏngjŏng*):[68] "External concentration-calmness is the practice of keeping one's resolution externally immovable as follows. First, one develops a great aspiration. One's unwavering aspiration lets one look but see nothing, or see no hindrance when myriad worldly affinities lie ahead, just as the pleasure of the royal palace or the suffering of the Himalayas did not stay in the mind of Śākyamuni once he resolved to attain the great Way. Second, one possesses great faith. This is to have no consideration or estimation of the myriad worldly opinions because of one's firm faith, just as Huike (AD 487–593) sought the dharma upon his resolution to receive the dharma from Bodhidharma without minding his body. Third, one develops zeal, that is, to be extremely zealous so that one will not be stopped by myriad surrounding obstacles, just as the twelve apostles were not stopped by the danger of death in order to protect the Way. If you

follow these three practices, your volition will be as firm as Mount Tai and not waver. Internal concentration-calmness is the practice of internally keeping the mind from being disturbed. First, one fosters the one mind by keeping disturbed thought from arising, by seated meditation, reciting the name of Buddha, or being at rest. Second, one keeps delusive thoughts from arising even for a second, maintaining right intentions while in motion, walking or standing, or while the six sense organs are at work. Third, one forgets the mental spheres confronting one and keeps the mind free from attachment or defilement by being free from the four false notions (*sasang*) and keeping the six mental spheres pure. If you attain these three powers, naturally the sea of your mind will be calm and peaceful and the evil passions will be permanently extinguished." (*CP* 6:66)

16. The Master said to a student, "It is said that you must enter into a great calmness in order to attain great wisdom. So I was training in calmness of no-thought at Wŏlmyŏng-am. However, Grand Master Sot'aesan warned me that I would be ignorant of affairs and facts if I practiced that way. Thus, you should train yourself in the practice of getting hold of and letting go of the mind together. You will practice perfectly only if you can do the practice of getting hold of and letting go of the mind as freely as inhaling and exhaling." (*CP* 7:33)

17. The Master said concerning the three great powers, "The power of cultivation of spirit can be measured by checking how often one's mind is drawn to external things while one is at rest and whether one's mind is drawn to things when one is in motion. The power of inquiry into facts and principles can be measured by evaluating one's mastery of the principles of self-nature, depth of understanding of the scriptures, and ability to make correct judgments on facts and things. The power of heedful choice in karmic action can be measured by checking one's daily diary to gauge one's adherence to the precepts and by examining one's ability to act in a timely manner according to circumstances." (*CP* 6:17)

18. The Master wrote nine articles of reflection as a commentary on the Essentials of Daily Practice[69] for the students at Yŏngsan: "When the mind-ground is not disturbed, the elixir of immortality (*yŏngdan*) will gradually grow greater; you will be endowed with the capacity to develop into a great person. When the mind-ground is not deluded, the light of wisdom gradually appears, and you will attain the wisdom of a great person. When the mind-ground is free from error, the power to do justice gradually expands, and you will be endowed with the blessings

and virtue of a great person. As you develop your faith, zeal, doubt, and devotion, all disbelief, greed, laziness, and delusion will be extinguished, and you will succeed in attaining the great Way. As you change a life of resentment into that of gratitude, grudges accumulated in former lives will gradually be dissolved and blessings and virtues will be abundant. As you change a life dependent on other-power to one that uses self-power, debts accumulated in your former existences will gradually be paid off, and blessings and income are gradually saved. As you change those unwilling to learn into those willing to learn and those unwilling to teach into those willing to teach well, you will always have rich knowledge in the endless future lives. As you change those lacking in public spirit into those full of public spirit, your virtue and influence will be boundless in numberless future lives." (*CP* 7:30)

19. The Master said, "If you apply faith, zeal, doubt, and sincerity to mind cultivation, you will succeed in the Threefold Practice. And if you apply them to the occupations of scholar-official, farmer, artisan, and merchant, you will succeed in your occupation." (*CP* 7:32)

20. The Master said, "The practice of inquiry (into facts and principles)[70] has three essentials. The first is to see correctly, the second is to know correctly, and the third is to be awakened correctly. Of these, the correct awakening is the final. The true realm of correct awakening includes the following: what you cannot discard internally though you try to, what you cannot forget though you try to, what you cannot hide though you try to, what fortune and misfortune cannot shake externally, what favorable and adverse conditions cannot tempt, and the thought that cannot be deflected by hundreds of mysterious things." (*CP* 7:39)

21. The Master said, "Do you spend your time with *hwadu* in your mind? Although it is right to practice *hwadu* in the orders of rational Zen, Tathāgata Zen, and patriarchal Zen, you should not continue *hwadu* practice all day long, as in the Zen monastery in the past. While you may spend your time with a *hwadu* stored away in your mind, you should inquire into it briefly when your mind is clear and calm. Then the gate of wisdom will open just as an egg transforms itself into a chick when the hen keeps and rolls it for a long time." (*CP* 7:38)

22. The Master said, "Great Master Hui-neng (638–713) and Great Master Shenhsiu (605?–706) both edified others on the triple discipline of concentration, wisdom, and precepts; however, their levels of edification differed from each other. Shenhsiu taught simply concentration, wisdom, and precepts, while Hui-neng taught the concentration, wisdom, and pre-

cepts of self-nature. The former practice was like going somewhere without knowing the destination, while the latter was like going with a clear destination. While a practitioner who is ignorant of the concentration of self-nature is troubled by as many evil passions as he tries to suppress, the one who is enlightened to self-nature finds that any evil passion thaws like melting snow. While one who is not enlightened to self-nature, which is devoid of birth and death, is frightened at death, the one enlightened to self-nature devoid of birth and death attains peace of mind when facing death. While one who is ignorant of the wisdom of self-nature is attached to what one knows, the one who knows the wisdom of self-nature attains the light of prajñā-wisdom of Irwŏn (Dharmakāya). While one who is ignorant of the precepts of self-nature will be intent on distinguishing between right and wrong and good and evil in daily affairs, the one who is enlightened to the precepts of self-nature will act like heaven and earth, knowing that the mind devoid of wickedness is righteousness and that righteousness is one's original nature." (HH 3:30)

23. The Master said, "By the mind 'neither deficient nor excessive' is meant that the mind devoid of wicked and wanton thought is Irwŏn; hence, one's action is neither wicked nor wanton if done without wicked or wanton thoughts. By 'not deficient' is meant that there is nothing deficient or wrong, and by 'not excessive' is meant that there is nothing to feel satisfied or proud of achievement." (HH 3:47)

24. The Master said, "In the Analects of Confucius, we read, 'When Yen Yüan asked the meaning of ren, the master replied: ren is the denial of self and response to the right and proper (propriety).'[71] The phrase 'keeping disturbances from arising' in the Essentials of Daily Practice is similar to 'denying the self' and 'maintaining concentration of self-nature' in 'response to what is right and proper (propriety).' "[72] (HH 3:94)

25. The Master said, "When one's reason is obscured by something, one is attracted to it; when attracted, one does wrong. What is wrong becomes sin and evil. Foolish people cannot see anything but their own ideas because they are obscured by their own self-importance, thus doing things wrong. When they criticize someone else, however, they are bright and sharp because nothing obscures them. If that brightness can be turned inward and used to correct one's own faults, one will attain great wisdom and blessings." (CP 5:26)

26. The Master said, "Seeing into nature has three stages. The first is to be enlightened to the realm where myriad dharmas have returned to unitary nature; the second is to be enlightened to the realm that is empty

of existence and nonexistence; and the third is to be enlightened to the realm where existence and nonexistence are complete. There are three stages of practice. The first is to differentiate good from evil; the second is to realize the emptiness of good and evil; and the third is to practice to attain the ability to deliver both good and evil." (*HH* 3:76)

27. The Master said, "Seeing the nature (attaining enlightenment) has five steps. The first is to show the evidence for how all dharmas (beings) return to one.[73] The second is to know the realm of true emptiness. The third is to see the truth of wondrous existence. The fourth is to keep the one mind from internal disturbances and external temptations. The fifth is to apply this mind to all situations magnificently." (*CP* 5:9)

28. A disciple asked about suddenness and gradualness, and enlightenment and cultivation.[74] The Master answered, "If you attain sudden enlightenment after gradual cultivation, you are a person of ordinary capacity. A man of ordinary capacity keeps up his practice under the direction of a good teacher and is suddenly enlightened to the principle of his own nature. This is the normal way for most people. If you take the path of gradual cultivation after sudden enlightenment, you gradually correct the old habit of your past lives with dharma power. This occurs because the habit force remains even after you are enlightened to your own nature by the power of wisdom. This is the way one follows if in one's previous lives there was enough training in wisdom but little in practice. If you take the path of sudden cultivation upon sudden enlightenment, you complete practice in wisdom and action at the same time because you attain the power of cultivation as soon as you are enlightened. Then you must have been a buddha or bodhisattva whose Threefold Practice has been perfect throughout innumerable incarnations. Such a buddha or bodhisattva recovers the light of wisdom all at once after being deluded in the human condition for a while." (*CP* 6:47)

29. A disciple asked about the samādhi and prajñā of self-nature and the relative samādhi and prajñā that adapts to signs.[75] The Master answered, "You enter the samādhi of self-nature if there is no sign of samādhi when you enter it in all mental spheres. You realize the prajñā of self-nature if there is no sign of prajñā when you are wise. If there is a sign of samādhi when you cultivate it, it is the relative samādhi that adapts to signs. If there is a sign of prajñā when you cultivate it, it is the relative prajñā that adapts to signs." (*CP* 6:48)

30. The Master said, "The practice of letting go of the discrimination

between oneself and others is done by maintaining the complete, perfect, and true realm of one mind while one is at rest and by remaining utterly fair and unselfish while one is acting.[76] (*HH* 3:22)

31. The Master said, "Reciting the name of Buddha has degrees of fruitfulness. Mere repetition of the name of Buddha or mere imagination of the image of the Buddha is a practice of those low intellectual capacity. Intoning the name of Buddha, when done by a true practitioner, is the concentration of the one mind on the uniform sound of the intoning while thinking of the power of the Buddha's aspiration, his mind, and his deeds." (*CP* 6:28)

32. A student asked, "Are recitation of the sacred name of Amitābha and seated meditation the only way for the practice of concentration?" The Master said, "Concentration of your mind without attachment to whatever you do is the way of practice of concentration. A prayer makes a way for practice of concentration, and you can attain great power of concentration if, with sound thought, you ascertain what should be chosen and forsake what should be forsaken, in accordance with the nature of the matter." He continued, "Seated meditation is the main path in the practice of concentration, and prayer is a shortcut to the practice of concentration. If your mind is concentrated while offering prayers, you attain both the great power of prayer and the power of concentration." (*CP* 7:14)

33. The Master said, "A judgment can be right only if it arises in the state of mind which is free from the false notions of good or bad, beautiful or ugly, one's self or others, and enlightened or unenlightened. You can be a perfect being of the Way only if you attain to the Truth with such judgment and practice it." (*CP* 5:24)

34. The Master said, "There are a few difficult barriers on the way toward buddhahood, which we practitioners must overcome. The first is the time when knowledge and views have started to advance. The second is the time when the public confidence and popularity have started to consolidate. The third is the time when the public acceptance has become highly visible. The fourth is the time when material things have come into one's possession. The fifth is the time when one has risen to power. The practitioner will ably accomplish a great practice only by foreseeing these barriers and not being troubled by them." (*CP* 7:21)

35. The Master said, "Those of low capacity cannot rise high because they are tied down by the desires of food, sex, and greed for wealth. Those of intermediate capacity cannot rise high because they are tied by the

desire for fame. And those of higher capacity cannot soar high because they are trapped by false notions (*sang*). If one is free from the five desires and the four false notions, one is of high capacity." (*CP* 7:22)

36. The Master said, "If you wish to become a noted calligrapher, you must model yourself after the style of penmanship of the master calligrapher and develop the stroke of your brush. Likewise, if you wish to attain to buddhahood, you must model yourself after the mental dharma of the Buddha and grow the Buddha-mind daily and hourly. We should become true disciples of Grand Master Sot'aesan by modeling ourselves after his mental dharma and thereby receiving the transmission of his dharma." (*CP* 7:23)

37. The Master said, "The national defense needs to protect in three areas, land, sea, and air. A practitioner needs to subjugate, using dharma power, the threefold evil (*māra*), that arises in the three mental spheres. The favorable mental sphere is subject to mental temptation; the adverse mental sphere is subject to mental offense. The mental sphere of emptiness is subject to mental laziness. Prior to the subjugation of evil (*māra*) by the power of dharma,[77] one must exert mainly to defend; after subjugation, one should make use of these mental spheres, as one does one's servant." (*CP* 7:41)

38. The Master said, "If you make an extreme effort to practice without taking care of your body and thereby hurt yourself, or if you neglect the practice only to take care of your body, you do not know how to do practice right. You will achieve a good practice without falling ill only if you know when to make an effort and when to let go, by checking your physical and spiritual capacity." (*CP* 7:42)

39. The Master said, "It is the wise one's way of practice to check one's capacity to cope with difficult mental spheres. If one can stand up to a mental sphere well, one will cope with it; otherwise, one should first avoid it and then, only after one has attained enough spiritual power through one's practice, stand face to face with it. If you try to overcome tough mental spheres without enough spiritual power, you will only trouble your mind and body without making any progress in practice, as often happens." (*CP* 7:43)

40. The Master said, "A patient recovers good health when the pulse is balanced by slowing it down if it is too rapid and making it strong if it is too weak. Likewise, our personal character will be healthy, with no moral illness, only if we have balanced our mind with the mean, to be neither excessive, nor deficient, nor partial. One whose nature is overly truthful and good does not know how to overcome an adverse condition

of even minor difficulty. One whose character is overly lively has the fault of being restless, of being too empty-headed. One who is overly courteous has the fault of being slow. One who is overly talented has the fault of being imprudent and scanty in virtue. One whose thought is overly lofty has the fault of being arrogant. One who is overly modest has the fault of having little courage for improvement. One whose thought is overly grand has the fault of being negligent in minor and close matters. One whose thought is overly minute has the fault of losing sight of the main point and of general principles. One who is overly zealous has the fault of readily hating someone who does better than he or she does. One who is overly humble has the fault of having no zeal at anything. One who is overly dignified has the fault of lacking a gentle attitude. One who is too gentle has the fault of lacking a dignified attitude. One who is overly upright has the fault of being disliked by people. One who is unreflectingly harmonious has the fault of not discriminating good from evil. One with an iron will has the fault of being cruel. One who is overly genial has the fault of wanting in the power of decision. We must know our characters and exert ourselves to balance them if our own character is disposed to lean to one side. While doing practice, we should not be attached to a particular part of it; while doing public service, we should not be attached to only a part of public service. We should not neglect public service when we are more inclined to do practice, nor should we neglect practice, when we are inclined more to public service. One who continues to practice in this way will be a person of merit, gradually achieving the perfect Way, one's character will be flawless and one's personality will be perfect." (*CP* 7:44)

41. The Master said, "Do not try to bind your mind too fiercely, but pursue the practice slowly without interruptions. You should pursue the practice with getting hold of the mind (*chipsim*), watching the mind (*kwansim*), and having no-mind (*musim*) alternately. The first stage of practice should concentrate mainly on getting hold of the mind; being somewhat skilled with this, you may practice mainly with watching the mind; being more skilled, you may practice with no-mind. Finally, you should attain the able-mind (*nŭngsim*)." (*CP* 7:48)

42. The Master said, "Though you accumulate concentration, do so without adhering to movement and quiescence. Though you cultivate wisdom, do so without attachment to being wise or deluded. Though you observe precepts, do so without being shackled by good and evil." (*CP* 7:52)

43. A disciple asked, "What is the correct way of mind cultivation

when there is a complicated matter to deal with? The Master answered, "No particular practice is necessary. Practice deliberating on the matter only then, and forget about it when it is done. (*HH* 3:25)

44. The Master said, "The soul, the original source of our being, is eternal and free from birth and death; however, our body and the elixir of the divine spirit that we have consolidated with great effort have their life span. Thus, the elixir of the divine spirit, though we have accumulated it, can crumble if we are careless." (*HH* 3:28)

45. The Master said, "The steps of practice to eradicate the three poisons of mind are generally as follows. Ordinary humans live their lives sunk in the sea of three poisons, but they do not know that they do. Listening to the teachings of the enlightened masters, they for the first time come to know that they have greed, anger, and delusions in their mind, and they begin to exert themselves to eradicate the three poisons. In the beginning it may take an hour for them to let go of the three poisons, then it may take less and less time until they reach the stage of practice where the three poisons are done away with instantly, eventually reaching the realm devoid of the three poisons. This is the process of going through *śravaka, pratyeka-buddha,* bodhisattva, and the Buddha. This process can be compared to the day breaking. The deep night before the rooster's crowing is the time for the living sunk in the sea of three poisons. The rooster's crowing is the time for knowing of the three poisons. Daybreak is the time for maintaining heedful practice. Sunrise is the time for one's practice maturing. And broad daylight is the time for reaching the buddha stage." (*HH* 3:34)

46. The Master said, "Even if the evil mind is cut off, there remain unnecessary delusive thoughts, which should be cut off. Do not be vexed by delusive thoughts and worldly thoughts that may arise. They will vanish of themselves if you do not adore them." (*HH* 3:26)

47. The Master said, "The reason human mind is called heavenly innocence or the will of heaven is that heaven and human mind are not two but one. Only if one knows this realm, one will stand in awe of the Truth and know how to accumulate hidden virtue and merits." (*CP* 5:29)

48. A disciple asked, "Are ascent and descent[78] dependent on how one practices?" The Master answered, "There are two causes of ascent and descent; one is natural and the other is human. Natural ascent or descent occurs in accordance with the degrees of the movement of heaven and earth. The human cause of ascent or descent is the karmic cause that

depends on one's practice and action." (*CP* 5:37)

49. The Master said, "There are six ways of ascent. The first is to make constant progress without becoming depraved. The second is to establish a firm faith that will not be shaken in either favorable or adverse mental spheres. The third is to establish a friendly and close relationship with a morally superior person, whom you should regard with deep respect and have faith in, devoting yourself to practice. The fourth is to accept with magnanimity those of inferior capacity and to protect and lead them to become superior to you. The fifth is to devote yourself to, always feeling deficient in, practice and public service. The sixth is to feel satisfied with your own daily commodities and to love to give generously to your poor neighbors." (*CP* 5:38)

50. The Master said, "The cause of ascent and descent of our practice lies in the greatness or smallness of our aspiration, harboring or not harboring self-conceit, and maintaining or not maintaining close relationship with the mentor of the lofty dharma. Hence, when we do the Buddhist practice, we must set ourselves a great and boundless aspiration, and exert ourselves on the path of practice with no self-conceit, and in close relationship with a mentor and dharma friends. Only then will we not be demoted but on the path of ascent eternally." (*CP* 7:7)

51. The Master said, "The person who is on the way of ascent has the characteristics of benevolence, modesty, diligence, humility with an empty mind, respect for others, magnanimity and virtuous influence, and consistency in his or her constant effort in the practice and in public service. The person who is on the way of descent has the characteristics of harshness, no respect for others, jealousy and envy, selfishness, and self-conceit about his or her superior knowledge, property, power, or skill. You should keep on the path of ascent by devoting yourselves to practice and public service. True ascent comes only if you do not abide in the idea of ascent when you are promoted. Whichever level of the six dharma stages[79] you are on, you can truly be on that level only if you do not abide in the idea of being there. Only then can you promote yourself to the highest position, attaining to the position and ability of the 'never regressing.'"[80] (*CP* 5:39)

52. The Master said, "Humans bestow blessings or commit transgressions with their body, mouth, and mind. Sages who know the Way put emphasis on the formless mind, while ordinary people are afraid of nothing but what is manifest. The perspicacious, empty dharma realm

responds to what happens in the formless mind. Hence, we should be careful about our words and deeds, and we should be more afraid of any evil karma committed by our mind, taking care of what is before its manifestation." (*CP* 5:47)

53. The Master said, "The practice of repentance[81] does not lie in the formalities of repentance, but in sincere repentance in front of the three precious ones (*triratna*) of Buddha, dharma, and sangha. By 'Buddha' is meant Dharmakāya Buddha, Irwŏnsang. Hence, one must reflect on whether one has attained cultivation, knowledge, and action that are as perfect as Irwŏn whenever one confronts any matter, so that one may foster spiritual power that is as perfect and complete as Dharmakāya Buddha. By 'dharma' is meant the *Canon* of this order, which is the description of the truth to which one is awakened. By reflecting on whether one has practiced in accord with the teachings in this *Canon,* one should be free from any deficiency. By 'sangha' is meant the community of good friends in the dharma who practice the dharma to be enlightened to the truth. The beginner ought always to follow their teachings well, report all things to them for appraisal of good and evil, right and wrong before taking an important action. In this way one can become a bodhisattva who has taken refuge in the three precious ones of Buddha, dharma, and sangha." (*HH* 3:50)

54. Concerning the practice of the phenomenal repentance (*sach'am*)[82] the Master said, "First, one should erase small greed with the great aspiration to realize buddhahood. Second, one should understand the benefits and harm of good and evil by examining the facts. Third, one should offer sincere prayers of repentance in front of the Dharmakāya Buddha. Fourth, one should do one's best to correct one's evil deeds and renovate oneself day after day." (*CP* 6:31)

55. Concerning the method of the noumenal repentance (*ich'am*)[83] the Master said, "First, one should be enlightened to the truth that everything is the creation of one's own mind. Second, one should comprehend that the causal law is the principle of the universe. Third, one should realize that one's own original nature is utterly devoid of evil karma. Fourth, one should attain the power of samādhi in motion and at rest by reflecting on the emptiness of one's own original nature." (*CP* 6:32)

56. Concerning the result of repentance the Master said, "The result of phenomenal repentance is, first, evil karma is daily extinguished; second, good karma is accumulated daily; third, worldly blessedness continues. The result of noumenal repentance is that one enjoys the pure paradise, which is realized, upon enlightenment to one's original nature, when the

six realms of existence are experienced as a pure, blissful taste." (*CP* 6:33)

57. Concerning the precepts[84] the Master said, "One should keep the precept of no killing, abstaining from harming or injuring living beings. One should keep the precept of no stealing, abstaining from taking unjust wealth. One should keep the precept of no adultery; even husband and wife should not be debauched or indulgent." (*CP* 6:34)

58. The Master said, "Even if taking a life has a due cause, it must be done with pity. If taking a life is done without pity, it creates two karmas: causing an atmosphere like war among the public and the taking of revenge for the killed. If the killing cannot be avoided, but is undertaken with pity, the karmic effect is singular. If the practitioner helps life on the principle of mutual benefaction by prohibiting people from taking lives and by encouraging them to keep precepts, the merit will be great." (*HH* 3:101)

59. The Master said, "Any matter or activity executed without adequate preparation can be hurried or go awry. Hence, the practice of propriety without preparation and cultivation can be inapt. If one is off one's guard or behaves recklessly when alone, one will be forming a bad habit, which will show in the presence of others. An ancient sage said, 'The superior man is watchful over himself when he is alone,'[85] because what is revealed and what is concealed are not two. Hence, anyone who wishes to practice propriety should be careful about this." (*CP* 2:16)

60. The Master said, "To flatter someone when that person prospers and despise the person when he or she is in a difficult situation is the deed of a mean person; to maintain friendship with someone more when that person is in difficult situation is the propriety of a superior person. To lose moral sense at times of gain and loss, or to practice propriety in the presence of others and not practice it in the absence of others is not to know the essence of propriety. To maintain moral sense and the principle of propriety regardless of gain and loss or what is concealed and revealed is to know and practice the principle of propriety." (*CP* 2:18)

61. The Master said, "An ancient saying has it that 'your mind should be as deep as the vast blue sea; your mouth should be as heavy as Mount Gunlun.' In other words, when you use your mind, keep it as deep as the blue sea so that no one can fathom it, and when you use your mouth, keep it as heavy as Mount Gunlun. The greater a person you become internally, the more difficult it will be to fathom the scope of your mind. A small vessel can easily be filled with water, and soon the water overflows; a great vessel always leaves a margin." (*CP* 7:53)

62. Upon completing his discourse on the *Diamond Sūtra* the Mas-

ter said, "The universe is based on emptiness, and its noumenal nature is devoid of any phenomenal differentiation. Since there is no difference of birth and death, the truth of cause-effect retribution is extremely clear. If we aim to cultivate the supreme Way, first, we should keep a mind that is as empty as the empty sky by keeping it from the four false ideas, the false idea of dharma, and even the false idea of no-dharma. Second, we should develop a perfect mind by disciplining it not to be attracted or dragged to what we see, hear, smell, taste, touch, or think. Third, we should use our mind perfectly without attachment to pleasure, anger, sorrow, and joy, and without favoritism based on distance and proximity or friendliness and estrangement. If we can do this ably, we will soon attain to the great Way and will have had faith, interpretation, performance, and realization of the teachings of the *Diamond Sūtra*." (*CP* 6:42)

63. The Master said, "'Empty and calm' are the characteristics of the mind in the tranquility of self-nature; 'numinous awareness' is the state of the mind when self-nature is the object of the mental function. In emptiness and calm and in numinous awareness are all the ways of practice. Heaven and earth are dark in stormy and cloudy weather, but dew falls when it is calm and clear. Likewise, a human mind is deluded if blocked and disturbed, but dew (saliva) becomes clear and sweet and mind becomes numinous and bright if the disturbing force calms down upon much spiritual cultivation. When one manages daily affairs, one can see and do them right only if one is not attracted to anything. One is apt to be keen at someone else's right and wrong but dull at one's own right and wrong because one is blocked and partial. Once upon a time, there was a general who was playing the game of *Go* with his nephew who was about to go to war. As the latter kept losing the game, his uncle said, 'You keep losing because your mind is drawn by the anxiety to win the war. From now on you should exert yourself to handle national affairs or any matter only justly without being concerned about victory." (*HH* 3:31)

64. Upon listening to a student's discourse on the *Heart Sūtra* the Master said, "The essential principle of the *Heart Sūtra* is contained in the phrase 'seeing clearly that the five aggregates (*skandha*) are all empty.' To see clearly is to reflect on with the light of one's own nature that is not thinking, measuring, or discriminating. It is an impartial, unselfish, and perfect intuition without attachment to any characteristics. The order of practice in this seeing clearly is as follows. The first is the practice of contemplation (*vipaśyanā*); this is to see straight and judge correctly the true nature of the universe and humanity without attachment to any

characteristics. The second is the practice of enlightenment; this is to attain great enlightenment by cultivating true emptiness and numinous awareness of one's own original nature while seeing things correctly and passing correct judgment on them. The third is the practice of putting into action; upon attaining enlightenment with no obstruction, one will attain emancipation and omnipotence by performing all actions as an enlightened person. If one makes an effort to achieve harmony in contemplation, enlightenment, and action and becomes an expert therein, one will by virtue of that effort have mastered the practice of seeing clearly and crossed the river of all sufferings and distress." (*CP* 6:43)

65. Concerning the actual practice of the *Diamond Sūtra*, the Master said, "What afflicts the human mind most is the four false ideas, the idea of dharma, and the idea of no-dharma. Hence, the practitioner must cut off the false ideas by reflecting on his mind. If the mind is attached to existence, one must face it with nonexistence; if attached to nonexistence, then one must face it with existence, and thus reach the absolute truth. One must take no false idea as the standard but not attach oneself to no false idea; one must take nonattachment as the substance without adhering to it; one must take marvelous application as the function without being tied to it. Whether one acts with or without knowledge of Buddha-nature depends on whether or not one traces light back to Buddha-nature. If one keeps on walking, standing, sitting, reclining, speaking, being silent, or resting with the spirit of tracing light back to Buddha-nature, this will be none other than following the teaching 'One should develop a mind that does not abide in anything.' "[86] (*HH* 3:91)

66. A disciple asked, "How can I let go of the four false ideas and attain the mind of equality?" The Master answered, "You have only to see into your original nature. In original nature, there is no distinction of mind, Buddha, and deluded beings. A deluded being has false ideas if he owns just a sack of unhulled rice. However, there is no increasing or decreasing in the mind of a buddha, whose capacity is boundless like the ocean, let alone a false idea, even when the whole universe is his own property. Since such a one knows the identity of the original nature of all sentient beings, a buddha never despises the deluded beings. One can know the principle of equality and transcend the cycle of birth and death if one understands the truth that 'all dharmas return to one.' "[87] (*HH* 5:5)

67. The Master said, "If you can keep your mind as empty as the empty sky, you can break out of the cycle of ascent and descent of the six paths. If you free yourself from grasping at false notions by basing

your mind on emptiness, you will always receive beneficence. Always do away with false notions of having bestowed favors on others or having suffered injury; always examine the insufficiency of your virtue." (*CP* 5:22)

68. The Master said, "In general, the mind of a person who makes no discrimination between oneself and objects, and oneself and others is empty of the four false notions, so that his mind is at leisure." (*HH* 3:23)

69. The Master said to his followers, "Become emptiness itself! The empty sky contains myriad things because it is empty. Your mind should become as empty as the empty sky if you want to be a great virtuous one. If you regulate yourself, your family, and the state with an empty mind, and if you treat your friends and all fellow human beings with an empty mind, then you can get rid of false notions, partiality based on distance and proximity, and hatred and love. You then become a Buddha-bodhisattva." (*CP* 5:23)

70. The Master said, "This 'I' is the source of both transgression and merits. An old saying goes, 'The ground is responsible for your falling; but you cannot get up without the ground.' It is because of this 'I' that either a transgression is committed or a meritorious act is performed." (*CP* 5:25)

71. The Master said, "If wicked thoughts take roots in your mind, meditate on Irwŏnsang in your mind, and make the effort to recover your original nature, which is empty, round, and right as Irwŏnsang.[88] Or meditate on Grand Master Sot'aesan's holy face and in this way make the effort to model after his fair, just, and compassionate mental Dharma. Make the effort to eliminate wicked thoughts by raising your self-awareness that you are the Buddha's disciple and minister of justice. Then, a vicious evil mind will turn into a wholesome mind." (*CP* 7:26)

72. The Master said, "Just as children take after their parents, the disciples of the Buddha must take after him. If you take after the Buddha in all the things you do and thereby take after Dharmakāya, Sambhogakāya, and Nirmāṇakāya completely, you have reached the stage of the *tathāgata*." (*CP* 7:24)

73. The Master said, "All speech and conduct in the world of the Buddha are governed by right thought; those in the human world by right thought and passions, half and half; and those in the triple evil world (animals, hungry ghosts, hell) by the power of passions. If the power of right thought increases in the human world, the triple evil world retreats; if the power of right thought decreases, the evil world comes nearer. If these points are carefully examined, one's future can easily be known. This does not mean that a person should annihilate passions; he should make

good and right use of them under the control of right thought." (*CP* 6:53)

74. The Master said, "Buddhas and bodhisattvas become what they are because their initial aspiration and later minds are uniform; common mortals fail to become buddhas and bodhisattvas because their minds are shaken in adverse circumstances and regress, contrary to their initial aspiration. You should therefore keep the mind to rejoice in the Way, and the mind for public well-being, uniform, from the time of your initial aspiration to your later mind." (*CP* 7:20)

75. Explaining mindfulness (*yunyŏm*) and mindlessness (*munyŏm*) in the practice of keeping a diary,[89] the Master said, "One who is mindful has numinous awareness and acts right without attachment, keeping a correct standard in situations where the mind can be off guard. A mindless person, being deluded by that to which he or she is attached, behaves foolishly, having no standard to follow." (*CP* 6:22)

76. The Master said concerning the practice of mindfulness, "The practice of mindfulness lies in constantly guarding one's mind while handling daily affairs. In this practice, one is constantly on one's guard and in the right frame of mind so that one's seeing, hearing, speaking, acting, or resting will be in accordance with correct standard. Thus, Grand Master Sot'aesan set up the method of constant training,[90] which requires one to examine one's mind by checking beans (white or red), by contrasting mindfulness and mindlessness, or by checking diaries, in accordance with the capacities of the trainee. These three methods are different in names; however, the aim is to create a discipline for mindfulness." (*CP* 6:23)

77. The Master elaborated on the practice of mindfulness, "Examples of the practice of mindfulness are as follows. (1) In order to bring success to any business, one's attention should be focused on it and one should study it with no distraction of mind. (2) In order to maintain the enterprise for a long time after achieving success, one must concentrate one's mind on it without handling it heedlessly, and study it continuously. (3) To be free from indigence and failure in adverse conditions, one should strike a balance between broad-mindedness and hurry, which balance one can secure only if one cultivates one's mind in advance. (4) In order to follow the mean and distinguish clearly right and wrong while one handles various human affairs, one must always be heedful to do the right and to forsake the wrong. (5) In order to learn a lesson for the future from what has happened, one must reflect on what has happened and examine oneself. (6) In order to keep oneself from drowsiness and delusions when one has nothing to do, one should have a heedful mind

to be rid of delusions. (7) In order to fulfill one's duties well, one should be mindful of them. (8) In order to requite the beneficence to which one is indebted, one should first be mindful of one's indebtedness to the beneficence. (9) In order to put one's pledge into effect, one must be mindful of being true to one's word. If one acts rashly without heedfulness in all these cases, one will bring about failure, ingratitude, and distrust in whatever one does and one will be rejected. Nothing is accomplished without mindfulness. How great the merit of mindfulness is!" (*CP* 6:24)

78. The Master said on the practice of no-thought, "The practice of no-thought lies in keeping one's mind from being attached to things during one's daily activities. In this practice one always removes delusions and attains true thusness (*bhūtatathatā*) by seeing with no attachment when seeing, hearing with no attachment when hearing, speaking with no attachment when speaking, acting with no attachment when acting, and getting into calmness with no attachment when getting into calmness. Hence, Grand Master Sot'aesan took the practice of no-thought to be the supreme Dharma when he talked about the true realm of practice, and the Buddha used the practice of no-thought as the standard when he explained the essence of morality." (*CP* 6:25)

79. The Master said, "Examples of the practice of no-thought are as follows. (1) One can attain the position of buddhahood only if one harbors no-thought of having attained to buddhahood. (2) One can become permanently a benefactor who devotes oneself to the public only if one harbors no-thought of having devoted oneself to the public. (3) One can enjoy permanently a comfortable life in the world only if one has no-thought of or attachment to the comfortable life. (4) One can maintain eternally the beneficence rendered to someone only if one has no-thought of having rendered it. (5) One can, upon attaining authority, maintain it eternally only if one harbors no-thought of having obtained it. (6) One can keep fairness in face of any matter of decision only if one's thought is free from attachment. (7) One can attain spiritual stability in motion and at rest only if one's thought is free from passion of love and desire. (8) One can keep oneself from being attached to dharma dust upon attaining the great Way only if one is free from the thought that one has practiced no-thought. Thus, if one acts with attachment to any thought, one will fall into wanton thoughts like endless ripples. All the great ways and great virtues of all things in the universe are based on this no-thought. Is not the merit of no-thought great?" (*CP* 6:26)

80. The Master continued, "Dear practitioners of the Way! You must understand that the practice of mindfulness is not apart from that

of no-thought, and the practice of no-thought is not apart from that of mindfulness. You must practice mindfulness where you should, and you must practice no-thought where you should, so that you may enjoy the true merits of both mindfulness and no-thought. If you do not know the way of mindfulness or no-thought, you will be mindless where you should practice mindfulness, and harbor false thought where you should practice no-thought, so that both will produce evil karma, sinking in the endless sea of misery. How pitiful that would be! It is imperative that a practitioner should know of this." (CP 6:27)

81. Yang Wŏn'guk asked, "I would like to know the relationship between one mind and justice on the one hand, and the relationship between delusions and injustice on the other, which we find in the statement about timeless Zen."[91] The Master answered, "The action done with one mind is justice; and the action done with delusive thought is injustice." (CP 6:30)

82. Upon the compilation of the Canon of Rites (Yejŏn), the Master composed a spiritual mantra called "Numinous Mantra" (Yŏngju), which he let his followers use:[92]

With the numinous force of heaven and earth
I concentrate my mind;
My mind penetrates all things according to my will,
I am united as one with heaven and earth,
Hence, my mind is as right as that of Heaven and Earth.

Thereafter, the Master composed a mantra for purification called "Purification Mantra" (Chŏngjŏngju) as follows:[93]

The Dharmakāya is pure and originally free from hindrances,
I recover the light of original nature and become just as pure.
When the great, harmonious, and perfect numinous force
   creates a unity,
All the evil demons and spirits and the evil paths vanish of
   themselves. (CP 2:21)

83. The Master said, "The 'Numinous Mantra' (Yŏngju) is chanted so that one may be unified with the substance of heaven. The function of heaven and earth is described in the following words from the Book of Changes (Yijing). 'In harmony in his attributes with heaven and earth; in his orderly procedure, with the four seasons; in his relation to what is fortunate and what is unfortunate, in harmony with the spirit-like operations

of (providence)."[94] The words 'in relation to what is fortunate and what is unfortunate, in harmony with the spirit-like operations' mean that we should transcend fortune and misfortune." (*HH* 3:46)

84. A disciple asked, "How is being stupid different from being foolish?" The Master answered, "One who is stupid is like a child who does not know right from wrong. One who is foolish knows right from wrong, but is shameless and ill-mannered. Among those of low spiritual capacity are found many stupid people, while foolish ones are more among those of intermediate spiritual capacity. Unless one emerges from the fog of stupidity and foolishness, one cannot rise to high spiritual capacity. When you write your daily diary for observing precepts, the principle against foolishness should be recorded as violated if you felt good at an empty praise. The root of foolishness is the desire for honor and fame; idiocy and stupidity are similar." (*CP* 6:21)

85. On a New Year's Day, the Master gave a sermon: "The path toward buddhahood or sagehood is not far away but nearby, in the religious practice of our mind. Hence, we must make it our task to correct our mind. In the New Year, let us exert ourselves, with a fresh new mind, to attain buddhahood." He said further, "The newness of the New Year is not in the day but in our mind. Hence, the true meaning of greeting the New Year lies in exerting ourselves with a fresh new mind in our religious practice and public service. If therefore we take care of our new mind, then every day is a new day and a New Year's Day; if we fail to take care of our new mind, we will not truly greet the New Year even though a New Year has arrived." (*CP* 7:27)

86. The Master said, "In ancient times, King Wu (1169–1116 BC) used to stand up and bow low whenever he heard of someone's good deed. People around him said, "Is it not beyond the norms of propriety to bow with no regard for upper or lower class rank?' To that King Wu said, 'It is not the social rank that I consider when I bow, but the good deed to which I bowed. To the good deed there is no distinction between upper and lower classes or the noble and the mean.' This can be the model for love of good throughout eternity." (*CP* 7:40)

VII

On Being Diligent and Truthful

1. Master Chŏngsan said, "Deluded people believe what appears as real but do not believe what does not. While they are absorbed in external glory, they are not even interested in searching for the internal truth. While they pay attention to even small increments of immediate gain and loss, they do not consider vices or blessings of the future; consequently, what they do falls into mere form and fabrication. Eventually, dancing with joy for daily false desires and greed, they fall into the pit of evil karma. How pitiful that is! We can learn from a fable. A deer loved her magnificent antlers but was ashamed of her ugly-looking legs. One day, being chased by a hunter, she was escaping danger through the bush; her magnificent horns impeded her escape but her unsightly legs ran well and saved her life. Although this is only a fable, if we reflect it on ourselves, we can say that it is a warning critique that truly depicts the world." (*CP* 10:1)

2. The Master continued, saying, "In keeping with the development of material civilization, this wonderful world becomes brighter daily.[95] However, if one wishes to enjoy exquisite, modern conveniences of all sorts to the full, one needs power and wealth. As public sentiment becomes overtaken by this reality, people grow arrogant and self-conceited if they obtain some of what they desire. Those who do not obtain what they desire using whatever contemptible means, commit all sorts of vices and sow various seeds of enmity. And when they are threatened one morning by the hunter of adversity, they are at a loss with fear, trying to

find the way out of danger with the power of concentration, know-how, and right conduct, which will be ineffective without daily practice. Moreover, being hindered in various ways by the distortions of fame, power, and wealth, they are forced into the jaws of death. How pitiful that is! Moreover, at death, which everyone faces eventually, the fame, power, and wealth that one has enjoyed are useless. Rather, in building up layers of karma and strengthening the attachment of evil passions, they cause one to lose freedom of spirit and hinder one's affinity for the good path. You should think through this thoroughly and bear it in mind, so as to devote yourselves to attaining the three great powers of cultivation, inquiry, and heedful choice, testing your actual mental power against any matter you face at any time." (*CP* 10:2)

3. The Master continued, saying, "Since you have entered this order for Buddhist practice, you may guess the essence of false and true. However, if you do not check your practice daily and hourly while residing in the order, you could, unawares, easily be attracted by external splendor. If as a Buddhist practitioner you possess vast knowledge, a good writing style, or eloquence, you may mistake it for true power of practice and be conceited. If you are praised or remunerated, you can easily be proud of yourself, as if you have achieved something great. However, true practice is not in what you say or write. It lies in the following Threefold Practice. First, it lies in the spiritual ability to be free from the six paths and four forms of birth, upon attaining spiritual freedom. Second, it lies in the wisdom to have no doubt about falsehood and truth, and right and wrong, upon awakening to the source of facts and principles. Third, it lies in the spontaneous observance of all precepts as the heedful choice is all in accordance with laws. Only with these three powers perfected can one be assured of having attained buddhahood. Therefore, in the moral religious order, one who, no matter how ignorant, lowly, or deficient in speech, has the root of faith in the dharma and pursues mind cultivation well is never regarded lightly but is expected to be a great, future vessel of the dharma." (*CP* 10:3)

4. He continued, saying, "Moreover, if you attain the true power of this mind cultivation, you can ably govern myriad things in the universe, and can make good use of fame, wealth, and treasure, and all knowledge. External splendor based on real power is like water flowing from a spring and a shadow caused by a real thing: the water and the shadow are also real. Consider! Who can belittle the fame of the Buddha-bodhisattvas and all sages from ancient times? Who can snatch the power from them? And

who would despise their grandeur? With the passing of time, their greatness grows more resplendent and lofty, as people are more enlightened. Their great aspiration is realized on the ground of no desire. I hope that you cultivate the realm of no desire and foster the formless true power, and thereby become a great worker for Grand Master Sot'aesan's grand task of spiritual unfolding." (*CP* 10:4)

5. The Master said, "One can easily make a name for oneself at a given time, but it is difficult for one to establish its true reality. It is easy to know apparent phenomenal features but difficult to comprehend their noumenal truth. It is easy to do a good deed that shows itself, but difficult to cultivate its good root. Name and known characteristics are like shadows; only the reality can be true gain and true fame." (*CP* 10:5)

6. The Master said, "A person of much arrogance loses people; a person with much show-off loses truth. To lose people is to discard the world; to lose truth is to discard one's own self. To lose these two and search for the Way is to lose the seed and search for harvest." (*CP* 10:6)

7. The Master said, "The good of a small-minded man is easily buried and the evil is easily exposed, as in the case of something dirty wrapped up with silk, the bad odor of which one cannot hide. And the fault of a man of virtue is easily buried and the good is widely recognized, it is as in the case of gold and jade, whose value does not change even if it is wrapped with rags. Therefore, the man of virtue does not care about outward appearances but performs internal moral cultivation thoroughly and strives for substantial cultivation of true ability." (*CP* 10:7)

8. The Master said, "Do not love ostentation in whatever you do. What is externally splendid but internally trifling is the cause of personal, familial, societal, and national ruin." (*CP* 10:8)

9. The Master said, "Rayon cannot pretend to be silk. Do not strive for ostentation, but cultivate only the real." (*CP* 10:9)

10. The Master said, "Falsehood disintegrates utterly when it does; truth cannot be destroyed even by heaven and earth." (*CP* 10:10)

11. The Master said, "An ancient saying has it that a personality is evaluated by his appearance, speech, writing style, and judgment. However, judgment is the most important of these, and what is more important than that is one's mind." (*CP* 10:11)

12. The Master said, "Common people often argue about character based on the appearance only, but in the order of morality character is judged on whether the seed of blessings and virtue is sprouting in the mind-ground. Common people often argue about character on the bases

of learning and good academic career, but in the order of morality, character is judged on whether one has the growing tendency to awaken to the truth. Common people argue on character on the bases of a person's present position and fame, but, in the order of morality, character is judged on whether or not the person's action is on the righteous path." (*CP* 10:12)

13. The Master said, "Such external illnesses as those that occur in the eye, ear, or limbs normally are not life threatening, but internal diseases, especially heart ailments, can cause death. Likewise, minor spiritual illnesses that appears externally and that are due to certain habits are not symptoms of critical moral illness; however, if one deceives one's own mind, especially one's conscience, and feels no remorse, then one's conscience is paralyzed and one will eventually fall apart." (*CP* 10:13)

14. The Master said, "One's appearance and academic circle make up one's external character, but one's conscience makes up the internal character. Compared to a tree, one's external character is like the branches and leaves, and the internal character is like the roots. Branches and leaves will be luxuriant only if the roots are well cultivated." (*CP* 10:14)

15. The Master said, "There are three kinds of learning. The first is to extend one's knowledge externally by learning various sciences. The second is to expand one's knowledge and wisdom with the self-awakening achieved through internal cultivation and thorough inquiry. The third is to apply in actual situations what one has learned and awakened to, so that knowledge can be accompanied by practice. Of these three, the practice in actual situations is the most important." (*CP* 10:15)

16. The Master said to students, "In ancient China, there was a gateman of a village and his name was Houying. Although he was only a gateman, his ability and talent was so magnificent that not only was his name well known throughout the world but the village gate also became famous. Likewise, if a figure of great ability and practice is produced out of you, this institute will be known worldwide accordingly. Now the world has put the age of empty formality behind. It will take true ability and practice above all, such that a person of true knowledge and true practice will be sought and employed in the world. Therefore, you should exert yourselves in the cultivation of true ability without being attracted to external formalities. From now on, you should demonstrate your own ability at your post, wherever you may be assigned, so that, I hope, you and your workplace become highly visible, as Houying made the gate known worldwide." (*CP* 10:16)

17. The Master said, "In the world to come, one can stand only if one has real ability, and the necessary condition of real ability does not lie in knowledge or talent. It lies in, first, one's being truthful; second, in one's being public-spirited; and third, in one's being virtuous." He said further, "The one who will minister to the world to come is the one who is on a high dharma stage, truthful, and beneficial to the general public." (*CP* 10:17)

18. The Master said, "By 'the world of Maitreya Buddha' is meant the world of diligent and truthful people. A religion will stand only if its doctrine is truthful and it is a religion of self-power. An individual, too, will be able to stand in the world only if he or she works diligently, with a vocation, and has the actual merit of having served the public with truthful morality." (*CP* 10:18)

19. The Master said, "Politicians are noisy, but the practitioners of the Way do great work silently. They manage the most important affairs of the world as if they were handling their family affairs after breakfast." (*CP* 10:19)

20. The Master said, "Grand Master Sot'aesan used to say, 'From now on, the life of anyone who advocates formality will be in vain.' In the world to come, one will rise in the world only if one is truthful and has self-ability; one will be employed only if one is faithful and public-spirited; and one will manage a great task only if one is virtuous and dynamic." (*CP* 10:20)

21. The Master wrote for Chŏn Ŭmgwang, "A person of wisdom regards faithfulness as treasure, a person of cleverness regards fame and gain as treasure, and a person of no wisdom regards material goods as treasure. The treasure of material goods is as vain as the floating clouds and as dangerous as a pile of rocks, and the treasure of fame and gain lacks true reality in spite of its seeming glory. The treasure of faithfulness, being unified with the Way, has infinite life, and it is replete with fame, gain, and material goods as it interpenetrates the internal and external." (*CP* 10:21)

22. The Master wrote in an album of single phrases at Sandong temple, "I have left it up to heaven whether it's going to be a 'rainy season' or 'the sky clearing up.'" Later, at Namwŏn temple, he said, "The verse is incomplete," and wrote, "Farming, sowing and reaping is up to man," saying, "These four Chinese characters should be added to make the two lines a living dharma teaching." (*CP* 10:22)

23. The Master had an apricot one day and said to Pak Chŏnghun, "Plant this pit somewhere in the precinct of the headquarters. The mind that loves planting trees is a virtuous mind." And he said further, "Even if one does not harvest the fruit in one's lifetime, one is sowing the seed of virtue for one's next life; this is the far-reaching state of mind of the practitioner of the Way. Love to plant trees." (CP 10:23)

24. A Confucian scholar who entered the order in his old age was residing in the precinct of the order without any responsibility, and the manager of the precinct was complaining. The Master said, "The mere fact that a scholar of such a status is residing here constitutes a covert encouragement for others to enter the order. And we should create a dharma affinity with him now so that he may perchance come into this order in his next life and do great work, shouldn't we?" (CP 10:24)

25. A student had a fit following a serious agony, and his mentor suggested sending him back home. The Master said, "When you suffer from an intestinal convulsion, the disorder is cured by a simple course of *sagwan* acupuncture. Likewise, when one suffers from a mental convulsion, it can be stopped if the closed mental spots are opened up with care. Hence, let's try to treat him with the mental *sagwan*." (CP 10:25)

26. A dormitory superintendent reported to the Master, "What should I do to a student who does not listen to me no matter how hard I try to give guidance to him?" The Master said, "You, as counselor, will not succeed in guiding anyone if you try to bend him in accord with your temperament. Your edification will be effective only if you slowly guide him after checking his intellectual capacity and temperament and understanding his aptitude and what he desires." (CP 10:27)

27. A student asked, "Wouldn't it be right to expel a comrade who has no moral sense?" The Master replied, "If you expel a comrade for the reason that he lacks moral sense, it hurts your own moral sense. Thus, it is minor justice. To forgive him and help him recover moral sense in order to realize the original vow together is great justice." (CP 10:28)

28. One of the devotees in the order was trying to split the order into petty factions by concentrating his power to attract the popular sentiment toward him. The Master said, "Popularity that you set out deliberately to win will be in vain when it crumbles. If you are endowed with the power of the Way and with public spirit and make no calculation of popularity, you will never fail in edification for lack of disciples." (CP 10:29)

29. One of the devotees in the order expressed his intention to step into the world of politics. To him, the Master said, "As you have already

taken the vow for the grand task to attain to buddhahood and deliver sentient beings, what other task would you prefer to this? The practitioners of the Way should be the mentors to guide politicians instead of being politicians themselves." (*CP* 10:30)

30. Some birds frequently pecked at and ate the ripe, red persimmons on a tree in front of the head dharma master's room. Seeing this, the Master said to his attendant, "Those birds, unable to render help to the foundation of a new grand order, should not get into debt against it. Shoo them away." When the attendant was not around, the Master himself shooed them away. (*CP* 10:32)

31. Kim Chin'gu, seeing Master Chŏngsan for the first time, described him with the words, "An unclouded moon, and a bright, warm breeze." Hwang Sŏngt'a said, "Gentle breeze and felicitous clouds." An Pyŏnguk said, "The best face I have seen in the world" and wondered, "How sincerely he must have accumulated moral discipline throughout his life, that his countenance is so replete with joy of peace, love, and benevolence!" (*CP* 10:33)

32. The Master said, "When someone becomes an eminent scholar, his writing style becomes simple; when one's practice of the Way gets deep, one's words and deeds become ordinary. Hence, a shallow intelligence cannot easily fathom the state of such perfection." (*HH* 1:78)

33. The Master said, "Concession leaves room for growth, where triumph does not. Confucius did not receive the recognition he deserved for his great teaching in his lifetime, though he was accorded due respect. The influence of his residual virtue, however, continues even up to today, so that he is enshrined in ancestral tablet halls for religious offerings. The sage kings Yao and Shun, on the other hand, enjoyed prosperity during their reigns, so they are respected now only with kindness. Just as water, in spite of flowing downward, forms great rivers and oceans, compromise and forgiveness gather and preserve myriad blessings eternally. Just as fire, blazing up, turns everything into ashes, leaving no trace, the temperament that wants to defeat and overcome others attracts all sorts of calamity, turning all the gains into nothing but a dream. Those who, though capable of defeating, let others defeat them are magnanimous people; those who, incapable of triumph, try to defeat others are mean-spirited." (*HH* 2:12)

34. The Master said, "A good person who is poor and suffers calamities in this life is paying off the evil karma of the past life, and hence preparing for blessings of the future. If one satisfies one's greed by viciously harming others, one may enjoy this life in accordance with meritorious

karma earned in past lives, but one will fall into the abyss of sin when those merits are all dried up." (*HH* 2:15)

35. At Yŏngsan Monastery, the Master asked his students, "What has been the most awful thing in the world?" The students mentioned demons, tigers, men, vehement desire, and abhorrence. The Master continued, "The most awful thing in the world is public reputation. If the public says of a man that he is good, his future will be auspicious, and if the public says of a man that he is bad, his future will be ominous. Following the funeral bier after someone's death, one can tell whether the deceased is on the path of ascent or descent. If all say of the dead that they lost a very good man, he will be on the path of ascent; and if they say that he is better dead, he will be on the path of descent." (*HH* 2:30)

36. The Master said to Sŏng Sŏngwŏn, "One, who has let go of the false idea of 'I,' has the sharpest eye; one who accepts advice well has the sharpest ear. These are those who have obtained the numinous eye and ear. Be amicable to others." (*HH* 7:3)

37. The Master said to Song Chŏnun, "An excellent practitioner is the one who is completely endowed with humaneness, trust, and the virtue of enlightenment to the Way." (*HH* 7:10)

VIII

Edification in Response to Capacities

1. Master Chŏngsan said, "The relationship between the mentor and the disciple or that between comrades is such that some disciples need frequent care and some do not need so much care by the mentor or comrade. The disciple that needs frequent care is not yet a close dependent, since there is a danger of causing a crack in the relationship if that person is not frequently taken care of. The disciple that needs no special care is a close dependent, with a mind and a spirit united with that of the mentor and comrades, fulfilling duties and showing humanity without being scrupulous about formalities. If the mentor has no need to use any device or expedience in treating the one who receives guidance, and the latter uses no deceit and fabrication in treating the mentor, then, naturally, a great cause is established and the vein of dharma is connected between the two. The more such members there are, the more easily the order will grow in prosperity." (CP 8:1)

2. The Master said, "Grand Master Sot'aesan said, 'Just as the field where many weeds grow requires the farmer's frequent weeding, a capricious practitioner requires much more of the mentor's effort in guidance.' This is not because the mentor practices partiality, but because such a practitioner will easily be lost if so much effort is not exerted. Therefore, the practitioner should not wish to monopolize the mentor's affection, but fulfill duties and show humanity, treating the mentor magnanimously." (CP 8:2)

3. The Master said, "One who wishes to be a person of great virtue should practice to love virtue; it is difficult for one to become a person of great virtue without loving the virtue of someone else. If you do not love the virtue of someone, you will not be close to that person; if you do not have that closeness, your sense of virtue will naturally fade away. If the sense of virtue fades away, you will not enjoy doing virtuous acts. Then, certainly, you will be farther away from the way of becoming a person of great virtue. Therefore, to love and speak for someone else's virtue is an important condition of practice for you to be a virtuous person." (CP 8:3)

4. The Master said to the students at Yŏngsan, "It is due to the effect of the karma that one has created in former and current lives that one suffers from external retribution of evil; the principle of the Fourfold Beneficence, being always thus, is immutable. Good awakens one to realize good, and evil awakens one to see what evil is; thus, both are good teachers that guide one well. If one thinks this way all the time, one will preserve peace eternally, wherever one goes." He then wrote in Chinese as follows, "Harmful effects originate in what one does; beneficence is fundamentally limitless. Both good and evil are one's teachers; both guide one to do the good. If every thought is like this, one can preserve eternal peace." (CP 8:4)

5. Yang Tosin requested the Master for a lifetime guide when she entered the order as a celibate devotee, and the Master wrote down four vows: (1) Since practice of the great Way makes the eternal treasure, while temporary glory or shame is like a patch of passing cloud, I shall transcend the immediate passion with this eternal hope. (2) Since both favorable and adverse mental spheres provide me with opportunities for practice, and since both good and evil people provide me with the way for practice, I shall always be happy and grateful to those. (3) Since diligence is the source of all blessings and love of learning is the foundation of wisdom, I will make diligence and learning be my lifelong enterprise. (4) I have entered the order of a great sage, something that one finds only with extreme difficulty through eons, and I have entered into the life of the selfless devotee in order to sacrifice myself for the whole world. With such an opportunity, I shall not waste even a moment and, with such a vow, I shall not be bound by small desires, and thereby ruin the eternal journey before me. I shall bear this rare opportunity and significant obligation in mind. (CP 8:5)

6. The Master wrote a teaching for Yi Chungjŏng: "Make a great vow. Since management of self-interest and egoism is like dew drops and

smoke, the vow to attain to buddhahood and deliver sentient beings is the greatest of all vows. Set a firm faith. Nothing is more mysterious nor is any treasure more valuable than the interior (mind) that is as firm as an iron pillar and the exterior that is as impregnable as a granite wall. Nourish a great zeal. It is said that if you sever the origin of profit its merit will be a hundredfold, and if you repeat it three nights and days, its merit will be ten thousandfold. Hold a great doubt in mind. The great doubt arises only from a great faith; the concentration of one mind can penetrate iron and rock. Act with great sincerity. If you are true to yourself, using no falsehood, there will be no duality between the interior and exterior of your personality, and if you maintain constancy from beginning to end, the merit will be the same as that of heaven and earth. Follow the great Way of Irwŏn to deliver immeasurable sentient beings, and emancipate your own self from the sufferings of eons." (*CP* 8:6)

7. The Master wrote a few lines and gave them to his students: "Pine and bamboo attain their integrity through frost and snow, and bodhisattvas foster their minds through forbearance. The practice of forbearance is like bamboo shoot at the beginning and like bamboo thereafter; it attains great power so that it cannot be uprooted, as a lofty mountain is rooted through all ages. The practice of broadening the mind is at first like a brook, then it is like a river, and finally it attains a mysterious capacity like that of a great blue ocean. Although defilement is turbulent and changes morning and evening, true nature is ever thus through eternity. One whose mind is not moved by material things is reckoned to be of high capacity and shining the light onto one's self-nature is none other than the path of the Buddha." (*CP* 8:7)

8. At a joint ceremony of the coming of age, the Master said, "One does not become an adult simply because one gets old and one's hair turns gray. One who tolerates others well and renders good to others is a real adult. One who tolerates others and renders good to others is an adult even if young; one who is always tolerated by others, always receiving favors from others, is always a minor. Since you have already come of age, you should be the one who tolerates others; you should not be the one who is tolerated. Be the one who takes care of others, not the one who is always taken care of. Be the one who blesses others, not the one who receives blessings from others. The law of victory is such that if you try to win only with toughness you cannot win the final victory; if you try to win wisely, with gentleness, you can win the final victory. Water is extremely soft, but it can easily make a hole through a mountain." (*CP* 8:8)

9. Seeing one day that the students were arguing one-sided opinions and not understanding their opponents, the Master said, "If you fail to observe both sides of a thing and attach yourself excessively to one view, you become one-sided and fail to be well-rounded. Hence, you should not be drawn to your fixed view; you should make an appropriate critique of it and a heedful choice, observing both sides of any matter in its particular context." (CP 8:9)

10. A student said to the Master, "In our order we have a system of the household priesthood, which I think is not in accordance with the life of the sacred monastery." The Master replied, "The dharma in the world to come will be a boundless one. In order for many sentient beings to receive the Buddha grace widely, we should try to provide ways for a husband and wife to devote themselves to proselytize in accordance with their wishes." (CP 8:10)

11. A student said to the Master, "In a communal life like ours, reward and punishment should be clear." The Master said, "A great reward subsists when there is no overt reward, and a severe punishment when there is no overt punishment. Hence, you should not be attracted to the overt reward and punishment, but maintain the standard of true and false in your mind." (CP 8:11)

12. Kim Sŏryong asked, "Can I get what I seek out of greed?" The Master said, "Where there is no mind that desires, what you seek comes to you abundantly." Sŏryong said, "Teach me the dharma that is the greatest and most perfect." The Master said, "It lies in finding the mind and cultivating and using it well." (CP 8:12)

13. Yi Myŏnghun asked, "I wish to learn and keep a skill. What is the greatest skill in the world?" The Master answered, "You should learn and keep the skill to make peace with others well." (CP 8:13)

14. Chang Sŏngjin asked, "How should I always keep my mind and how should I speak and act?" The Master answered, "You should always be broad-minded and speak and act generously." (CP 8:14)

15. A student requested, "Would you please teach me a method of constant practice that anyone could follow?" The Master responded, "It is the Way of keeping the middle way that is neither excessive nor deficient in everything one does." The student asked again, "Which practice is the most difficult?" The Master answered, "To use the ordinary and constant mind is the most difficult." (CP 8:15)

16. Chŏn Ich'ang asked, "Who made the greatest discovery of all time, past, present, and future?" The Master replied, "The sage who

discovered beneficence[96] made the greatest discovery." She asked again, "From what kind of relationship is the worst enemy produced?" The Master said, "People easily become formidable enemies to each other when they are close to each other; hence, you should be careful with those who are close to you." (*CP* 8:16)

17. An Ijŏng said to the Master, "Since I am assuming the responsibility of edification for the first time, I would greatly appreciate it if you give me a few words of advice." The Master said, "You should practice first what you preach." (*CP* 8:17)

18. Hwang Chunam asked, "How can I be endowed with the great power of heaven and earth and render distinguished service with them?" The Master answered, "You can render great service if you are free from evil." (*CP* 8:18)

19. A student asked, "What is the most urgent of all urgent things humans should do?" The Master said, "To find one's own fault and correct it is the most urgent." (*CP* 8:19)

20. Yi Chesŏng asked, "What is the correct way of doing great practice?" The Master said, "There should be no distance between the mentor and the student." He asked further, "What should be done in order to remove the distance?" The Master said, "If the student's faith in the mentor is sincere, the distance disappears naturally." (*CP* 8:20)

21. A student asked, "When I practice to eliminate the five desires, the three poisons, attachment, and false notions, will it be right if I mindfully eliminate each one after another individually, and little by little?" The Master said, "It will be alright; however, various vicious thoughts will not arise of themselves if you keep eliminating evil thought as soon as you see it in the bud." (*CP* 8:21)

22. A student asked, "Are the five desires bad for humankind?" The Master answered, "The five desires are neither good nor evil in their own essence. However, desires beyond one's lot lead one to transgression and suffering; satisfaction of the desires within one's means leads to worldly blessings and happiness." (*CP* 8:22)

23. Yi Kwangjŏng said to the Master, "When I try to concentrate on whatever I do with one mind, the effort to do so interferes with one mind." The Master said, "Only at the beginning do you keep in mind the standard to do it with heedfulness. Once you have started the task, you keep one mind by letting go of the heedfulness." (*CP* 8:23)

24. Kim Inchŏl asked, "Is it a good idea to confront and fight to the last a wicked mental sphere that is beyond my ability to overcome?"

The Master answered, "You treat it as you would skillfully avoid a stupid but violent villain who provokes you to a quarrel and then later give him admonitions. On the path of practice some crises are unavoidable; it is a good idea to find a way out of the difficulty instead of trying to get over it by force." (CP 8:24)

25. The Master said, "Only upon going through an adverse mental sphere, will you come to know the real ability of your practice, develop a new ability, or have your ability fortified." (CP 8:25)

26. A student asked, "How should I control my mind in ordinary times?" The Master said, "Make it a general standard to leave good thoughts alone and to let go of wicked thoughts. Try to have occasions to keep your mind clear of any thought, good or evil." The student asked further, "What should I do when thoughts of a good thing that I failed to take care of in the past come into my mind while sitting in meditation?" The Master said, "Let go of it after making a note of it in your mind, then take care of it later." (CP 8:26)

27. A student asked, "How can I cultivate public spirit?" The Master answered, "You should realize that your body is the public property of the Fourfold Beneficence, and hence the requital of beneficence is your duty. You should know that the true value of human life lies in benefiting others; and you should know thoroughly the consequences of self-interest and those of public interest." (CP 8:27)

28. A student asked, "I would like to know about the mastery of the Way (tot'ong), the mastery of laws (pŏpt'ong), and the mastery of spirit (yŏngt'ong)." The Master said, "The mastery of the Way lies in seeing into one's own nature; the mastery of laws lies in establishing religious and moral laws in accordance with principles; and the mastery of spirit lies in attaining numinous brightness." He said further, "One must attain the mastery of the Way and the mastery of laws first; one who attains the mastery of numinous spirit first runs the danger of falling into wickedness and keeping his practice from growing." He said further, "Occult supernatural power is a minor concern for a sage.[97] If the main skillful means used by a presiding sage is his or her occult supernatural power, who will take care of humanity and justice? In the New World, the enlightened master will not need to use occult supernatural power, for scientific methodologies will be the occult supernatural power." (CP 8:28)

29. The Master said to Yang Tosin, "To maintain one mind in motion and at rest is to be in concentration (samādhi) and to manifest

right action through the six roots with one mind is none other than the mastery of occult supernatural power." (*CP* 8:29)

30. The Master said to a student, "A huge evil on the way of religious practice is pride in one's accomplishments, thinking 'I must be quite good.' This is the indigestion of dharma food." (*CP* 8:30)

31. The attendant asked, "Shall I deal with all affairs only after informing you of the matter?" The Master said, "Inform me prior to taking care of the matter except for daily trivial affairs. The matter will be done well when I know of it, so our spiritual energy will have no blocking between us." The attendant asked again, "What should I do when I notice a fault in a mentor?" The Master said, "If you notice a fault in the mentor on whom you cannot but depend, grieve only over your misfortune. If the suspicion is not dispelled, then let him know directly of your suspicion and get it dispelled." (*CP* 8:31)

32. A student asked, "Does the Buddha act in accordance with friendliness and estrangement or closeness and remoteness?" The Master answered, "The Buddha is not without friendliness and estrangement or remoteness and closeness; he looks all around and deals with all affairs only fairly, without being partial. Grand Master Sot'aesan said, 'I feel more affection to the one who is public-minded and good-natured.' " (*CP* 8:32)

33. A student said, "I'm concerned that if one is contented with one's lot, one may not make any progress in the world." The Master said, "Contentment with one's lot does not lie in lack of motivation or being lazy; it lies in doing things in an orderly manner and coolly. Hence, one should make progress in accordance with one's own ability." (*CP* 8:33)

34. A student asked, "What is the compassionate way to treat a person who is persistently unrighteous to the last?" The Master answered, "If an unrighteous person will not listen to any admonition, to reform him with extraordinary means is also compassion. To ignore good and evil is not true compassion; to prevent transgression and suffering is the compassion of a living buddha. However, an admonition can never be compassion if it is given in hatred and with intention to harm." (*CP* 8:34)

35. A student asked, "Can one practice mutual benefit[98] only with material things?" The Master said, "To become a model of practice for others by right speech and right conduct is also an excellent practice of mutual benefit." (*CP* 8:35)

36. The Master wrote an aphorism for Yi Ŭnsŏk and Kim Chŏngyong: "Make both angular and round behavior be in accordance with the Way."

He wrote an aphorism to Yi Chungjŏng: "Follow the way of the mean and righteousness." He wrote an aphorism to his attendant: "Exert yourself in the practice and do not be wicked." (*CP* 8:36)

37. The attendant said to the Master, "I found a line in my dream, 'No confrontation, decency, and modesty.' " The Master said, "No confrontation with one's external conditions is the basis of harmony; to be decent and modest internally is the basis of cultivation of virtue. It's a fine aphorism; keep it well. Generally, one with overly unyielding character should first exert on the practice of being modest and smooth-tongued. Only then one will attain great success in the coming era of harmony among people." (*CP* 8:37)

38. The Master wrote an aphorism for Pak Changsik: "The essence of nourishing self-nature lies in being broad-minded, generous, and free. Train your mind for an adamantine self-nature." (*CP* 8:38)

39. The Master said to Yi Sŏngsin, "If your mind is broad and great, all the mental spheres will calm down of themselves; this is the way toward paradise. If your mind is narrow and small, all the mental spheres will threaten you from four directions; this is the way toward the sea of misery. Suffering and happiness depends on one's perspective." The Master then wrote, "If one cultivates morality with utmost devotion, one's future will be on the level road." (*CP* 8:39)

40. The Master wrote an aphorism for Kim Chŏnggwan: "Movement and quiescence should be in accord with laws." He gave an aphorism to Yi Chŏnghwa: "If my mind is right (*chŏng*), all the minds under heaven respond to me with justice, and if my mind is peaceful (*hwa*), then all the minds under heaven respond to me with peace." (*CP* 8:40)

41. To the students who committed faults, the Master said, "Repent of your faults to the public and in front of Dharmakāya Buddha." He then wrote a line, "Be true to yourselves, and do not deceive yourselves. Take a vow that you will not commit the same fault twice." (*CP* 8:41)

42. The Master wrote an aphorism for Ryu Kihyŏn and Han Chŏngwŏn: "To reduce all thoughts to no-thought is the practice at rest, and to become conversant with myriad human affairs is the practice in motion. If both thought and no-thought are right, the great Way will be broad and long with no obstruction."[99] (*CP* 8:42)

43. The Master wrote an aphorism for Chŏng Chonghŭi: "Cultivate the Way, nourish virtue, and make a fresh start every day"; he wrote an aphorism for Yun Chuhyŏn: "Only if every one strives to cultivate the Way, will the whole world return to the Way." (*CP* 8:43)

44. The Master wrote an aphorism for Mun Tonghyŏn: "The difference between staying home (laity) and leaving home (priesthood) does not lie in the body but in the mind; the difference between bodhisattvas and deluded beings does not lie in the body but in the mind. Let every thought be of supreme enlightenment and let every step transcend the three worlds." (CP 8:44)

45. The Master wrote some words to a student who left the order for home: "If you think of the Buddha and practice, a long distance is but a short distance. If you turn your back against the Buddha and immerse yourself in worldly dirt, a very short distance is nothing but a very long distance." (CP 8:45)

46. The Master wrote a verse for a student who was getting married: "Faith is the root of myriad good deeds. Harmony is the fundamental source of myriad blessings." Later, he wrote another line: "Sincerity is the ancestor of myriad virtues." (CP 8:46)

47. Sending his students to their assigned work places in Seoul, the Master said, "Be patient, diligent, honest, and generous. Be heedful not to be carried away by worldly tastes." (CP 8:47)

48. To the staff members of the Tonghwa Clinic, the Master said, "The business of medicine is also a holy mission saving sentient beings. Hence, make kindness, dedication, and honesty your creed." (CP 8:48)

49. When the road to Kaesŏng was blocked for several months after the liberation of Korea (from Japanese occupation, in 1945), the Master wrote a verse to Yi Kyŏngsun, asking her to memorize it and pray: "Dharmakāya is originally pure, so is the taste of Zen. Kaesŏng is originally without barriers, hence there will be no obstruction to those who are enlightened. The public Way is broad and long of itself and so is of service to the public. All buddhas of the three time periods act in this way." The Master continued, saying, "Do not make any enemies wherever you go; render virtue even to a cat. Live by giving the impression that you have nothing though you do, and that you do not know though you do. This will be a secret to escape the calamity of war." (CP 8:49)

50. To some youths about to leave general headquarters after being drafted for the national militia force during the Korean War, the Master said. "Handle all affairs always with Dharmakāya Buddha and Grand Master Sot'aesan watching over you; live with the same frame of mind as if you were in the precinct of the general headquarters even though you are far away. When you are confronted with a difficult situation, offer a prayer with a sound frame of mind; and then deal with the matter with the

insight that comes to your mind first. Live by knowing that you are under my tutelage even though you are far away from my guidance." (*CP* 8:50)

51. During the Korean War, the Master admonished his disciples, "Always speak in such a way that you give no cause for enmity, take actions leaving margins for humaneness, and offer sincere prayers so that our brethren who have fallen into the misery of hunger and cold may recover peace and lead comfortable lives." He said further, "If you offer prayers at dawn and night without any selfish motives, then, first of all, your mind will become that of the Buddha so that its benefit will return to you ahead of others. Second, your wish will be realized so that the benefit will return to the public." (*CP* 8:51)

52. Some members of the order took advantage of the chaos after the Korean War and became self-indulgent, violating rules of the order. So the majority of the order requested the Master several times to see to the matter. One day, the Master quoted the sacred saying of Ch'oe Sihyŏng,[100] who said, "I am not a clot of blood: why should I not have brute courage? I have five viscera and six entrails; how could I have not emotions? It is only because I may hurt the heavenly mind that I do not blame him." Quoting this, the Master said, "It is not because I do not know justice that I do not discuss the rights and wrongs. It is only because I should not cut the dharma affinity off or give up on those whom Grand Master Sot'aesan himself brought up. How can I block the future of even a single disciple? Grand Master Sot'aesan never gave up on even a leaf of grass or a tree." (*CP* 8:52)

53. For the ceremony of the tenth anniversary of founding Han'guk Poyugwŏn (the Korean Orphanage), the Master sent a congratulatory message: "Form a circle harmonizing with ten thousand people, and penetrate heaven with one mind." (*CP* 8:53)

54. When Hwang Chŏngsinhaeng took a trip to the United States of America, the Master wrote her a line: "Through tens of thousands of miles by water, land, and air, may your trip—going and coming—be peaceful." When Pak Kwangjŏn was going to America, the Master added one more line: "When you transmit the light of Dharma in accord with your affinity, may the beginning and end be as you wish." (*CP* 8:54)

55. For the celebration of Im Ch'ilbohwa's sixtieth birthday, the Master sent the following dharma words: "In the secular world, gold, silver, lapis, crystal, coral, agate, and pearls are called the seven treasures. The seven treasures in the order of religious practice are faith, zeal, doubt, sincerity, stability, cultivation, and resolution. I pray that you take these

seven spiritual treasures as fundamental, and thereby own all wisdom and blessings through eternal life." (*CP* 8:55)

56. At the ceremony of Yun Sŏgin's sixtieth birthday, the Master delivered a sermon: "In heaven and earth there are rain and dew; however, only those who farm making use of rain and dew are more blessed. Likewise, in the world there are good laws (dharma); however, only those who accomplish charitable work making use of these laws are more blessed. The commemoration of a sixtieth birthday can increase more in glory if it helps establish new laws in the world and accumulate charity, making use of the rules of propriety of this order, than if the day is spent in insignificant external splendor, wasting a great deal of money. The requital of the beneficence of parents by the offspring will also be many times greater." (*CP* 8:56)

57. The Master wrote a letter to Kim Hyŏngwan: "When people produce karma, good or bad, deluded beings do so for fame, power, and personal gain, but Buddha-bodhisattvas do so with faith, duty, and compassion. Hence, true fame, power, and gain return to Buddha-bodhisattvas, while deluded beings wander around looking for unreal fame, power, and personal gain." (*CP* 8:57)

58. The Master wrote a letter to Song Chamyŏng: "Though bodies are separated by mountains and rivers, our minds are in the one place of dharma meeting. Although myriad affairs differ from one another, if the spirit based on one thought of faith and devotion keeps striving, then this is the practice without leaving me and the way you can reach the buddha stage." (*CP* 8:58)

59. To his attendant in convalescence, the Master wrote, "Although the human body gets ill, the fundamental mind does not get ill. If you treat your sick body with a mind devoid of sickness, your body can recover health. I ask you to practice this." (*CP* 8:59)

60. To Kim Paengnyŏn, who was critically ill, the Master wrote a letter: "There is neither birth nor death, nor is there purity or impurity. Practice peace of mind, and rejoice eternally in the Buddha land." (*CP* 8:60)

61. During his long period of convalescence, the Master experienced frequent changes in his appetite. And he said, "If you have a good appetite, simple food consisting of vegetables without meat is sweet and becomes good nutrition for the body. But if you have lost your appetite, even good food with delicate flavor tastes bitter and causes indigestion. Likewise, if you follow the Way, you can enjoy blessings and happiness by

handling well even the adverse mental sphere; however, if the Way is not in yourself, you sometimes produce the source of calamity by mishandling even the favorable mental sphere. Therefore, whether you find the worldly life happy or unhappy depends not just on the external mental spheres, but, in reality, on the existence or nonexistence of one's own power of and appetite for the Way." (*CP* 8:61)

62. A disciple asked, "Am I under a false impression if I see one person as cold-hearted and another as warm-hearted?" The Master answered, "If a third person feels the same way, then your perception is not wrong. A person appears cold if that person lacks in virtue or if you have no affinity with that person." The disciple asked again, "Then how should I create a close affinity?" The Master answered, "You must cultivate a warm influence; virtue is warm. Hence, the repeated warm contact will do it. There is nothing that does not produce heat with repeated rubbing. The earth grows all things because it has the virtue of warmth." The disciple asked further, "Wouldn't it be hypocritical if I behave like that superficially only, with an unwilling heart?" The Master replied, "If you keep making an effort for a long time, the form produces substance. Hence, you must produce warm energy ceaselessly. How can one be a practitioner if one does not produce warm influence?" (*HH* 5:13)

IX

Dharma Admonitions

1. Master Chŏngsan said, "The physical life is a side job; the spiritual life is one's primary occupation." (*CP* 11:1)

2. The Master said, "Precepts (śīla), concentration (samādhi), and wisdom (prajñā) are the clothing, food, and shelter of our spirit." (*CP* 11:2)

3. The Master said, "If one is enlightened in one's youth, does deliverance work in middle age, and becomes emancipated in one's last years, then one's life is perfect." (*CP* 11:3)

4. The Master said, "The one who, while residing in the precinct of the dharma practice, does not know the preciousness of the dharma is harder to deliver." (*CP* 11:4)

5. The Master said, "Observe precepts, beginning with trivial ones, with utmost care. People in the secular world will regard this dharma as of great significance only if we observe it with utmost care." (*CP* 11:5)

6. The Master said, "Observe the precepts for yourself like a Hīnayāna practitioner, and edify the world like a Mahāyāna practitioner, so that you may practice both Hīnayāna and Mahāyāna Buddhism together." (*CP* 11:6)

7. The Master said, "In ancient times, it is said, a Confucian scholar read the *Xiaoxue* his whole life. If you read and put into practice the *Essentials of Daily Practice* your whole life, then that will be sufficient for attaining to buddhahood."[101] (*CP* 11:7)

8. The Master said, "The great way under heaven is simple and easy. One who has found the correct way of practice drills oneself in

the *Tripitaka Koreana* and, summarizing its essential principles in a few words, puts them into practice." (*CP* 11:8)

9. The Master said, "Make your resolution unique, but your conduct should be commonplace." (*CP* 11:9)

10. The Master said, "Dozing while hearing the dharma is like eating rice cake in a dream, and hearing the dharma aimlessly is like looking at rice cake in a painting." (*CP* 11:10)

11. The Master said, "Knowledge is different from self-awakening; if knowledge is not accompanied by self-awakening, one will be no more than a slave to one's knowledge." (*CP* 11:11)

12. The Master said, "If you do not stop practicing with faith, you will eventually attain to complete enlightenment." (*CP* 11:12)

13. The Master said, "True Buddha-dharma is the Buddhism that includes the Buddhism of faith, the Buddhism of scholar, and the Buddhism of the practitioner." (*CP* 11:13)

14. The Master said, "Superstition lies in a faith based on ignorance and nowhere else." (*CP* 11:14)

15. The Master said, "In your daily greetings, do not just inquire about the physical well-being, but say, 'Let's do our mind cultivation well.' This will become the true greeting of the practitioner of the Way." (*CP* 11:15)

16. The Master said, "An ancient sage taught his disciples to become salt. I encourage you to become a lotus. Though a lotus has its root deep in mud, its leaves do not get dirty and its flower is beautiful and fragrant; it will be the symbol of the practitioners of the New World." (*CP* 11:16)

17. The Master said, "To hold your ground against greed, anger, and delusion, you need integrity, fairness, and brightness. Integrity replaces greed, fairness anger, and brightness delusion." (*CP* 11:17)

18. The Master said, "If you can willingly submit to advice, your practice will make steady progress daily and monthly." (*CP* 11:18)

19. The Master said, "Who has the sharpest eye? The one who examines one's mind thoroughly for any fault does. Who has the sharpest ear? The one who willingly submits to earnest advice does." (*CP* 11:19)

20. The Master said, "It is difficult to expound the deliverance sermon[102] to a person in his or her last moment who does not think of death. Likewise, it is difficult to give advice to someone who does not check his or her mind for any fault." (*CP* 11:20)

21. The Master said, "An eye cannot see itself and a mirror cannot reflect itself. Likewise, deluded beings, being blocked by a false notion of

the self, cannot see their own faults but only see someone else's fault. The practitioner of the Way, however, examines him- or herself, transcending self and others, and therefore knows correctly the right and the wrong of self and others." (*CP* 11:21)

22. The Master said, "Anyone who has neither aspiration nor zeal for advancement is a living corpse." (*CP* 11:22)

23. The Master said, "Aspiration and greed look similar, but there is a huge difference between the two; aspiration is the mind that seeks on behalf of the public, while greed is the mind that seeks on behalf of the private self." (*CP* 11:23)

24. The Master said, "The most urgent thing for a dying person is to take care that his or her last one thought be pure; the most important thing for a person making his or her start in the world is to set up the first great aspiration. The best of all aspirations is that of becoming a buddha and delivering sentient beings." (*CP* 11:24)

25. The Master said, "Just as a traveler has a destination, the Buddhist practitioner's destination is the stage of buddhahood." (*CP* 11:25)

26. The Master said, "Although it is true that right will prevail of all affairs in the end, in fact it is true that all affairs end up as destined. Although it is said that calamity extends to one's offspring, in fact it is true that calamity lies in oneself." (*CP* 11:26)

27. The Master said, "A small measure of depravity can cause failure in the great task of eternal life. Those who changed heart halfway and became corrupted are your teachers." (*CP* 11:27)

28. The Master said, "Those who, being pulled by greed and attachment, are not afraid of transgression, are like fish that, being attracted to bait, do not know what it is to be killed. Those who think that truth can be cheated or avoided are like the fish in the net that take the net for a hiding place." (*CP* 11:28)

29. The Master said, "The mind that, being innocent, is devoid of evil is the heavenly mind, and judgment of the heavenly mind is the heavenly judgment. If one judges one's own good and evil with one's own heavenly mind, then one will see the heavenly judgment." (*CP* 11:29)

30. The Master said, "No matter how far science can advance, what should be done by heavenly principle will be done by heavenly principle, and what should be done by humans will be done by humans." (*CP* 11:30)

31. The Master said, "Because it is the principle of heaven and earth that whatever reaches its extremity changes, an individual, a family, a

party, and a nation should all be careful at times of extreme prosperity."[103] (*CP* 11:31)

32. The Master said, "The Chinese character for the word *virtue* signifies greatness. Since the foundation of what can ably influence all the beings on the six paths and the four forms of birth is this 'virtue,' what can be greater than it?" (*CP* 11:32)

33. The Master said, "Humaneness can be an attachment if it is excessive; it is none other than virtue if moderate." (*CP* 11:33)

34. The Master said, "If you handle all human affairs with peace and gentleness, you can overcome harshness and accomplish your task without hurting anyone. However, if you cannot accomplish the task only with peace and gentleness, you will have to use harshness." (*CP* 11:34)

35. The Master said, "When the strong help the weak make progress, the strong can take either of two contrary ways, following the principle of agreement or that of opposition. Progress by the way of agreement occurs when the strong help the weak improve themselves; progress by the way of opposition occurs when the strong oppose the intention of the weak to become zealous for progress." (*CP* 11:35)

36. The Master said, "A truly virtuous person can show his brilliance where he should and can appear totally ignorant where he should." (*CP* 11:36)

37. The Master said, "Virtuous people take more care of those inferior to them." (*CP* 11:37)

38. The Master said, "It is difficult for the junior to take good care of the senior, but it is more difficult for the senior to take good care of the junior." (*CP* 11:38)

39. The Master said, "There is a saying 'Mouth is the gate of calamity'; in fact, however, the mouth is the gate of both calamity and blessings." (*CP* 11:39)

40. The Master said, "Saying a single word can occasion a calamity or blessing between people. Hence, do not say even a single word rashly." (*CP* 11:40)

41. The Master said, "Speak cordially, but manage affairs efficiently." (*CP* 11:41)

42. The Master said, "A practitioner who loves to receive favors but does poor practice falls into the evil path; a practitioner will get into less debt if he or she practices while receiving favors as little as possible." (*CP* 11:42)

43. The Master said, "Do not love to receive favors from others, and do not take favors from the faithful rashly. In the event of even a small lapse of attention, it will be like picking popped rice to eat after setting fire to a grain stack." (*CP* 11:43)

44. The Master said, "Footprints remain on the ground; mental functioning leaves traces in empty space; the traces of one's life remain in the world as the merit and virtue one has bestowed on the world." (*CP* 11:44)

45. The Master said, "Sages such as Buddha-bodhisattvas freely enjoy calamity or blessings by transcending their fate; deluded people and sentient beings are ruled by calamity and blessings, being dragged by their fate." (*CP* 11:45)

46. The Master said, "It is difficult to be patient, but, if you bear and forbear for a long time, then your numinous elixir is consolidated. It is difficult to do a thing unremittingly, but if you do it again and again, then spiritual power is accumulated, so you will attain the freedom to do all things." (*CP* 11:46)

47. The Master said, "The power of concentration of mind is great. When the nine disciples of Grand Master Sot'aesan worked in icy water to construct the embankment in 1918, none of the members caught cold, even the virulent influenza of the winter of that year." (*CP* 11:47)

48. The Master said, "True practice of patience by changing one's mind is significantly different from the mere verbal practice of patience. If you persevere with a difficult situation successfully several times, the next situation becomes easier to handle." (*CP* 11:48)

49. The Master said, "Zhuxi said, 'A bramble grows again even after it is cut back, but iris and epidendrum die easily even if they are raised with care.' And it is difficult for us to do good and easy to do evil. Cut back an evil as soon as its bud takes form in your mind. Strive to foster the good in your mind and not lose it, so that buddhahood for innumerable lives can take good root deep in your mind." (*CP* 11:49)

50. The Master said, "A sage can argue right against wrong and can hate or love; however, the sage discriminates right against wrong only for the sake of public interest and even hates or loves with the mind that is not attached to anything." (*CP* 11:50)

51. The Master said, "Good becomes prominent because of evil; evil can be corrected because of good. However, the highest good manifests itself as good by transcending relative good and evil." (*CP* 11:51)

52. The Master said, "Deluded beings do not do any major good because they get caught up in minor good and cannot attain great wisdom because they are caught up in minor wisdom. But a sage does great good with small good and gets great knowledge beginning with small knowledge." (*CP* 11:52)

53. The Master said, "Do not hate a bad person; though you may take pity on that person. Do not be jealous of a good person; though you may respect that person." (*CP* 11:53)

54. The Master said, "A person of high capacity is naturally endowed with good nature; someone of medium capacity does good only after learning of it, and someone of low capacity is unable to do good even after learning of it." (*CP* 11:54)

55. The Master said, "Even though you have won here and now, you will lose next time if you are arrogant and careless. Even though you have lost here and now, you will win if you are humble and exert yourself." (*CP* 11:55)

56. The Master said, "Deluded beings get further and further into debt because they only have many things to demand, while sages see the cause of blessings accumulate because they only have many things to do as duties." (*CP* 11:56)

57. The Master said, "Being resentful without knowing the great beneficence for the reason that one is partially harmed, is like regarding food as an enemy because one had an upset stomach after a meal." (*CP* 11:57)

58. The Master said, "Deluded beings feel grateful for a minor favor or for the first favor, but do not feel grateful to great beneficence and continued favors. And one cannot do the true requital of beneficence[104] unless one knows what the fundamental and great beneficence is." (*CP* 11:58)

59. The Master said, "One who lives only the life of gratitude will always be helped by the Fourfold Beneficence;[105] one who lives only the life of resentment will always be harmed, even by a microbe." (*CP* 11:59)

60. The Master said, "Not a single thing will have grudge against you if you hate not a single thing." (*CP* 11:60)

61. The Master said, "Not a single thing will be accomplished if one is careless." (*CP* 11:61)

62. The Master said, "Success lies in not being careless; hence, secure a successful outcome by not stopping in the middle." (*CP* 11:62)

63. The Master said, "Do not use the expression 'It has no use for anything,' because using that expression cuts its affinity to the task and the thing." (*CP* 11:63)

64. The Master said, "Heaven does not bestow blessing on anyone that does not create it, and one is not punished for the evil one does not commit." (*CP* 11:64)

65. The Master said, "Set your aspiration on what is great and accumulate merit on a small scale. If you exert yourself in meritorious work without being concerned with remuneration, then a great reward of virtue and remuneration will return to you." (*CP* 11:65)

66. The Master said, "By the time one leaves the world, having lived a life in this world, one must have justice in abundance, virtue in abundance, and aspiration in abundance." (*CP* 11:66)

67. The Master said, "Do not lament that the world does not recognize you. Truth, being fair, does not let your merit come to nothing. Hidden virtue and the virtue of no-thought are the highest virtues." (*CP* 11:67)

68. The Master said, "There are three kinds of courage. To resort exclusively to force with no knowledge of the order of things is brute courage. To attack injustice for the sake of justice is courage for righteous cause. And to strive to practice constantly without compromising one's righteous intention, being externally soft but internally firm, is the courage of the Way." (*CP* 11:68)

69. The Master said, "There are three kinds of shame. To be ashamed of asking something one does not know is a foolish shame. To be ashamed of exposing one's deficiency and faults is an outward shame; and to be ashamed upon checking one's conscience and fostering a righteous mind endlessly is the inward shame." (*CP* 11:69)

70. The Master said, "It is said that there are four occasions of joy in the secular world. How wonderful it will be when an old disease cures itself! How wonderful it will be when one can administer a miracle drug widely! How wonderful it will be when all dharmas are brightly interpenetrated! And, how wonderful it will be when all sentient beings turn to one for refuge!" (*CP* 11:70)

71. The Master said, "An ancient loyal subject said 'Upon death, I will become a pine tree and be alone and as green as ever.' We should become pine trees while we are alive, and all together be as green as ever, using all our strength to be loyal to our order and the world." (*CP* 11:71)

72. The Master said, "If there is something in the way, it blocks the way, and if there is nothing, then the way is open. If blocked, the way is dark; if open, it is bright." (*CP* 11:72)

73. The Master said, "One who practices the ordinary and constant mind well is the true person of the Way. One can be a great practitioner

of the Way only if one keeps the mind of the Way constantly, whether one is poor or rich, noble or humble, or suffering or happy." (*CP* 11:73)

74. The Master said, "The mind of the masses eventually follows the virtuous one; the mandate of heaven eventually returns to the selfless person." (*CP* 12:64)

X

The Destiny of the Way

1. The Master said, "The order of a correct dharma looks insignificant in its formative stage; however, it will emanate a great power all at once at the right time because it is the right power to be in charge of the world. If one acts with truthful and public spirit under the sign of Won Buddhism, one can bring about success in what is initially a wearisome and difficult task, and one will be protected and welcomed wherever one goes. For the auspicious power this order received is transmitted to the person and his work. If, however, one manages one's private interest under the pretense of public interest, not only will one's business fail, but also one's future will be blocked, though one may be unaware of it. Such a person will be disliked and hated by the public, and slide gradually into the pit of calamity. Therefore, exert yourselves with utmost devotion and earnest public spirit to receive the order's auspicious fortune so that you may be the minister that can ably receive and move the awesome power of heaven and earth." (CP 13:3)

2. The Master said, "Although a great new fortune is arriving, it depends on the frame of one's mind whether or not one will receive it. This is analogous to the fact that one cannot hear the news on the radio if one does not turn on the receiver, even though the news is on the air, or the fact that a farmer will have nothing to harvest if he does not sow the seed and cultivate at the right time, even though there is a good omen for great harvest at the beginning of the farming season." (CP 13:4)

3. The Master said, "The new fortune of the way is that which only a truthful dharma can claim. One who is honest, candid, and calm, with true ability inside, will be recommended in accord with the time and situation. However, a person will not stand in the world if his conduct is not as good as his words, his reality is less than his name, his hidden character is not as good as his appearance, and his vanity and falsehood are revealed. The new fortune of the way is that which the dharma of harmony can lay claim to. An individual, an organization, or a nation will be successful if they harmonize with others by being simple-hearted, as if they were unskilled, but generous and virtuous. If, however, a person is sharp, judgmental, and heartless, and thus often conflicts with others, he will face difficulty in accomplishing anything. The new fortune of the Way is that which the dharma of justice can lay claim to. To the person who, being earnest, public-spirited, and diligent, renders benefit to the masses in many ways, all positions and power will return, even if he does not try to lay claim to them. However, the person who, being selfish and greedy causes harm to the masses, will never stand in the world, no matter how hard he tries." (CP 13:5)

4. The Master said, "In the past, practitioners of the Way, wearing rags, submitted themselves to poverty and a lowly station in life, living in rural retirement. In the future, however, the higher dharma stage you are in, the more riches and honors will follow you. What a foolish practitioner of the Way one would be if one worried about food, clothing, or a lowly station in the world. True practitioners of the Way, meanwhile, regard ascetic practice as nobler than wealth and fame, so that they, praising honest poverty over luxury, will unreservedly decline even a position that they deserve in favor of another person, and will use the material things given to them for the public well-being. In other words, the new fortune is that of great morality, which is perfect and unselfish. Since the foundation for receiving the fortune of the Way is the morally sound mind that is perfect and unselfish, I ask all of you to become the masters of this rare, great fortune by exerting yourselves to reform your mind." (CP 13:6)

5. A student asked, "What kind of dharma will be most advocated in the world to come?" The Master answered, "The most perfect, right, and realistic doctrine will be the one most advocated. In the past, all religions arose in localized areas and had their doctrines structured to fit the public sentiments of their times; these religions could lead public sentiment even though their doctrines were not comprehensive. In the future, however, with the great improvements in transportation and communica-

tion and the lively exchange of ideas of the times, any religion will find it difficult to guide the general and public sentiments of the world unless its doctrine is so perfect and right that it can hold good throughout the world. In the past, since human beings were unsophisticated, all religions used mostly practical expedients or solemnity to impress their followers. However, in the future, as human beings are gradually enlightened, any religion will find it difficult to guide the human mind unless its doctrine can correctly expound the truth of facts and principles, and unless it can be applied practically to actuality." (CP 13:7)

6. The student asked again, "What kind of a person will be the most honorable in the future?" The Master answered, "A truthful human of great public spirit will be the most honorable person. In the past, heroes and extraordinary men gratified their desires and ambitions by winning over the public sentiments by trickery, and even today people occasionally get high positions by schemes and underhand means. From now on, however, as human intelligence will in general be brighter, trickery will be exposed, so that there will be no one to be deceived. Only the true and honest person will be well received by the public. In the past, as social life had various limitations, and human knowledge was limited, such ideologies as selfishness and putting one's family first governed the public mind. However, in the future, as the fortune of the Way opens for the ideology of one family under heaven, anyone operating from selfishness or putting his or her family first will find it difficult to rise in the world. It is because only the person of great public spirit will be welcomed by the masses and will become prominent in the world." (CP 13:8)

7. The Master said, "The realm where all religions will be united is Irwŏn, and the standard of government is the mean. If you are enlightened to the truth of Irwŏn and analyze it, you will realize that the realm where all religions are united is Irwŏn. Although the way of government includes many particulars, an analysis of the essential points of all governments will show that the standard of all governments is the government based on the principle of the mean, the principle of neither excess nor deficiency. The chaotic world will recover stability only if religions return to Irwŏn and governments operate on the principle of the mean. And, as the world gets gradually enlightened, the principle of Irwŏn and the mean will stand in the world." He said again, "Of all the ways, the way of Irwŏn is the best; of all the governments, the government based on the mean is the best. Irwŏn is the substance of truth, and the mean the functioning of truth." (CP 13:9)

8. A student asked, "What kind of energy is the vital force of the 'earlier heaven'?" The Master answered, "By the 'vital force of the earlier heaven' is meant the spirit that is opposed to the new era. Just as the leaves of the last year inevitably fall and the leaves of the New Year gain power, the obsolete spirit of selfish desire and superstitions of the past will find no ground to stand on in the New World." He said further, "The ancient sages of the Orient, being superior figures of thorough knowledge, explicated the fortunes of the earlier and later heavens in the *Hedu luohsu.*" (*CP* 13:10)

9. Song Chŏnun said, "I want to know about the 'yin world and yang world.'" The Master said, "The yin world and yang world are like the night world and the day world. Because night is dark, it is difficult to discern things right in the nighttime, and even if you can, you can only recognize things within a limited area. Just as people close their gates and sleep at night, the yin world is blocked, narrow, inactive, and leaning to one side. The yang world, on the other hand, is like the broad daylight, when human knowledge will generally advance, ideology and the dharma they advocate will become bright and perfect, people will open their doors to each other and frequent each other's houses and act with energy and alertness. This will be a world of great civilization." (*CP* 13:11)

10. The Master said, "In the past world, one could manage world affairs with the principle of pandemonium, the principle of mutual opposition. However, in the future, nothing will be accomplished unless one follows the way of 'releasing the devil.' This is because the great fortune of heaven and earth has reached the age of 'mutual benefaction by resolving grudges.'" (*CP* 13:12)

11. The Master said, "The master of the body is the mind, and the master of all religions is the one that explicates the principle of the mind best. Since Buddha-dharma explicates the principle of the mind best, a religion that has revived the flow of Buddha-dharma correctly will be the dominant religion in the New World." (*CP* 13:13)

12. The Master said, "In preparation for opening this order, Grand Master Sot'aesan was born several times in this land (Korea), making many dharma affinities in advance, some overt and some covert." He said further, "The legend that Mount Kŭmgang (Diamond Mountain) is Dharmamodgata's monastery predicts that a new dharma to save the world will arise in this country. And the legend that Bodhisattva Salāpralāpa comes to meet Dharmamodgata from the west means that westerners will come to the east to seek the dharma." (*CP* 13:14)

13. The Master said to his students, "You are bearing a very heavy duty, the duty to make this country a first-class country. You will not create a first-class country with money and power; if you make it with morality, this country will become the heart of all countries." (*CP* 13:15)

14. The Master said, "In the past, because transportation was inconvenient and people were ignorant, Buddha-bodhisattvas appeared now and again, taking charge of districts in the east, west, south, and north and opening their orders to a few. From now on, however, as the world has shrunk until it is now like one family, all Buddha-bodhisattvas gather together in one order, opening an order on the grand scale." (*CP* 13:16)

15. The Master said, "Because the world will be more enlightened in the future, it will be easy for people to move to other parts of the world and to go and come anywhere; there will be no boundary between countries, so people can move from this region to other regions. And a virtuous and able person can be the leader of a country if supported by the people of the country, regardless of national and racial differences, just as, within a country, a person from another province can be a governor of a district." (*CP* 13:17)

16. The Master said, "When the world enters the era of new opening, workers following the natural order, and workers going against it, standing opposed to each other, make progress, promoting the construction of a good world." He said further, "It is said, 'One who causes a rebellion is a sage, and one who suppresses the rebellion is also a sage.' The one who causes a rebellion at the right time and suppresses it at the right time is called a sage. The one who fails to do so is called ungrateful. Since every matter has its order to be followed, to understand the order of the essence of the matter, and to apply skillful means correctly for it—this is the compassionate, skillful means of a sage." (*CP* 13:18)

17. The Master said, "Can an equal society be realized with materialistic supremacy? It will be realized only when the spirit of public interest is realized generally in the minds of the society. Can world peace be realized by relying primarily on struggle? A truly peaceful world can only be realized when people become aware of beneficence in each other." (*CP* 13:19)

18. The Master said, "Can this order become a major religion of the world by propaganda and advertisement? This order will be developed well only if many trustworthy devotees arise, bringing Grand Master Sot'aesan's spirit to light; if this order becomes the focus of the minds of people; and

if the order is authenticated by the world for the prominent achievement of every individual's practice and of its missions."[106] (*CP* 13:20)

19. The Master said, "Today people who are intoxicated with material civilization may not fully understand it if you mention spiritual culture. However, people in the world to come, with their spirits being greatly brightened, will come to know well the blessings and offenses of their own making, the details of their original nature, and the events of their previous lives as if they were the events of their youth in this life. The world to come will be that of material civilization and spiritual culture perfectly balanced. Wait just a little more and see! A truly good world is on its way." (*CP* 13:21)

20. The Master said, "There are three great ways under heaven. The first is the way of mutual understanding, the second is the way of mutual concession, and the third is the way of impartiality. If these three ways are followed, peace will be realized for individuals and the whole world." (*CP* 13:23)

21. The Master said, "Nowadays, the term *universal harmony* is used often in many areas, and this truly is good news. If all the people of the world cherished the spirit of universal harmony in name and actuality, what will be so difficult under heaven? Therefore, if, facing the affairs of the world, we do not attempt to monopolize power, profit, fame, or favor, universal harmony will be realized of itself, and world peace will naturally be realized." (*CP* 13:25)

22. The Master said, "World peace is realized by everyone's harmonizing mind; thus, the harmonizing mind is the meridian of world peace." (*CP* 13:26)

23. The Master said, "When Yao and Shun conceded the world under heaven to each other, and feudal lords conceded the nine towns to each other, a harmonious spirit filled the whole world. When this event was represented as music, it is said a Chinese phoenix danced to it. Harmony among people is realized by concessions, and when harmony is at its acme, the spirit under heaven pervades everywhere accordingly." (*CP* 13:27)

24. The Master said, "It's because people are not aware of being indebted to beneficence, or because they do not requite it even if they are aware of being indebted to beneficence, that world peace is not realized, though it is desired by individuals and by the whole world. Therefore, Grand Master Sot'aesan has opened the Way for true world peace by revealing the grand Fourfold Beneficence and by letting all people lead the life of beneficence requital and gratitude." (*CP* 13:28)

25. The Master said, "By 'broad-minded' is meant having one's mind unobstructed. If the mind is free from attachment to hatred and love, from the limitations of national boundaries, attachment to favorable and adverse mental spheres, and the entrapment of suffering and happiness, then the mind is broad and great." He said further, "The great doctrine that will save the world should be accessible from all directions, with no barriers, either geographical, which are the visible barriers, or mental, which are the invisible barriers." (CP 13:29)

26. The Master said, "In the past, one tried to put the world at peace by means of statecraft; in the future, however, one will try to put the world at peace by means of statecraft based on the principle of world peace. The way of governing the world is statecraft, the way of world peace is to rule by the Way and its virtue." (CP 13:30)

27. The Master said, "The quintessence of Buddhism is emptiness. If one approaches it erroneously, one falls into false emptiness. The quintessence of Confucianism is the scale. If one enters it erroneously, one ends up being narrow-minded and inflexible. The quintessence of Taoism is non-ado and spontaneity. If one approaches it erroneously, one becomes self-indulgent. The quintessence of science is accurate analysis. If one approaches it erroneously, one will be caught up by existence and attached to material things. If one makes a good application of these fourfold quintessence without approaching them erroneously, one will accomplish the perfect system of truth in oneself and a perfect personality." (CP 13:31)

28. The Master said, "When people were ignorant and narrow-minded, stuck in their times and within their boundaries, their minds were controlled by selfish individualism, the ideology that one's own family comes first, the ideology that one's own society or nation is above all others. Even now, the remnants of such ideologies can be found surviving in various places. From ancient times, Buddha-bodhisattvas and sages inspired people with great spirits to regard the world as their main concern by transcending all those boundaries. The so-called great compassion and great pity of the Buddha is cosmopolitanism, the spirit of benevolence and righteousness of Confucius is cosmopolitanism, and the spirit of universal love of Jesus Christ is cosmopolitanism. All these sages, regarding the whole world as one household and all humans as one family, advocated great moral principles with which to save the human race. Buddhism in particular has advocated that the great spirit is concerned not only with the human race but also with all beings of the six paths and four forms of birth in the ten directions. Thus, Buddhism can be recognized as the most cosmopolitan of all." (CP 13:32)

29. The Master said, "To judge from the great fortune of the world today, human knowledge is about to make great advances, and all limitations are about to be overcome. And we are at the initial stage of a grand cosmopolitanism that will govern the hearts of the people under heaven. This is a sign that a magnificent world with a new civilization, a world of great morality, is about to unfold. The new principle is so perfect and fair that, clearly transcending all obsolete limitations, it will let all sentient beings of the six paths and four forms of birth coexist and prosper mutually in a supreme paradise. This principle, however, does not imply that individualism, the family-centered ethic, parochialism, or nationalism should be abolished. It rather means that all these principles will help build a cosmopolitan paradise if they are applied correctly in accord with the cosmopolitan principle. At this propitious time, we, the founding apostles of an unexcelled great religious order, should firmly establish the spirit of the world as one family in everyone's mind. Then we should take a vow to render the spirit of cosmopolitanism worldwide, so that all sentient beings may rejoice in a vast and limitless paradise on the earth. Thus, I am entrusting to you that you refresh your mind daily and monthly and exert yourselves on this practice and public service so that you may be the guide of the grand cosmopolitanism that is perfect, complete, utterly fair, and unselfish." (CP 13:33)

30. In April 1961 (WE 46), the Master said, making public the ethics of triple identity (samdong yulli), "The concept of the ethics of triple identity is the threefold principle of grand harmony for all human beings of the world. This is the fundamental principle for the whole human race to follow in order that they may work and rejoice together in a peaceful and comfortable world: namely, as one household, as one grand family, keeping the one grand house by transcending all boundaries. To judge from the great fortune of the world today, human knowledge is about to increase greatly and all limitations are about to be overcome one by one; thus, a grand spirit of harmony and unity is about to govern the whole world. This is the opportunity for all nations and all peoples of the world to rise together to build one grand world. Soon, all humans will gladly accept the spirit of the ethics of triple identity and exert themselves to realize it, establishing organizations to realize it together, so that this spirit will be realized worldwide, building a grand paradise on earth. Therefore, I say to the assembly of this order, which is meeting here at this propitious time, that you should refresh your mind daily and monthly, and exert yourselves all the more in this practice and this public service, so that you may guide the building of a good world." (CP 13:34)

31. The Master continued, saying, "The first principle of the ethics of triple identity is the principle of one origin. This implies that all people of religion must harmonize with one another, with the knowledge that the fundamental origin of all religions and religious sects is one. In the world, there are deemed to be three major religions, namely, Buddhism, Christianity, and Islam, and other well-established religions such as Confucianism and Taoism. Moreover, in modern times, numerous other religions have arisen in this country and in various regions of the world. All these religions with their differing criteria for belonging have different missions in accord with their different doctrines and different abilities. Although their doctrines are expressed in different names and forms, a careful inquiry into their fundamental sources will show that the fundamental tenets are not contrary to the truth of Irwŏn. Therefore, all religions are generally of identical origin.[107] If all people of religion in the world were awakened to this connection and harmonized with one another, all the religions of the world would form one grand household, with their followers adapting themselves to one another and keeping company with one another. Thus, we must realize the spirit of the great Way of Irwŏn, the fundamental source of all religions, and firmly establish in our mind the spirit to regard all religions as one. We should accordingly take the initiative in the grand task of uniting all religions with Irwŏn." (CP 13:35)

32. The Master continued, saying, "The second principle of the ethics of triple identity is the bond of one vital force. This principle implies that all races and all sentient beings should be united in grand harmony by awakening to the truth that they are all fellow beings bonded together by the one vital force. In the world, there are the so-called races of four colors living in various regions, various nations making up one race, and various clans making up one nation. If we inquire into the origin of all people, we see that the fundamental source of life is imbued with one vital force. To those who take heaven and earth as their parents and the universe as their own household, all people are related; even birds, beasts, and insects are related by one great vital force. Thus, when all people in the world, awakening to this relationship, harmonize together, all races and all nations will unite as one family and cultivate universal friendship and harmony, influencing all sentient beings by virtuous example. Therefore, by realizing the principle that all human races and all lives are related by the one vital force, we must firmly establish in our mind the grand spirit to view all races and lives as one. Furthermore, with this spirit, we should take the initiative to unite all races on the principle of equality." (CP 13:36)

33. He continued, saying, "The third principle of the ethics of triple identity is renewal with one aim. This implies that, being awakened to the truth that all enterprises and proposals help toward the renewal of the world, all should unite in grand harmony. Today in the world, there are two great power blocs[108] each with separate claims and systems, and each managing various enterprises. Besides these, there are various entrepreneurs who have launched all sorts of enterprises according to their areas of specialty and within the boundaries of business. Although their claims and expedients are sometimes challenged and sometimes accepted by others, their original aims, as an inquiry into their fundamental sources shows, are all to make this world a better place; even the evil has the power to help one awaken to the good. Thus, in general, all enterprises are essentially in one, identical line of business. When all the entrepreneurs in the world, being awakened to this relationship, understand each other and harmonize together, all the enterprises of the world will form one household. They will encourage each other and make advances side by side, eventually being united into the way of fairness. Hence, we, clearly realizing the spirit of this fairness, should establish the grand spirit to view all enterprises as one, and from that point, we should take the initiative to unite all enterprises and do so with fairness." (CP 13:37)

XI

On the Korean National Destiny

1. One day in November 1944 (WE 29), Master Chŏngsan copied for his attendants a poem from ancient times and said, "The destinies of the nation and Won Buddhism will be like this:

When on Mount Ji has the mist cleared,
Its lofty height and the luxuriant forest lie revealed.
Though the wind has stopped, ripples roll on the mirror-bright water.
Lament not that spring is over and that the lovely flowers fade away,
Another season awaits the harvest of lotus seeds in midstream." (*CP* 3:1)

2. In July of the following year (1945), the Master went to the Chŏryang Temple in Pusan. There he wrote and hung on the wall of the dharma hall the following: "This is where the Fourfold Beneficence[109] is reciprocally produced; here are the triple jewels[110] enshrined." The Master then prayed for the settling of the national situation. (*CP* 3:2)

3. One day a Won Buddhist asked, "Didn't Grand Master Sot'aesan say anything special about the March First Movement in 1919?" The Master replied, "Grand Master Sot'aesan said, 'It is the scream pressing the New World to unfold. We should hurry. Let us finish the embankment project and offer prayers.'" (*CP* 3:3)

4. After Korea was liberated from Japanese occupation on August 15, 1945, the Master wrote a treatise on national foundation and expressed his opinion on the foundation of the nation as follows: "Since August 15, 1945, I have heard declarations of various leaders and seen the methods of leadership, and perceived the drift of public sentiments. I was sometimes pleased and at other times worried; sometimes I had an idea for a better future for the nation. I have briefly described those natural ideas in this booklet, which I have titled *A Treatise on National Foundation* (*Kŏn'gungnon*). The gist of it is to take the spiritual as the roots; government and education as the trunk; national defense, construction, and economics as branches and leaves; and the way of improvement as the fruit, so that the nation should have the national power with a healthy root through eternity." (*CP* 3:4)

5. On the spirit of national foundation, the Master said, "The first spiritual foundation on which to build the nation is spiritual union. It is a matter of natural principle that union makes things strong and division makes them weak, and that united we stand and divided we fall. A perfect and strong nation that plans to prosper for tens of thousands of years cannot be founded unless the fundamental spirit of the people is strongly unified. Hence, the foundation of the nation lies in the unity of the people, which is possible only when our mind is bright. But our mind cannot be bright unless the walls surrounding our heart are destroyed. The walls consist of many things. They are (1) lack of harmony among the people, who are attached to their own views and biased against impartial views; (2) lack of respect for others, because of self-conceit and greed for fame; (3) disregard of the righteous and correct views, due to a burning greed for political power, (4) disturbance of the minds of the masses by the stirring up of jealousy and conflict or by crafty means; (5) movement by impulse and loss of the power to make correct and fair judgments, due to an improper understanding of a matter's right course; (6) attachment to localism and factionalism, losing the spirit of grand harmony, and the exposure of someone else's minor faults and lack of capacity for tolerance based on personal hatred and old enmity; (7) placing one's own gain and profit before anything else and lacking in spirit for the national independence, (8) rejecting the true heart of a genuine patriot, and (9) shifting the responsibility of unity onto someone else without examining oneself. If we demolish all of these walls, our unity will be quite natural. However, if the walls remain in our hearts, there will be no unity, no matter how

loudly the people speak out for it. Thus, this fundamental problem should be solved as part of the foundation of the nation." (*CP* 3:5)

6. The Master continued, "The second of the spirit of national foundation is the establishment of national self-sufficiency. While we should be thankful to the nations that recovered for us our national liberty, we should maintain friendship also with other friendly nations on the spiritual basis of fairness and the spirit of independence. We should not attach ourselves to an ally against another power group because we take the former to be the source of our own ideology and power. An examination of our present situation of affairs shows that we cannot stand unless we follow the middle way, and our national reconstruction will be difficult without the common aid of the United Nations. Hence, national unity and self-sufficiency should be taken as our first national priority." (*CP* 3:6)

7. The Master continued, "The third of the spirit of national foundation is loyalty, justice, and dedication to the public. By loyalty is meant the truthful and sincere mind; by justice, fairness and impartiality; and by dedication to the public, serving with loyalty and justice both society and nation. For any age, therefore, an enterprise, a society, or a nation where there is no loyalty and justice is no more than a show of beautifying deceit and will eventually fall. Thus, we must examine ourselves to check whether we are loyal and just; we must expand loyalty and justice if we are and, if we are not, we must cultivate loyalty and justice in ourselves. If the general public is loyal and just, checking evil inclinations and indolence against justice, the enterprise of founding our nation will succeed, and the foundation of our nation will be as solid as Mount Tai." (*CP* 3:7)

8. The Master continued, "The fourth of the spirit of national foundation is regulation and rectification. In the national structure, there should be leaders and those who are led, and those who are respected and those who respect. If the leader loses the authority to lead and those to be led have no intention to be led, or if those to be respected give no grounds for respect and the people have no intention to respect anyone, everyone will behave as the head. This will be contrary to the spirit of founding a nation and it will be difficult to establish an orderly government. Yesterday's leader can be today's follower or vice versa; we should follow the leader even if he was a follower yesterday; yesterday's leader who is today's follower should follow the new leader. As to the matter of veneration, a new leader who is right for the times and for that position should be given due respect and cooperation, regardless of closeness

and remoteness, friendliness and estrangement, or ideological agreement or disagreement. Here lies, I think, the right way for civilized people to found a nation." (*CP* 3:8)

9. The Master continued, "The fifth of the spirit of national foundation is an insightful view of the general situation. Immediate gain or temporary greed should not be one's guiding principle in handling one's various affairs; one should take measures to approach the situation by observing international and national circumstances. A personal reputation should not be put in front of the national reputation. One should help the nation's strength grow without fighting for one's own political power. One should consider national interests and not devote oneself to one's own interests. One should not do anything base in front of a foreigner, understanding that one person's actions can have a favorable or unfavorable effect on the nation's prestige. One should understand that what looks good now could be the cause of public worries. Understanding that what is a gain now could be a big loss in the future, one should calculate carefully for long-term gain. One should understand that change is part of the principle of the universe so that one should, without adhering to just one kind of law, set up laws and rules properly for the times. Finally, one should not lean to one side, understanding that anything excessive leads to vice." (*CP* 3:9)

10. The Master said on government, "The government should guarantee equal political rights to everyone and help everyone practice their rights. While the administration should be based on easiness and promptness, matters of great importance should be resolved in accordance with laws and public opinion. The people, high or low, should abide by the laws. Once a national consensus is established, the whole nation should be trained for patriotism and public morality. Leadership should be based on the moral principle of faithfulness, so that the leader can be trusted by the people. The nurturing of talent and economic development should not be neglected, so that the nation should become economically and politically independent and self-sufficient. For the spiritual guidance of the people, the state and religion should cooperate." (*CP* 3:10)

11. The Master said on religion, "If people do not have firm faith in truthful religion, spiritual control and the cultivation of the people's conscience will be ineffective and, as a consequence, the crime rate will rise as some people will do as they please. Some people with religious faith occasionally become superstitious, attaching to a partial view, so that they cannot lead the life of an honorable citizen with sound morality. As

a way of guiding the people, the state should encourage proper religion and let the administration, judiciary, educational bodies, and religion do their assigned work. This will be an essential element of national planning for ages to come." (*CP* 3:11)

12. The Master said on education, "People evolve through education; hence, compulsory education should be instituted and the educational system should be expanded. In the past, science education was emphasized and moral education was neglected; this should be corrected and replaced by a balanced education with a sound curriculum based on patriotism and public morality. Education on matters of propriety should be improved in order to spread and unify the rules of propriety. In order to raise the national morale for work, labor together with practical training should be the first means adopted for the national encouragement of industry and as the driving force for the cultivation of diligence and sincerity in the nation." (*CP* 3:12)

13. The Master said on the principle of progress, "The first task is to honor those who serve the public altruistically. Due recognition and honor should be given to those with outstanding achievements in government or the national defense, those with remarkable achievements in religious edification or in education, those who provided financial support for the public interest, and those who have rendered a great service to the development of the nation and society with inventions or discoveries. The second task is to encourage education. Special education for the gifted should be supported by individuals, organizations, and the state toward the attainment of new knowledge; research institutions should be aided so that excellent means of national construction and social development can be developed by them. The third task is to abolish heredity and inheritance. Honors of any kind should be limited to the one person concerned, lest descendants rely on the influence of that person. Inheritance should be limited to the amount of funds necessary for living; the rest should be contributed to enterprises for the public so that both parents and children may accumulate merits. For national and social development and for an individual's personal development, everyone should lead a life of self-reliance." (*CP* 3:13)

14. Concluding the *Treatise on National Foundation* (*Kŏn'gungnon*), the Master said, "The central point of my teaching on the founding of the nation lies in the following. People of all classes should be equally protected, attaining individual liberty and stability in their lives. Before undergoing an external change, everyone should undergo a spiritual

change. Rich people should without prompting be generous to donate so as to increase organizations for the public so that the national living standard can be balanced. Private enterprises should not be treated differently from governmental enterprises so that both can cooperate for the national construction. And everyone, in both private and public life, should follow the way of progress, with a clear reward system for persons of merit, which may require a moderate degree of limitation on how one lives." (CP 3:14)

15. The Master continued, "The most urgent thing at this critical moment is for everyone to examine one's own mind and to strive to improve it, and for the leaders to give correct guidance to the people. For even the best ideology that they advocate will bring about evil consequences if their mind is not good. To infringe on someone else's rights or to try to gain unrighteous profit is against the principle of equality. The true value of equality will be realized only if people, becoming enlightened to the great way of the universe, cultivate an altruistic spirit and the spirit not to acquire clothes and food without due labor. To refuse sanctions of any kind against a life of indolence is contrary to the principle of liberty. The value of true liberty will be realized only if one's life does not violate public morality and the norms of social control, does not restrain the opinions of others, and does not infringe on someone else's rights." (CP 3:15)

16. The Master said further, "If we examine public sentiment these days, we see that a number of people cause disturbance in the mind of others, provoking a storm in the midst of dead calm or treating their fellow countrymen as enemies. They fancy themselves as contributing greatly to the reconstruction of the nation by such activities. The real power for reconstruction arises from the harmonious cooperation of people of all classes, by calming down any existing storm and changing any enemies into sources of beneficence. The reconstruction of the nation will be realized if people from all occupations cooperate following the right ways, which the rich, the poor, officials, or the masses should follow without losing orderliness while being equal, and without violating rules and laws while being free. Ideologies, equality, freedom, and rights can truly be enjoyed only after the nation is firmly established. If people put egoism before patriotism, individuals and the nation will both perish; but if people put patriotism before egoism, then individuals and the nation will both be saved." (CP 3:16)

17. The Master said, "Things have roots and branches; human affairs have beginnings and ends.[111] The reconstruction of the nation will fol-

low its due course only after people know what the right order is. The nation will earn international trust only after domestic unity is achieved, and international diplomacy will be successful only after international trust is gained. The national sovereignty will stand only after international diplomacy is successful, and equality and freedom will be enjoyed only after national sovereignty is established. Anyone who hopes for equality and freedom but disturbs national unity is like a person who wishes to live but does things that bring about his or her own death." (*CP* 3:17)

18. The Master said, "Even the best ideology can be stained by impure heart, and even the best effort can be wasted if what is undertaken is not right." He said again, "If you propagandize for yourself extensively and target others with strategic attacks, you can incite people for a while but can never achieve lasting success." He said further, "Traitors are none other than those who do things from greed knowing they are wrong; patriots are those who correct themselves the moment they find themselves in the wrong." (*CP* 3:18)

19. The Master said, "If one dances for joy without knowing the just and righteous cause, one's life will be worthless even if one is alive, and one's death will be a worthless death should one die." He said again, "If one compromises one's conscience by going along with the situation, one will never escape long-lasting shame, despite a false impression of temporary protection." He said further, "If one seeks one's own interests under the pretext of public interests, all of one's words become lies, and all of one's actions nothing but fraud." (*CP* 3:19)

20. The Master said, "Human conflicts start with ideological differences and move to a power struggle, and then to a war of hatred, eventually resulting in senseless fighting with unjustifiable harm to the public." (*CP* 3:20)

21. The Master said, "Someone else's clothes will not fit you even if they are good; only the clothes of your size can be yours." He said again, "At this time of cultural exchange it will be senseless obstinacy to hold only to one's own; and it will be stupid to be fascinated by someone else's things. Hence, one should be independent internally, and be harmonious externally with others, adopting another's good points and forsaking their weaknesses. This will be the best policy at this time." (*CP* 3:21)

22. The Master said, "If anything goes to extremes, it changes; and anything excessive leads to evil. Hence, the essential way to deliver the world lies in leaning to neither." He said again, "There is a huge difference between snatching and being snatched, on the one hand, and giving and taking on the other. The former produces enmity with the hidden

seed of anxiety, while the latter produces the harmony of beneficence and generous feelings, constructing peace." (*CP* 3:22)

23. The Master said, "To encourage people to do good and to honor their established merits make a great way for progress; if people neglect the good or look down upon established merits, they are on the way of retrogression." He said, "People should be prohibited from living beyond their means and encouraged to contribute to the public cause. If inheritance is limited by law, then people will be inspired to contribute to the public cause and the assets for the public will increase, thus resulting in the happiness of the people." (*CP* 3:23)

24. The Master said, "Without sufficient training one can carry out hardly anything; without preparation nothing can succeed. Hence, there should be periods for training and preparation." He said further, "When you bend a tree, you should do so slowly; for if you bend it abruptly, there is a danger of breaking it." He said, "You cannot teach the *Great Learning* (*Daxue*) to a child; you cannot entrust an egoist with public affairs." (*CP* 3:24)

25. The Master said, "If the head is disturbed, the rest of the body gets disturbed following the head; if the head is right then the rest of the body will be right accordingly. Hence, the leader takes the total responsibility." He said, "A grave vice cannot be forgiven by the heaven; but one's great public spirit is rewarded by heaven." He said, "That 'right prevails in the end' is the principle of the universe; hence, a human sentiment that is in accord with heaven has its proper direction." (*CP* 3:25)

26. A politician asked, "At this early stage of national reconstruction, the state of national affairs is unstable, with many problems waiting for solution. There can be a religion only after the nation is founded. I request, therefore, that you work for the reconstruction of the nation." The Master replied, "Although I have little ability, I am exerting all my efforts toward national affairs through this religious order. What do you mean by asking me to work for the national reconstruction?" The guest said, "I mean that you should participate in a political party and initiate a national movement." The Master said, "When you build a house, a foundation stone, a pillar, and a beam, each has its role, so that unless each in its given position cooperates, the house cannot be built. Likewise, when you found a nation, the government, religious edification, and domestic production each have their role and obligations, such that the nation cannot be founded unless each carries out its duties and cooperates. The foundation of the nation depends on how well the politicians conduct national affairs, how well the religious leader edifies the people, how well

the producers produce, and how well these three sectors cooperate. If today's state of national affairs is yet unsettled, as you said, then proper guidance of public sentiment is more urgent than anything else for the national foundation. Hence, the foundation of the nation can be helped if the government looks over all religions and support those religions for better religious edification, which will be of service to the national foundation. This religious order has not won over a large mass of people because of its short history. But I believe that this religious order has rendered some unpublicized service to the foundation of the nation by the proper guidance of public sentiment and other efforts, including relief work immediately after the national liberation in 1945." The guest said, "Do you intend, then, to limit yourselves to nonpolitical service and not have anyone represent your order in politics?" The Master said, "The clergy are devoting themselves to the affairs of the order and cannot bear two burdens; but the laity can participate in the politics. I think that in the future only those with good religious edification can make good politicians." (*CP* 3:26)

27. The Master said, "I hear that these days much noise is being raised in the world on whether we are on the left or right; but this question is raised by those who do not understand what a religion is all about. A religion, or sound morality, is the substance or the central principle of politics; and politics should be a function of morality. One of our four pillars, namely, 'Serve the public selflessly,' is also the fundamental principle of moral government and is valid anywhere and anytime. Whoever unselfishly serves the public with a thorough awakening to the principle of selflessness can be said to have a true ideology; and no one who acts rashly, chasing after fame and power, can be the main figure of the national reconstruction. The root of politics is morality, and the root of morality is mind; hence, our duty is to know and nourish this mind so that we may practice following our original nature." The Master said further, "When you build a house, you start with the foundations on which carpenters erect the house, and then walls are added, which are covered with wallpaper. After that the owner of the house moves into the house to live. Likewise, the parties on the left and on the right lay the foundation; the government does the carpenter's work; and after that the moral order does the work of laying tiles and applying wallpaper. In this manner, a perfect nation will be established." (*CP* 3:27)

28. The Master said, "This nation is in a difficult situation after its liberation; however, the general trend for the future is bright. The day dawns slowly, and spring does not come in one day; there are processes

and order to be followed." He said further, "Now is like the early spring, with ice here and there, though it has started thawing; soon the ice will melt away without being noticed." He said, "The more the world is enlightened, the more the bellicose ones will perish. From now on, whoever attacks first either among individuals or between nations will lose." (CP 3:28)

29. The Master said on New Year's Day 1951, during the Korean War, "Consolidate your faith while you are greeting the New Year. You reap what you sow, either blessing or punishment; hence, you should have firm faith in yourself and in the truth that the empty space devoid of sound or smell has the mighty power that cannot be deceived or transgressed. Do not lose hope. A reflection on the eternal world reveals that those who do not despair or lose hope in desperate situations will find room for progress. Keep your mind peaceful; do not seek peace from afar but in your own mind. Only those who can keep their peace of mind in the most difficult situation can bring about peace in the world." (CP 3:29)

30. The Master often gave guidance to his followers during the Korean War and said, "Can you devote yourself to this religious practice and public service even if you are the only one left? Would you protect and keep this religious order even if all others slander and persecute you? In the past, the opening of a new religious order produced numerous martyrs; but this order is governed by the law of mutual benefaction for the New World, hence, there will be no such martyrs. You do not need to be concerned. The faithless are far away even if they stay with me; and the faithful are with me even though they are a thousand miles away. Be altruistic and take care of the order wherever you are, then you will find refuge there." (CP 3:30)

31. The Master said, "Once, when Confucius and his followers were surrounded by a gang of bandits for seven days without food, he sat calmly and said, 'One appreciates the integrity of pines and large cone pines only after freezing weather. And one attains the real power of practice only after experiencing severe hardships.' Hearing this, his followers were calm and peaceful, conversing and singing in peaceful voices. The gang of bandits were marveled at the scene and retreated, saying 'These surely are heavenly people.'[112] This can be an eternal model for peace of mind." (CP 3:31)

32. At Sandong Temple, the Master composed a line: "After the noise of thunder and a shower in the dawn, the house doors will open one by one." He then said, "The recent war had its beginning with the

Kabo Uprising (AD 1894); since the war started in this country, the beginning of peace will be in this country. How could we dictate to the whole world with economic or military power? The destiny of the New World will depend on the leadership of sages, buddhas, and bodhisattvas. With the new grand moral and religious doctrines of this country the whole world eventually will form one family." He said further, "The global force is now turning toward Southeast Asia; hence the countries in Southeast Asia will gradually develop. And this country will be the spiritual center of the world." (*CP* 3:32)

33. Seeing *mugunghwa* (rose of Sharon) and the *T'aegŭkki* (Korean national flag) in front of the Sandong Temple the Master said, " '*Mugunghwa*' is a good name; '*mugung*' means limitless and changeless. *Mugunghwa* indicates that this country will be the origin of the great moral and religious order of the New World. *T'aegŭkki* has a profound principle in it; '*taegŭk*' (*taiji*) is the principle of the universe and the parents of all things of the universe. *T'aegŭk* is *mugŭk* (*wuji*) and *mugŭk* is Irwŏn; *T'aegŭkki* indicates that the great way of Irwŏn will be the refuge of the whole human race, and this country being its origin will be the spiritual parent-country for all sentient beings." (*CP* 3:33)

XII

On Birth and Death

1. Master Chŏngsan said, "There are three stages in resolving the grand matter of birth and death. The first stage is to awaken oneself to and know the realm where there is originally no birth or death, and birth and death are not two. The second stage is to model after and keep the realm where there is originally no birth or death, and birth and death are not two. The third stage is to bestow and apply the realm where there is originally no birth or death, and birth and death are not two. One can be said to have resolved the grand matter of birth and death only if one has acquired the capabilities of these three stages." (*CP* 14:1)

2. The Master said, "There are three different spiritual capacities to go and come through the path of birth and death. The first is the capacity to go or come, being attached to love and lust. This capacity, being attracted by grudges and hatred, is depraved, and falls into the evil path because it cannot hold the right view on the path of going and coming and, being always confused, leads a life of befuddled and dreamy indolence upon getting any form of life, and makes no discriminations. The second is the capacity to go or come with the power of adamantine aspiration. A person of this capacity joins the Buddha's order, either going or coming, just as metal pieces are attracted to a magnet because those with this capacity practice with an unwavering faith in the order of correct dharma and thereby can keep the last one thought pure. The third is the capacity to be free at birth and death, having great spiritual power. This is the capacity of Buddha-bodhisattva and sages who can go and come

231

through the six paths freely with the three great powers perfected as the result of thorough discipline." (*CP* 14:2)

3. A student asked, "Please, explain the following propositions: 'Fixed karma cannot be escaped' and 'One can break through the heavenly destined karma.'" The Master said, "By 'Fixed karma cannot be escaped' is meant that, since the authority to bless or punish in accord with fixed karma rests on an outside party, one has to receive the result of the karma: there is no way to escape it. By 'One can break through the heavenly destined karma' is meant that, since the one who receives the result of the karma is one's own self, a person who has attained freedom of mind is not troubled by blessings or punishment but is peaceful and hence can manage the karma freely. Hence, such a person can break through the heavenly destined karma."[113] (*CP* 14:3)

4. The Master said, "The more greed and attachment one has, the less one's numinous consciousness can rise from falling into the evil path, just as a turbid or heavy thing sinks low. The less greed and attachment one has, the higher the departed spirit rises, to be born in the good path, just as a clear and light thing rises high." (*CP* 14:4)

5. A disciple asked about Buddhist fasting and the preparatory memorial service one arranges in anticipation of one's death. The Master answered, "The purpose of Buddhist fasting is to make a pure, unadulterated progress by reducing one's expenses, thus lessening one's debt, and doing without meals to save for charity. The original purpose of the preparatory memorial service before one's death was to cultivate one's mind and do things that result in blessings. Doing without meals without making true progress in practice is useless. A lavish service before one's death will earn no merit for blessedness unless one has accumulated truly meritorious deeds." (*CP* 6:56)

6. The Master said, "If one's numinous consciousness leaves with pure mind, clearly taking care of the last one thought without adhering to anything, it will not be deluded on the path of going or coming. The spirit that cannot do so faces many a delusion on its path, and hence needs a deliverance service." (*CP* 14:5)

7. The Master said, "The expression 'to resolve the grand matter of birth and death' does not mean to resolve the matter of death only, but to resolve both birth and death. To resolve the matter of birth well is to resolve that of death well and to resolve the matter of death well is to resolve that of birth well." (*HH* 2:21)

8. The Master said, "A human being can only be formed if numinous consciousness combines with vital force and matter. These are cases of the numinous consciousness entering the baby when it comes out of the mother's womb, but this can happen only in the case of a powerful soul. Before the entrance of numinous consciousness, the fetus consists of vital force and matter. The rebirth of a human being depends on the conditions of heaven, earth, and humanity, but a great sage is born with the whole endowment of heavenly and earthly vital forces." (HH 2:22)

9. The Master said, "The pure one thought becomes the field; the one thought of the vow, the seed; and the dharma words of deliverance the fertilizer." (HH 2:25)

10. The Master said, "When a human being dies and gets a new body at rebirth, what kind of rebirth one will get depends on which side is heavier in the scale of thinking and passion.[114] By 'thinking' is meant the vow and aspiration one has, transcending one's own self, to take care of one's parents, fellow-beings, and society, state, and the world. Its vital force, being clear, soars high. By 'passion' is meant the selfish desire to take care only of oneself. Passion descends, as its vital force is heavy with attachments. Thus, if thinking predominates, the person ascends to paradise; and if passion predominates, the person descends to the hellish realm. Common practitioners' thinking and passions are in balance; some advanced practitioners have more thinking than passions; and a buddha has only thinking. Ordinary humans have more passions than thinking, and beasts are endowed with passions only. However, ascent and descent do not apply only to human birth and death; at every moment, your mind passes through various stages; hence, you must practice checking its balance in order to follow the path of ascent, maintaining thinking and letting go of passion." (HH 2:27)

11. The Master said, "When the soul transmigrates, it first follows attachments, and then gets a body in accord with karma. Thus, attachment is like bone and karma is like flesh. If one decides on a burial site and becomes attached to it, thinking, 'I shall be buried there on death,' then the soul dashes to it as fast as an arrow, as soon as it is unleashed at one's death. It may get a human body if there is any chance to be born as a human being in the surroundings; but if there is no such chance, one will be born in the world of beasts or some other lower realm of the six paths. It is because, just as water has the nature to flow downward, the soul has the nature to receive a body as soon as it leaves the body

at death. The one who has accumulated good karma abundantly will be born to a rich house, if one were to receive a cow's body, and live in a rich warehouse, were one to receive a mouse's body. Thus, it is important to produce good karma and, what is even more important, to attain the power to cut off the chains of attachment and thereby to be free from the cycle of birth and death while enjoying one's merit as a human among the six paths. To attain freedom, it is necessary for one to gain the insight that one cannot attain freedom if one has the three poisons in the mind and suffers in the bitter seas of misery." (HH 2:28)

12. The attendant said, "When we perform a ceremony, we address ourselves to the Dharmakāya Buddha or to the spirit of the deceased; in either case, the formless mind has to face the formless realm. From the point of religious belief no objection seems necessary; however, from the point of view of actuality it seems hard to understand that formless beings can respond to each other." The Master answered, "The origin of all beings in the universe is the substance of the Dharmakāya Buddha, and it is the function of the Dharmakāya Buddha that a vital force in the substance circulates, causing kaleidoscopic changes. Amid the substance and function is the numinous awareness of the Dharmakāya Buddha, which is formless, soundless, odorless, and hence ineffable, and yet eternally empty and aware, majestically controlling both substance and function. Substance, function, and numinous awareness are but three aspects of the Dharmakāya Buddha and our body, vital force, and mind are also but one element of the Dharmakāya Buddha, these two forming one thing by mutual interpenetration. Because of this nonduality, karmic retribution and the cycle of birth, old age, illness, and death follow without fail the way of the Dharmakāya Buddha. Because of nonduality, one can attract the mighty influence of the universe when one prays to the Dharmakāya Buddha with the ultimate state of the one mind. Because of nonduality, the spirit of the deceased can be influenced by mutual interpenetration and be reached by the mighty power if the concentrated one mind is in its ultimate state when the ceremony is performed and directed to the spirit of the deceased, wherever it is. This is the boundless truth of Irwŏn. Because of mutual interpenetration of energy, we can hear a voice from thousands of miles away by wireless telecommunication. Even senseless plants can take up fertilizer because of mutual interpenetration of energy. If the principle of nonduality is thoroughly mastered, and if the principle that all phenomenal reality is based on what is formless is understood,

it wouldn't be so difficult to grasp how the formless mind can penetrate the formless realm." (*CP* 2:9)

13. The attendant asked, "How does merit accrue to the departed spirit by the performance of various rituals?" The Master replied, "The purposes of performing rituals are as follows. The performance is to lead the deceased to have affinities with the truthful religious order. The karma tiers of the deceased can be melted away in accordance with the principle of the nonduality of the Dharmakāya Buddha and our original nature if the sponsor for a Buddhist deliverance service, the officiator, and the participants pray sincerely. The reading of scripture by an enlightened master or a sermon can indirectly open the way toward wisdom for the deceased. If the offering is used for public service, the happiness of the deceased in the other world can be increased. The hidden virtue will reach the spirit of the deceased if the descendants and relatives contribute substantially to the public in addition to their contribution for the deliverance service and if they follow the right path or a descendant attains eminent dharma power in the religious order of the correct doctrine. Such influence takes place in accordance with the natural principle of inaction; hence, it should not be judged by what appears in front of us." (*CP* 2:10)

14. The attendant asked again, "In Yŏngmojŏn, memorial tablets are enshrined in such a way that, except for the tablet for Grand Master Sot'aesan, one tablet stands for a group of ancestral spirits and another for another group, and so on. How could so many ancestral spirits stay at one tablet?" The Master answered, "To enshrine a tablet does not mean that the ancestral spirit resides at the tablet; rather, it means that the ancestral spirit will respond from anywhere without any hindrance. The spiritual response will not be hindered by the distance of thousands of miles, and thousands of spirits can respond to one place with no obstructions. Hence, the realm of ancestral spirits will not be disturbed by the enshrinement of a shared tablet." (*CP* 2:14)

15. The Master said, "Deliverance is to help the departed spirit (*yŏngga*) leave suffering and attain happiness, stop evil and cultivate good, and drive out delusion and obtain awakening. True deliverance is achieved when deliverance reaches the realm where deliverance is no longer necessary because of the pure one thought. Although our mind is formless, its one thought unites with the great spirit of the universe. Therefore, if practitioners of the Way gather at a pure precinct of Buddhist practice and offer prayers with utmost sincerity, the root of the spirit receives the

influence and the spirit of the deceased can be delivered. The deliverance service is one of the most important things the descendants or posterity should do for the deceased. However, the ceremony of the deliverance service is not sufficient; what is most important is for one to exert oneself to deliver oneself at ordinary times. Another important condition for deliverance is that the descendants, without stopping after the deliverance service, should pray and accumulate merit for the deceased, so that the merit and virtue of the deceased can reach far and wide in the world for a long period of time." (*CP* 14:6)

16. The Master asked, "What could be the capital that could be used to save oneself from falling into the evil path?" Cho Chŏngwŏn answered, "Deep faith, a good understanding of Dharma, and a mind that is not attached to suffering and happiness or hatred and love, could be this important capital." The Master continued, "Could anything be added to that?" Yi Tongjinhwa replied, "There should be a self-awakening." The Master asked again, "Could anything else be added?" His attendant replied, "The consolidated power of aspiration and the one mind could be the important capital." The Master then said, "All three answers are correct." (*CP* 14:7)

17. Pak Chegwŏn asked, "What is the most important condition of deliverance?" The Master answered, "It is the one mind of one's vow and the one pure thought." She asked again, "What sort of a thing is a vow, and what should be done to purify the thought?" The Master answered, "An aspiration with no desire is the vow, and no attachment to hatred or love is purity." (*CP* 14:8)

18. The Master said, "There are three treasures that one should possess before the approaching nirvāṇa. The first is charity, the second is the good affinity of mutual support and the third is the one pure thought. The most important of these is the one pure thought because all the charitable work one has accumulated and the many good karmic affinities one has entered, no matter how extensive, can easily be fuel for self-conceit and attachment if one has not practiced at ordinary times. What could be a greater treasure than keeping one's last one thought pure upon a thorough awakening to the principle that one comes and goes with empty hands?" (*CP* 14:9)

19. A student asked, "How efficacious is the deliverance service for the spirit of the deceased?" The Master answered, "For the spirit that had no affinity to Buddha-dharma it can establish one. For the spirit that had faith in Buddha-dharma, it can consolidate a vow. And for the

spirit of advanced practice it is not particularly necessary, but it can help fix dharma affinities with the general public attending the deliverance service." (*CP* 14:10)

20. The Master said, "Once fall is past, fruit trees have no flowers or leaves, and yet fertilizer is applied to their roots and solutions are sprayed on their trunks so that in the spring they may bear healthy flowers, leaves, and fruits. The same principle is true of the deliverance service for the spirit of the deceased. The body of the deceased has returned to earth, water, fire, and air at death. The deliverance service for the spirit is like applying, with sincere effort and dharma power, fertilizer and solutions to the root of the spirit so that the spirit can receive great help on its way toward obtaining a new body. In our ordinary practice, too, we should carefully prepare for any matter of importance in advance so that we may apply it well as required." (*CP* 14:11)

21. The Master said, "Funeral and burial services are held in order to complete the life and send off the spirit of a person at death. This is the time when sorrow of the close relatives is profound and the deceased discards this body and receives a new one, and hence needs to receive a correct deliverance. What is primary in this ceremony is the deliverance of the spirit, and expressions of sorrow and sympathy and other formalities should be secondary. The Buddhist memorial service, as a rite to be performed for deliverance of the spirit of the deceased, is to help the spirit focus on the one thought, dissolve any remaining attachment, and, by the reading of scriptures and prayers, influence the spirit's affinities so that when it is reborn it will be on a good path. It also aims at increasing the happiness of the deceased by the offertory at the service and by letting the relatives observe the rules of mourning. None of these elements should be neglected." (*CP* 14:12)

22. The Master composed "The Final Farewell Address" while he was compiling the *Yejŏn* (Canon of rites). It is as follows: "O spirit of the deceased! The four elements of earth, water, fire, and air of your physical form have already been dispersed, and the six roots of eyes, ears, nose, tongue, body, and volition have already lost their mental and physical characteristics. The wealth, sex, fame, and profit you enjoyed have already turned out to be a mere dream, and you are separated from your families and relatives, so that you can never see them as you did in the past. What good could there be in thinking of them, and what use could there be in being attached to them? The life of the dead person, whether it was one of suffering, happiness, prosperity, or poverty, has already ceased; so do

not concern yourself even a bit with the worldly attachments of the past. I pray and beseech you to attain buddhahood without fail in your future lives by discovering the original true source where there is no birth and death or going and coming, and delusion and afflictions do not exist. I beseech you also to benefit the general public and accomplish the mission of the Way by meeting in the paradise of Buddha land all the good affinities that you met in this life." (*CP* 14:13)

23. On his sickbed, the Master composed a verse and asked his attendant to write it down and pass it on to posterity. It runs, "Human sufferings and happiness are all devoid of reality. To gaze on self-nature is to be in a vast and magnificent peace." (*CP* 14:34)

24. On his sickbed, the Master composed a verse: "Void and calm, numinous awareness, this is one's own self-nature. Front, back, left, and right are originally peaceful and composed." He wrote another verse: "In the center of self-nature, everything is originally equal. Since there is no going and coming, how could there be suffering and happiness?" (*CP* 14:29)

25. The Master said, "If people commit themselves, with utmost sincerity, for their next lives, such commitments are sometimes realized. If one's spirit leaves at death after making many good friends among the people without deciding on any particular affinity, then, since one was kind, one will get reincarnated to any one of the good affinities. If, however, one decides on an affinity but with attachment, and fails to meet it in the next life, it is easy for that spirit to obtain a lower reincarnation close to that affinity, in accord with that attachment." (*CP* 14:31)

26. To a layperson who offered a live carp for medical use, the Master said, "Wasn't there a dead one?" After he returned, the Master said, "Return it to a pond and let it live." (*CP* 14:32)

27. On his sickbed, the Master said, "When you use medicine, do not make it by destroying life." He said further, "This life should not be handled recklessly; the matter of eternal life should be considered with even more care." (*CP* 14:33)

28. The Master delivered a sermon at the final deliverance service for his younger brother Song Tosŏng (1907–1946), "On a sad day like this, I have not much to say, since everybody grieves over your death more than I do. However, I can clearly see their affection for you. Seeing everybody in such continual and profound grief over your death, I feel that it is good not only that you are missed so dearly but also that the

order has thus received an auspicious sign. A few days ago, a comrade in the dharma said, in tears, 'Grand Master Sot'aesan left us at the critical moment of growth of our order, and now Chusan[115] has also gone. Is this not a misfortune to us?' To this I replied, 'Have you ever been to a huge construction site? The general contractor of a huge construction is not tied to one construction site from the beginning to the end, but goes to another project before the first one is finished, preparing something necessary for the new one, taking rest as necessary. Likewise, the major masters of a religious order have things to prepare in a hurry in the east or in the west, or take rest for a while. In the grand view, however, there is just one project on a single work site. Hence, do not lament too much.' Thus, the future of our order will be bright through eternity if, believing that Grand Master Sot'aesan and other senior members have not left us for good but only temporarily for the new preparation, we devote our effort with earnest and pure feelings to the development of the great task they have left behind to our care." (*CP* 14:14)

29. When Yi Myŏnghun's illness got critical, the Master composed a verse of praise:

As you pay off old karma, you will be pure when you return.
As birth and death are identical, there is no ceasing or resting.
As the Buddha affinity is deep and firm, there is nothing to
    worry about.
The treasure for eternal life is one's faith and vow.
With noumenal repentance and factual repentance,
The precinct of Buddhist practice is purified. (*CP* 14:15)

30. At the memorial service for Yi Myŏnghun, the Master gave a sermon. "It is sad when a plant breaks before it is full grown, and what a pity it is for a human being to leave her life halfway, without fulfilling her great vow and aspiration! Viewed from the immeasurable realm of truth, however, there is an immortal life with no birth and death, or going and coming. Although this was a premature death of someone who was young, there is something to be blessed in the realm of truth, as she had made sacred vows and possessed deep-rooted faith, the eternal treasures. Moreover, she finished her life as a celibate devotee; her life therefore cannot be compared with a hundred-year-long, worthless life. For this reason, not all of us comrades may end up feeling sorrow for or grieving over

her death; we should decide to realize her unfinished will by cultivating our power to continue the work she intended to do. This is the mind that truly cares for the departing comrade." (*CP* 14:16)

31. At the memorial service for Pak Ch'anggi (1917–1950), the Master delivered this sermon: "It is difficult for a human being to make a correct start during childhood; however, he gladly gave up the splendid city life and grew up under the guidance of Grand Master Sot'aesan. It is difficult to abjure luxury in an affluent living environment, but he declined new shoes and new clothes, contributing instead to the public. It is difficult to do justice in face of danger, but he lost his life while protecting a comrade at the risk of his own life. I believe therefore that the path of his spirit will be full of wisdom and blessings. The way of true deliverance lies in regarding everything as the result of heavenly karma, in consolidating his vows, and in keeping his numinous awareness from delusions in the realm where one holds no grudge against opposition." (*CP* 14:17)

32. At the combined memorial service for the spirits of the victims of the Korean War, the Master delivered a sermon containing these aphorisms: "One pure thought lets karmas cease of themselves and mutual support and mutual harmony produce prosperity with myriad blessings." He then said, "When a storm arose, the four seas were in turmoil; when the turmoil subsided, the world was calm. Our mind being like this, one disturbed mind is followed by all sorts of karma. When the one thought calms, the whole world will turn into a Buddha world, where all sentient beings will rejoice. O all spirits of the deceased! Be awakened to the true Buddha world of no resentment and no quarrel; rejoice in the true paradise!" (*CP* 14:18)

33. On the same day, the Master preached again, "Thinking of a few of the comrades who lost their lives during the Korean War, I am filled with sorrow. There were some who came to take the life of the sixth patriarch, such a great man of the Way, on account of his karma, so we hear. How could there not have been some karma of mutual destruction throughout innumerable kalpas of rebirth? Thus, this tragedy became the occasion through which you paid off an ancient and heavy debt. So, if you accept this with a satisfaction and determine never again to enter the karmic debt of mutual destruction, the path of your spirit will be bright. If, however, you intend to pay back with more conflict, the evil karmic affinity will continue endlessly. O all spirits of the deceased! Let go of all the grudges and attachment and take refuge in the great way of the Buddha, the perfect way of no obstruction and mutual support! If you

change your mind for the better, a way of mutual support will open for mutual harmony, but if you have wrong thoughts, all will perish on the path of mutual destruction. All sentient beings are brethren born in the one truth and in one world, and it depends on us whether we create hell or construct a paradise. If we must create a world, then, why shouldn't we create a comfortable paradise? Even if you spirits of the deceased still have some unresolved evil karma, those debts will be gradually erased if there are no resentments or grudges in your mind. If, however, there are resentments or grudges in your mind, the evil karma will remain against you. O all spirits of the deceased! Whether you were happy or unhappy, resentful, or suffered injustice, forget everything about the past and obtain perfect freedom and deliverance, having a pure mind and fulfilling the great principle of mutual support, so that you can appear, smiling broadly, in a blissful world." (*CP* 14; 19)

34. As his father's death was near, the Master asked him to prepare for nirvāṇa with this exhortation, "Aspire to attain to buddhahood and deliver sentient beings; take refuge in one pure thought." (*CP* 14:20)

35. To the departed spirit of Song Hyehwan (1905–1956), the Master said, "Though the body of Kongsan[116], our comrade, has gone, the true Kongsan has not. Kongsan's earnest spirit for public service and the merit of his contribution to this order will shine forth in eternity along with the expansion of this order. I believe and pray that the power of his aspiration, consolidated with one thought and deep comradeship even to the last moment, will bring about thousands and tens of thousands of Kongsans." (*CP* 14:21)

36. Receiving at Changsu the news of the death of Pak Chebong (1888–1957), the Master said, "O spirit of Chesan,[117] our comrade! In our original nature nothing can be said to have come when it has come, nor can anything be said to have gone when it has gone. Hence, there is nothing now to grieve over or to be pleased about. In the phenomenal world, however, it is clear that something has come when it has come, and it is clear that something has gone when it is gone. And accordingly, it is a pleasure to meet with someone and a sorrow to part with someone. I am deeply saddened at the news of your death, and it is regrettable that I cannot come and fully express my deep sorrow at the funeral service. If we keep our original aspiration and devotion for the realization of this grand task whenever we visit this order throughout endless rebirths, then our coming and going will be none other than this task. And hence there is really nothing to be pleased about and nothing to grieve over. O spirit

of Chesan, our comrade! May you come back, where there is neither going nor coming!" (*CP* 14:22)

37. To the departed spirit of Ch'oe Tohwa (1883–1954), the Master said, "Human body is the aggregation and dispersion of causes and conditions of earth, water, fire, and air. Human mind is the rising and ceasing of the seven feelings of pleasure, anger, sorrow, joy, love, hate, and desire. These are all false body and false mind. Among these are a true body and a true mind which, being numinous and pure without rising and ceasing, are the noumenal essence of all things. This is what we call the light of self-nature. O spirit of Samt'awŏn![118] Do you know this? I pray that, relying on this, you renew your vows for the future, and find and enter future beings." (*CP* 14:23)

38. To the departed spirit of Ch'oe Ŭnhyehwa, the Master said, "Birth and death are accompanied by pleasure, worry, sorrow, and joy. The original nature does not change through going and coming. Go with one straight mind and come back with one straight mind, and be a truly devoted worker in the order of the Buddha." (*CP* 14:24)

39. To the departed spirit of Song Ch'anghŏ, the Master said, "An ancient sage said, 'One thought of a pure mind is the enlightenment site (*bodhimaṇḍala*), and is superior to building seven-jeweled stūpas as numerous as the sands of the Ganges. Those jeweled stūpas will finally return to dust, but the one thought of a pure mind produces right enlightenment.'[119] O spirit of Chinsan![120] Keep your great aspiration with the one pure thought." (*CP* 14:25)

40. To the departed spirit of Cho Songgwang (1876–1957), the Master said, "If the prior thought is pure, the thought that follows will be pure. Take the one pure thought as the road toward yin and yang." (*CP* 14:26)

41. To the departed spirit of Yu Hŏil (1882–1958), the Master said, "It is difficult for one's initial thought to be right for whatever one does in the world, and it is also difficult to take good care of the last one thought at the end of one's life. If one's initial thought is right, then everything one does will turn out right, and if the last one thought is right, one's eternal future will be right. Hence, if you come and go with the right thought, then you will return to the Buddha's order without losing your way in the maze. This is what you have always aspired to, it is what you are to follow, and it is what all of us wish. Hence, may you take the vow to save sentient beings and rely on the right and pure one thought!" (*CP* 14:27)

42. To the spirits of the students sacrificed at the Student Uprising on April 19 (1960), the Master said, "In the world there are people who

are dead though alive, and also people who are alive eternally though dead. And this depends on whether or not their mind and noble spirit are alive. The students who were victims on this righteous uprising had short lives; however, their noble and altruistic spirit for the sake of the nation and the world will never perish. This is your great and immortal life. I pray that you should not regress or hold resentments but will progress further, so that you can be good leaders of the public throughout eternity." (*CP* 14:28)

43. As the Master's illness became more serious, his attendants asked whether they should offer a special prayer. The Master replied, "The one whom the dharma realm knows will be taken care of at its discretion. Hence, do not offer any further prayers." (*CP* 14:30)

XIII

The Last Instructions

1. Master Chŏngsan on his sickbed asked, "Do you know what our original intention is?" The attendant informed the Master of his view: "It is to create one household under heaven with the Way and its virtue." The Master said, "You are right. To create one household under heaven with the Way and its virtue is our original intention." (*CP* 15:1)

2. The Master said to Kim Taegŏ (1914–1998) and the attendant, "This is the age of opening and the age of exchange; hence, things are exchanged and adapted. If any parts in our scriptures can be construed as specific to any district or to any sect, adjust them at this time so that Grand Master Sot'aesan's original sacred intention can fully be brought to light. And there should remain no damage to the dignity as the main scripture of the New World. The main points are already determined there. Make any points more explicit if necessary or, otherwise, leave them as they are. The doctrine formulated there is the great dharma for all ages, as long as the tenets of the Fourfold Beneficence, the Four Essentials, the Threefold Practice, and Eight Articles are clearly brought to light."[121] (*CP* 15:2)

3. The Master said, "The Old World is changing into a New World, it is a constant truth that old things go and new things stand. We should become new persons; hence, examine yourselves to see how old you are compared with the vigor of the New World." (*CP* 15:3)

4. The Master said, "The Old World was narrow and limited, the New World is much wider and more open. The arena of the world affairs

is getting larger and it is rare to encounter a world like this. The 'great and bright position' that Grand Master Sot'aesan referred to means the world that is great and bright." (CP 15:4)

5. The Master said, "We have entered an era when East and West communicate fully; we must therefore use one dharma to make all the different doctrines adaptable to each other. Material civilization is the primary product of the West, while spiritual culture is the primary product of the East. Hence, let us take material civilization and exchange it with our spiritual culture at the opportune time, and let the West take our spiritual culture in exchange for their material civilization. This world will then be an exquisite place. Grand Master Sot'aesan was endowed with the great fortunes of both East and West. His Way and its virtue will preside over the world, and the merit of his opening of the New World will have influence in all the ten directions. The great way of Irwŏn will be the charity for the universe." (CP 15:5)

6. The Master said, "The world of great peace is coming; however, such a world will not be realized by the power of one or two people. It will be done only when the power of many people is united, and it will be done more easily if we put it into practice first. This is the time to remove all the barriers in the world, and the person of the Way has the frame of mind that communicates in all directions. Exert yourselves to resolve any grudge or regret without being tied down by partiality. Then everyone will become a benefactor and a world of true peace will be realized of itself." (CP 15:6)

7. The Master said, "We have been engaged in this business[122] for all the worlds and all our lives since time immemorial. Buddha-bodhisattvas come from the East or from the West, again and again, engaged in this business." (C 15:7)

8. The Master said, "Since our ideology is cosmopolitanism, let us realize this ideology. A figure of great enlightenment such as Grand Master Sot'aesan is the first and probably the last, so let us concentrate all things on him, and exert ourselves to limitless practice and limitless public service." (CP 15:8)

9. The Master said, "Since this is the time when the whole world is becoming one household, any leader, from now on, will be successful only if the leader carries out the ideology of cosmopolitanism. The person who manages world affairs should care for the people of each country equally, and assume responsibility for world peace throughout world after world and life after life." (CP 15:9)

10. The Master said, "On achieving great enlightenment Grand Master Sot'aesan decided to take Śākyamuni Buddha as the original source of his enlightenment, and thereby established the great cause of this order, providing the starting point for its development throughout eternity. And this order will thrive for ever only if the great cause of the flow of the dharma is firmly established, and this in turn can only be established if we relate our origin to our affinity with the continuing flow of the dharma." (CP 15:10)

11. The Master said, "It is said that one dies if one's pulse stops. In an order of the Way, if the flow of the dharma is stopped, the order will wither away. This order will flourish eternally only if the flow of mind-dharma continues between mentor and disciple and if the flow of the friendly feelings continues between comrades." (CP 15:11)

12. The Master said, "Regard the faults of a comrade as your own and thereby check yourself for any faults, without resenting or hating the comrade. If you forgive and awaken each other, you will connect through friendly feelings and hence the dharma will continue to flow, linking you to one another. Render the spiritual power to the one who is the head dharma master, asking him or her questions, making confessions, and taking dearly to your heart the dharma you hear. Only then will the mind-dharma, understood by you and the other, continue to flow eternally." (CP 15:12)

13. The Master said, "The correct transmission of Buddha-dharma through endless generations is the lifespan of the dharma. Mentors should train well the disciples who will succeed them, and the disciples, generation after generation, must receive the transmission of the dharma correctly; only then will the lifespan of the dharma be endless. In this order, to receive the spirit of Grand Master Sot'aesan completely is to increase the lifespan of this dharma. If one is to increase the lifespan of the dharma, one will be a great ancestor of the dharma only if one receives it completely and transmits it completely. The lifespan of the dharma in our order is the wisdom-life of the great Way of Irwŏn." (CP 15:13)

14. The Master said, "Just as water flowing from its spring lasts a long time, the mind-dharma of Grand Master Sot'aesan will be transmitted and the pulse of dharma will not stop, if we venerate and hold him, the origin of dharma, in esteem. This order will develop as long as we earnestly believe in Grand Master Sot'aesan and the high mentors under him. We are burdened with responsibilities as the successors of the original masters, to transmit the dharma to our next generations." (CP 15:14)

15. The Master said, "In an ancient text, the following phrase can be found, 'What looks real but unreal, that is paulownia fruit.' When children play in groups, they are clamorous all day long, as if they were doing something tremendous. But at the end of the day, there remains nothing real. Likewise, people are always in a hurry, making a lot of noise, as if they are doing something special. But how trifling many of their achievements are! If therefore there is to remain something worthy in a family or in a society, there should be something real rather than mere form. Once something real is established, it should be kept going forever. In our order, too, there should be figures who, with firm faith and authentic practice, will be consistent through the three time periods, so that this order will see endless progress, instead of looking 'real but unreal.'" (*CP* 15:15)

16. The Master said to his attendant, "In ancient times, someone wrote, 'A willow has one thousand strings hanging green, and peach blossom has ten thousand pink flowers' and was satisfied with it. His teacher, seeing this, said, 'Why should there be only a thousand strings to a willow, and why should peach blossom have only ten thousand flowers? Say, 'Every string of a willow tree is green, and every flower of a peach blossom is pink.' It is said that, doing so, the teacher gave new life to the two lines. This is a story that anyone who records dharma words or edits them should take notice of." (*CP* 15:16)

17. Upon listening on his sickbed to his students singing hymns, the Master said, "When I was a child, it came to my mind, as if they were heavenly words, 'With music, I will save the world.' An ancient sage also once said, 'For correcting public morals and changing the manners and ways of the age there is nothing as effective as music.'[123] Do not regard hymns merely as songs. There is truth contained in hymns, so sing them piously, appreciating the meaning of the words." (*CP* 15:17)

18. The Master said, "On numberless occasions in our past lives, we were not only members of a household through the dharma affinity of priesthood, but also as the members of a family through biological affinity." (*CP* 15:18)

19. The Master said, "Though the biological affinity of parents and their offspring is extremely important, the dharma affinity of mentor and disciple is no less important. We are always members of a household; hence, we share hardship and joy together, not only in this life but also in eternal life. Let us live together for this whole life and for eternal life." (*CP* 15:19)

20. The Master said, "The most important of all valued things in the world is the warm relationship between comrades. Our comradeship will last billions of years. Hence, never betray justice between comrades. Never lose a faulty comrade entirely, and lay emphasis on the importance of friendship among comrades." (CP 15:20)

21. The Master said to his attendants, "You are not strangers, but friendly brothers and sisters through many previous lives. Treat each other as dearly as gold; take care of each other like jade." (CP 15:21)

22. The Master said, "It is easy for you to complete a great task if you have good affinities around you. If you do not have good affinities around you, you will face many difficulties throughout your whole life." (CP 15:22)

23. The Master said to Yi Tongjinhwa, "Benevolence and righteousness are the foundation of morality." He said again, "Anyone who violates the rules of morality or anyone who has no self-power will not stand in the New World." (CP 15:23)

24. The Master said to Yi Kyŏngsun, "From now on, the Way of impartiality will be the framework of morality." He said to Song Yŏngbong and others, "The ethics of triple identity is the morality for the world and for all ages." (CP 15:24)

25. The Master said to Hwang Chŏngshinhaeng, "Dharma affinity can continue only with firm faith." He said further, "We are coworkers for all ages." He said again, "Be a noble person! The noblest person is one who is devoid of greed." (CP 15:25)

26. The Master said to Sŏng Sŏngwŏn and others, "Practice in accord with the functioning of your own self-nature, the Buddha-nature. Take this self as the standard of your practice." Later, he said to Yi Chang-sun and others, "Do your own practice in accord with the functioning of your original self, the Buddha-nature, and bring about world peace in accord with the functioning of universal harmony." (CP 15:26)

27. The Master said to Song Chamyŏng and others, "In the past, it was difficult for women to enter world affairs. You have become workers for world affairs thanks to the foresight of Grand Master Sot'aesan. Devote yourselves to this task wholeheartedly, forgiving each other, and taking care of each other, world after world and life after life. Be a great person of the world, preserving your purity as a celibate woman." (CP 15:27)

28. The Master said to Yi Powŏn, "A person with much wisdom can still be deficient in blessing." He said again, "From now on, people will accomplish things on the basis of concession, but never by force. People

will be treated in accord with their conscience and never in accordance with an untruth." (*CP* 15:28)

29. The Master said to Song Sunbong, "Everyone has the aptitude to become a great person. Exert yourself in the practice to become a great person by fostering your mind and by broadening your boundaries. You are a great figure if you have a great mind, even if your physical frame is small; you are a small person if your mind is small even if your physical frame is big." He said again, "The secret for one to become a great figure is to follow all affairs with tolerance." (*CP* 15:29)

30. The Master said, "We are all descendents of Irwŏn. From now on, people will not discriminate between people on the bases of race or clan, but they will live together as the descendents of one family." (*CP* 15:30)

31. The Master said, "Enlarge the scope of the Parents Association, and do your duty as the children of the world. All plans should have broad reach. Organize a community association in every village, so that villagers help each other and foster public morals, and the peaceful world will not be far away." (*CP* 15:31)

32. Greeting the physicians, the Master said on his sickbed, "Be fine doctors to cure people of physical illness, and we will be fine doctors to cure people of the spiritual illness, so that we can all better the world." He said to nurses, "A good world is on its way; so let's be great workers for the New World by keeping our minds good." (*CP* 15:32)

33. The Master said to his attendant, "Remove the fish tank, and you will see the fish swim freely in a pond. Remove the flower vase, and you will see the flowers as they are in bloom in the garden. Open the bird cage, and you will see the birds flying in the wood." (*CP* 15:33)

34. The Master said to his attendant, "Three chiefs and five successors[124] will preside over the opening of the New World, and thereafter, the world will be governed on the principle of impartiality eternally." He continued, saying, "There is an oriental legend that 'at the opening of the earlier heaven, three sovereigns and five emperors,[125] coming one after another, took charge of the construction work of the opening.' Likewise, at the opening of the later heaven, three chiefs and five successors will come, one after another, and preside over the opening project for the East and the West. And thereafter, great, impartial figures will govern the New World on the principle of impartiality and the world of peace and prosperity will last forever." The attendant said to the Master, "The three chiefs have already been, as Grand Master Sot'aesan has authenticated. When

will the five successors come, and who will acknowledge them?" The Master said, "They will come only at the right time, and people under heaven will venerate spontaneously only those who do the job at the right time; the whole world will spontaneously authenticate their identity." (*CP* 15:34)

35. The Master let the attendant read the draft of "the Scripture of Sot'aesan" and as a rule sat up to listen to it, letting him stop reading before he became tired and lay down. (*CP* 15:35)

36 In December 1961 (WE 46), the Master asked on his sickbed, "Do you remember the four plans I made earlier?" The attendant replied, "They were the preparation of teaching material, the establishment of organizations, the cooperation of state and religion, and understanding the essentials and illuminating the root." The Master said, "Explain the details." The attendant reported, "By 'the preparation of teaching material' is meant the complete compilation of the *Canon* and the *Scripture of Sot'aesan* and the editing of the *Canon of Rites* and *Hymns,* so that all the materials for edifying people shall be ready. By 'the establishment of organizations' is meant the laying of the foundations for educating talented youth, securing financial independence, and serving the public by establishing facilities for edification, education, charity, and production. By 'the cooperation of state and religion' is meant striving together to construct the peaceful world by working in concert with the leaders of the nation and world through the two channels of statecraft and religious edification. And by 'understanding the essentials and illuminating the root' is meant keeping the focus on the fundamental goal by illuminating it. In other words, practitioners should not neglect their own practice but should attain a thorough mastery of their original concern as a practitioner, while exerting themselves in all these public services. This is the way I understand the four grand plans of yours." The Master said, "What you said is correct. Now, have we realized as much as half of these plans?" On December 25, the Master, sighing, gave a special injunction to Kim Taegŏ, Yi Kongju, Yi Wanch'ŏl, Pak Kwangjŏn, Yi Un'gwŏn, and Pak Changsik, to supervise the editing of the *Wŏnbulgyo kyojŏn* (Scriptures of Won Buddhism) and other scriptures, pressing Yi Kongjŏn to hurry its compilation. (*CP* 15:36)

37. In January 1962, as his illness got more critical, most of the personnel from the order's organizations and from local temples gathered in the headquarters. On January 22, after taking a brief bath, the Master said to the crowd, "We are people who did practice and public service together for many previous lives; we are not the people who have met

for the first time in this order. We are people who will frequently meet again and work together in the future." He said further, "Someone may explain 'the ethics of triple identity.'" Accepting the request of the attendant, Kim Taegŏ explained: "By 'the principle of one origin' you mean that all religions in the world are of one identical origin and one identical principle. By 'bond of the one vital force' you mean that all living beings in the world are one family in one household. By 'renewal with one aim' you mean that all enterprises in the world share one workplace and one workforce. This is the great cosmopolitanism based on the great way of Irwŏn that was advocated by Grand Master Sot'aesan. As you, our mentor, said, this is the morality for the whole world and for all ages." The Master said, "What you said is right. The general trend of the world is gradually coming round to this way; hence, keep this way well and spread it widely, so that our dharma shall be the great Dharma under heaven and for all ages." (*CP* 15:37)

38. After having it explained once more, the Master said, "If there is anything to ask, do so." After a while, the attendant, accepting the inquiries of the crowd, asked, "Should we take the statement of the ethics of triple identity as the mentor's *gāthā*?" The Master said, "Do so. In the past, all the dharmas of the world were divided. However, now is the time for all the dharmas to be united. Strive to make the whole world into one household with the great Way of Irwŏn, the ideology of the cosmopolitanism." Thereafter, the Master told the crowd to disperse. In the afternoon of the same day, the Master composed his *gāthā*, "With one principle within one fence, as one family within one household, as coworkers on the one workplace, let us construct the world of Irwŏn." On January 24, 1962, Master Chŏngsan entered nirvāṇa with ease. (*CP* 15:38)

Part Three

Other Selected Writings

I

On Irwŏnsang

A. Introduction

Why we enshrine Irwŏnsang as the Buddha is explained in the *Treatise on the Renovation of Korean Buddhism* (*Chosŏn pulgyo hyŏksillon*). Hence, we must study it and experience its essence.[1]

Anyone in today's society who has little practice in Buddha-dharma will think it strange to look at Irwŏnsang, or will regard it as insignificant. Even some members of this order may not understand the principle of worshiping and offering silent prayers to Irwŏnsang. It is regrettable, I think, that the truth of Irwŏnsang is not yet widely understood at this early stage of this order. Hence, although my study is not very clear and bright, I will expand on the central meaning of the treatise with the following points. It is my hope that this may be of help to our practice.

B. The Truth of Irwŏnsang

What is the truth that is contained in Irwŏnsang? Irwŏnsang is, in essence, that which refers to the totality of beings in the universe and the empty dharma realm. It refers to the original source of the Fourfold Beneficence (heaven and earth, parents, brethren, and laws), and the form of our original mind, where there is no birth and no death, or discrimination and attachment. It also signifies the middle way of fairness and independence, and the way of what is neither excessive nor deficient. Thus, Irwŏnsang contains both being and nonbeing and identifies substance and function, so that myriad facts and principles are all based on this, the greatest, the most revered, unique, and supreme truth. In ancient times, Buddha attained sudden enlightenment to this Irwŏn and called it Buddha-nature, Dharmakāya, or True Mind, and the enlightened masters of successive generations elucidated the Buddha-nature. Not only did the sages develop the theory on Irwŏnsang, but they also focused on Irwŏnsang when they expounded the realm of the sole absolute truth. For instance, Confucius's "one all-pervading principle,"[2] Mencius's theory of "nourishing the vital force,"[3] and Chou Tuni's "An Explanation of the Diagram of the Great Ultimate" (*Taiji dushuo*)[4] all refer to it in different terms. Thus, the truth of Irwŏnsang was known to those of supreme intelligence long ago, being the same realm of Buddha-nature to which all sages were enlightened. Grand Master Sot'aesan of this order set out the method of enshrining the Irwŏnsang, thereby instituting a reform in the traditional practice of enshrinement of the Buddha statue. In this way he brought the concealed truth to light through the symbol of Irwŏnsang. And he showed the public thereby the Buddha-nature that only a few understood, so that all the laity could easily be enlightened to the true Buddha, letting go of the fake Buddha. How could this not be a skilful means to expand the great Way? Therefore, we should awaken to an understanding of the essence of Irwŏnsang in order to have faith in Irwŏnsang, to worship Irwŏnsang, to model ourselves after Irwŏnsang, and to use Irwŏnsang while walking, standing, sitting, reclining, speaking, being quiet, moving or resting, without leaving the Irwŏn-Buddha even for a minute. I think this is the right way to practice Buddha-dharma.

C. The Method of Faith in Irwŏnsang

How can we have faith in Irwŏnsang? Faith in Irwŏnsang can be explained as follows. First, traditional faith in a particular object is reformed as faith in the totality. Second, superstitious faith is reformed as realistic faith. Third, faith in forms is reformed as faith in truth. A brief explanation of these points is in order. People have faith in particular objects if they believe that the calamity and blessings of their life are determined by only one object. Examples are Buddha statues, a god (a divine power), a natural feature (mountains, rivers, trees, or rocks), or a spirit (a demon, a guardian spirit of the house, or a ghost). To have faith in totality is to take refuge in the great nature of the universe. One arrives at such faith by discerning the unity of the world and understanding that, since all things in the universe and the empty dharma realm are, taken together, of the Buddha-nature, the sources of transgression and blessings are not one, but all things, everywhere.

Superstitious faith is where people offer irrational prayers to the object of their faith without knowing whether that object is relevant to the cause of their weal and woe. One has this kind of superstitious faith if, for example, one prays to insentient things when the matter is related to human beings, or prays to a formless spirit for success in human affairs that can only be achieved by one's own effort. Realistic faith lies in finding out the real source of weal and woe while handling myriad things, in accord with which one can make realistic prayers and arrange things for success.

By "faith of forms" is meant a faith in which one believes that one cannot obtain the power of faith without dependence on a certain name or form to which one is bound, being ignorant of the supernatural principle. By "faith in the truth" is meant a faith in which, without limiting one's faith to names and forms, one is confident that one cannot deceive the law of cause-and-effect karmic retribution even for a moment. And one cannot because one is aware that the natural principle contained in Irwŏn is utterly fair, bright, numinous, and ubiquitous without any limit.

My intention with these words is to help set up a truthful and right religious faith, by critically analyzing the truth of Irwŏnsang. Anyone enlightened to this truth can be said to have attained the power of right faith.

D. The Method of Irwŏnsang Worship

How should we worship Irwŏnsang? We should worship Irwŏnsang as described above, namely, by reforming worship of particular objects into worship of the totality, superstitious worship into realistic worship, and worship of forms into worship of truth. A brief elaboration is in order.

By "worship of the particular" is meant a worship in which people do not include in their worship the whole source of their livelihood, but limit themselves to a particular object of worship. By "worship of totality" is meant worshiping, as the Buddha, of the myriad things of the universe and the empty dharma realm, keeping a worshipful mind anywhere and anytime. The expression "Never lack reverence" in the *Book of Rites* (*Liji*) is a succinct statement of this point.[5]

By "superstitious worship" is meant a worship in which people are not only ignorant of the sources of their suffering and blessing but perform absurd rites, offering, for example, food to insentient things or burning clothes and other articles as sacrifice. Realistic worship is performed when the method of worship is in accordance with the reality of the object of worship. The worship of heaven and earth lies in adapting to the principles of heaven and earth by modeling after their ways. The worship of parents lies in providing them with mental comfort and serving them faithfully as well as following the principle of protecting the helpless. The worship of fellow beings lies in practicing the principle of benefiting oneself by benefiting others. And the worship of laws lies in not violating any rule of laws with clear knowledge of right and wrong. These are none other than the articles of beneficence requital in the *Six Essential Principles of Treasury Scripture* (*Pogyŏng yuktae yoryŏng*).[6]

By "worship of forms" is meant the kind of worship in which people are worshiping when they rely on a mere name or form and no longer practice faith when that name or form is not present. In other words, their sincerity and respect are not constant, for things and affairs change. The "worship of truth," however, is such that people's respect and sincerity toward things and affairs are constant, when they are in the presence of the names and forms or they are concealed, so that there is no difference in constancy between being alone or in the public. In the *Great Learning* there is a phrase "watchful over himself when he is alone,"[7] which refers to the care one takes when alone. This practice of exerting oneself in carefulness is none other than the worship of things and affairs. This is an analysis of the worship of the truth of Irwŏnsang, which may help one attain the correct method of worship.

E. How to Model after Irwŏnsang

How should one model oneself after Irwŏnsang? The purpose of modeling is to reflect on one's original nature. As noted above, our mind is originally clear and truthful, free from birth and death, going and coming, or discrimination and attachment. When the six sense organs (*indriya*), becoming conscious, responding to the six external objects (*viṣaya*), one becomes subject to innumerable delusions and passions, eventually losing one's true nature. Hence, the practitioner must be resolved to accept as truth that he is endowed with such nature and take this resolution as the supreme standard of practice: to subdue the six sense organs, eradicating delusions so that the true realm of Irwŏn can be restored. Our daily chanting, sitting in meditation, and other practices for mental concentration at other times are none other than our effort to be enlightened to this true realm of this nature. If we wish to practice this strictly, we must always possess a deep awareness of Irwŏnsang (the realm of no delusive thought)[8] and should not forget it even for a short while. To give an example, if our mind is agitated with vehement desire, then we must recognize it at once, and exert to change our mind by reflecting, "Ah! I have forgotten Irwŏnsang!" When anger or delusion has arisen in the mind, we must practice like this. If one does not lose sight of the mind's standard day or night by reflecting and checking often, this is the way of modeling oneself after Irwŏnsang. If one continues this practice for a long time, one will finally reach the realm of no discrimination, so that one will peacefully reside in the realm of no phenomenal characteristics where truth and falsity are both void, and subject and object are identical. Anyone who has realized this can be identified as having clearly recovered Irwŏnsang and attained Dharmakāya of Tathāgata.

F. How to Utilize Irwŏnsang

How can we utilize Irwŏnsang? This is the practice of mastering the truth of Irwŏnsang for doing all things as perfectly as Irwŏnsang. To do the practice of Irwŏnsang, one must handle myriad affairs fairly, rightly, moderately, and honorably. This is the function of conscience arising from the original nature, and right actions done in accord with truth, and this is the essential way of self-cultivation, regulation of a family, ruling a country, and bringing about a peaceful world. To utilize Irwŏnsang, the practitioner, being always alert and unobscured, must act without passion and with an independent spirit in myriad mental spheres. Our practice of recording a daily diary and checking on mindfulness and mindlessness are all for this practice.[9] To illustrate the point with some actual examples: "To prepare and train oneself for a state of affairs in accordance with the situation prior to handling it"[10] is to train oneself not to stray from the right road in this teaching. "To be heedful to choose the right and forsake the wrong upon a sound thinking in handling daily affairs"[11] is to practice not to deviate from this great teaching. "To check whether or not one has practiced what one has resolved to do and what not to do"[12] is to verify whether one has not deviated from this great teaching. If one consistently follows such thorough practice, then one will always be with Irwŏn, attaining eventually the sagehood of myriad supreme good.

G. An Outline

The gist of the above discussion can be given as follows. The practice is divided into applications of self-power and other-power. Faith in and worship of Irwŏnsang endows one with other-power from Irwŏn; and modeling oneself after and utilizing Irwŏnsang endows one with self-power.

In the practice of Irwŏnsang, self-power contains other-power and other-power contains self-power, so that one realizes innumerable facts and principles with the balanced practice of self-power and other-power. Faith in Irwŏnsang gives rise to the efficacy of faith; and the worship of Irwŏnsang, the efficacy of worship; the realization of Irwŏnsang gives rise to the efficacy of realization; and utilization of Irwŏnsang, the efficacy of utilization. As a result, one can promote public well-being and attain buddhahood. This is the supreme, consummate teaching, and a practical and realistic teaching.

If, however, one limits one's faith and worship blindly to the circular sign with no knowledge of this truth, then it will not be any different from worshiping the Buddha statue. If, on the other hand, one neglects worshiping Irwŏnsang, saying that it is nothing but a mask, then one does not understand the original purpose of enshrining it. Understanding both sides of this, one must think of the principal face of truth while enshrining Irwŏnsang and imagine the whole universe while worshiping it.

When one offers silent confession and prayer, one must believe that One Mind contains in it the mysterious power to influence the material world. While doing the practice of modeling oneself after Irwŏnsang, one must not fall into enervated consciousness,[13] saying that Irwŏnsang is perfect and calm with no differentiation or attachment, but without knowing the moments of entering and coming out of samādhi and the state of no attachment in attachment.

In the practice of utilizing Irwŏnsang, one should not regard strict adherence to a path and self-protection as the Mean by claiming that a perfect adaptation of Irwŏn is free from attachment to joy, anger, sorrow, or pleasure; or remoteness, closeness, friendliness, or estrangement, but without knowing the middle way of expedient adaptation to circumstances.

In observing Irwŏnsang, therefore, one must always understand coherently the nonduality of equality and difference, form and formlessness, the absolute and the phenomenal, and substance and function. Only then, can one be said to have grasped the whole aspect of Irwŏnsang and realized the root and branches of the Way. (*HH*, 212–19)

II

Truth, Faith, and Practice of Irwŏnsang

A. The Truth of Irwŏnsang

Irwŏn is the inherent essence of all things in the universe, the original nature of all buddhas and patriarchs, and the Buddha-nature of all common mortals and sentient beings. It is the realm where there is no differentiation of noumenon from phenomenon or being from nonbeing, the realm where there is no change of arising and ceasing or going and coming, the realm where the karmic retribution of good and evil has ceased, and the realm where the verbal, audible, and visible characteristics are utterly void. In accordance with the light of empty and calm, numinous awareness, the differentiation of noumenon from phenomenon, and being from nonbeing appears; wherewith the distinction between good and evil karmic retribution comes into being; and the verbal, audible, and visible characteristics become clear and distinct so that the three worlds in the ten directions appear like a jewel on one's own palm, and the creative wonders of true emptiness-cum-wondrous existence freely conceals and reveals itself through all beings in the universe throughout incalculable eons without beginning. This is the truth of Irwŏnsang.

B. Faith in Irwŏnsang

The faith in Irwŏnsang is:

To believe in Irwŏn as the inherent essence of all things in the universe;

To believe in it as the original nature of all buddhas and patriarchs;

To believe in it as the Buddha-nature of common mortals and sentient beings;

To believe in it as the realm where there is no differentiation of noumenon from phenomenon, and being from nonbeing;

To believe in it as the realm where there is no change of arising and ceasing, going and coming;

To believe in it as the realm where the good and evil karmic retribution has ceased;

To believe in it as the realm where verbal, audible, and visible characteristics are utterly void;

To believe that, in accordance with the light of empty and calm, numinous awareness, the differentiation of noumenon from phenomenon and being from nonbeing appears in the realm of no differentiation;

To believe that the difference between good and evil karmic retribution comes into being;

To believe that, owing to the verbal, audible, and visible characteristics becoming clear and distinct, the three worlds in the ten directions appear like a jewel on one's own palm; and

To believe that the wonder of true emptiness-cum-wondrous existence conceals and reveals itself through all things in the universe throughout the incalculable eons without beginning.

C. Practice of Irwŏnsang

One is to establish the model of practice by having faith in the truth of Irwŏnsang. The method of practice is for one, being enlightened to the truth of Irwŏnsang, to know one's own mind, which is as perfect and complete, and utterly fair and unselfish as Irwŏn, namely prajñā-wisdom; to foster one's own mind, which is as perfect and complete, and utterly fair and unselfish as Irwŏn, namely, prajñā-wisdom, and to use one's own mind, which is as perfect and complete, and utterly fair and unselfish as Irwŏn, namely, prajñā-wisdom. Herein lies the practice of Irwŏn.[14]

III

Ode to the
Consummate Enlightenment

Consider the past and future of eternity throughout the vast universe,
Where change and immutability are the natural law:
Endless change in the circulation of heaven and earth,
Causing the changes of day and night, the cycle of the four seasons.
When spring changes into summer,
Innumerable changes burgeon.
When summer changes into autumn,
The chill withers myriad things to repose.
When autumn changes into winter,
Mountains and rivers lie under wind and snow.
When winter changes into spring,
The myriad things rise and live.
As there are the changes of heaven and earth,
So all things naturally change.
When all things change,
How could human life be unchanging?
As human life changes,
The world changes of itself.
Sentient beings are wrapped in changes!
Understand this! Pierce through the four cardinal directions,
See through east, west, south, and north,

And prepare for whatever is approaching.
In the universe of waxing and waning,
How is everything in this world?
Since the rise and fall of life reverse,
Riches and honors, poverty and lowliness are fleeting.
Since the strong and the weak change places,
Discrimination of class should be banished.
All beings subject to birth, old age, sickness, and death follow the cycle
  of the six paths;
Human nature, with its joy, anger, sorrow, and pleasure, rises and falls
  in weal and woe.
Young boys and girls!
Do not love to idle away your time;
If you waste your time thoughtlessly,
You will sigh for grief when your hair turns gray.
Friends replete in riches and honors!
Be not so happy with them.
If your happiness is unbounded,
Unexpected poverty will surely come your way.
Friends desiring for sensual pleasures!
Do not desire momentary pleasures.
If you wander thoughtlessly,
Eternal pain is sure to come.
Friends searching for freedom!
Do not love to do things as you please.
If you behave wantonly, without self-power,
Restraints will surely return to you.
Friends searching for profit!
Take no delight in deceitful gain;
If you indulge even in small measure,
Great loss is sure to return to you.
Friends wishing for warm reception!
Do not seek esteem that makes you feel good.
If that esteem is not earned,
How long will it last?
Friends who have won authority and power!
Do not abuse that authority and power;
If you wield coercive power for long,
Authority and power will surely depart.

Friends in high positions!
Guard against pride;
If you indulge in disrespectful pride,
Your high position will surely be lost.
Friends with talents!
Guard against frivolity.
If you are talented but frivolous,
Failure is sure to visit you.
Friends of high learning!
Guard against complacency;
If you are complacent,
You will sink back into ignorance.
Friends in business!
Do not rely on luck for quick success;
If you succeed quickly in an unrighteous business,
That quick success will yield to quick ruin.
Friends with successful businesses!
Guard against laziness.
If you surrender to laziness,
That success will vanish.
Haughtiness invites calamity, and the humble reap benefits!
This is true throughout all ages under heaven.
Do not insult friends of humble and low class!
If one makes up one's mind in poverty,
There will be a day of prosperity.
Do not deride a friend suffering in agony!
If one attains religious awakening in suffering,
The blissful world is sure to come.
Friends with gray hair!
Though old age is a matter of regret,
Death is the root of birth,
Why should there not be a new season of youth?
Dear friends! Observe these changes.
How can one clearly talk about thousands and tens of thousands of
    changes?
Since only a few examples are given of what humans should do,
Let us inquire to discover roots and branches, and beginnings and
    ends.
No matter how much one knows,

No one can attain knowledge without learning.
Consider the myriads of people,
Some changes are for the better, some for the worse;
Those changing for the better are on the road of ascent,
Those changing for the worse on the road of descent.
Friends who know ascent and descent!
Take the road of ascent by changing for the better.
If you wish for the glory of gray hair,
Be careful during your youth.
If you value riches and glory,
Understand the cause of poverty.
If you want to enjoy a pleasurable life,
Bear due suffering.
If you wish for freedom and liberty,
Constrain your mind first.
If you wish for great profit,
Do not lose justice and trust.
If you wish for warm reception,
Cultivate truth and good conduct.
If you aspire to authority and power,
Do not wield unfair authority and power.
If you aspire to a high position,
Develop the sense of yielding.
If you are endowed with talent,
Behave as if you were incompetent.
If you wish to expand your learning,
Augment your knowledge by studies.
If your wish is to succeed rapidly in business,
First maintain peace and stability of mind.
If your wish is to preserve your business,
Lose not the sense of awe.
All the sages and eminent ones from the time of antiquity
Grasped the principle of changes,
And established the moral principles.
Traveling throughout the four seasons,
They used endless circulation as their measure,
And were neither partial nor dependent.
How pitiful! Pitiful!
How pitiful a faithless person must be!

If one has no faith in this principle,
How can one know the matters of past and future?
If one knows nothing of past and future,
How can one know right from wrong in the present?
With no knowledge of the principles of the three time periods,
How can one know the principle of weal and woe, and the noble and
    the mean?
With no knowledge of weal and woe, the noble and the mean,
How can one aspire for eternity?
Without aspiration for eternity,
How can one know the principle of practice?
With no knowledge of the principle of practice,
How can one know the way of public service?
With no practice and public service,
How can one know the way of humanity and justice?
With no knowledge of humanity and justice,
How can human life be different from that of beasts and birds?
With life not different from that of beasts and birds,
One lives in the bitter seas of misery.
Those drowning in the bitter seas of misery!
Are they not to be pitied?
Since all sages elucidated this principle,
Let us be enlightened to it; let us observe carefully
And master the immutable truth through eternity.
I have come to know the principle of consistency;
It is immutability and eternity.
Immutability is the principle of no birth and no death.
Consider the myriad things in the universe;
They are invariable, spontaneous, remaining as before.
Because they pass through spring, summer, autumn, and winter,
There is nothing but the immutability of neither going nor coming.
Consider the going and coming of birth and death;
Their identity is clear and numinous.
Consider fortune and misfortune;
They follow the laws of cause and effect.
As the law of change dictates change of fortune,
One's fortune changes in accord with decree,
And this law is the same, past and future.
While various theories are divergent and confusing,

This fundamental principle is ever such.
As change and immutability go in each other's company,
Change is immutability and immutability is change.
As the law of change and immutability is universal and spontaneous,
No human power can deny it.
As it cannot be denied,
Do all things in accord with reason.
Doing all things in accord with reason,
Let us unify ourselves with heaven and earth.
If you wish to be unified with heaven and earth,
Learn the principle of seeing into self-nature.
Upon learning the principle of seeing into self-nature,
Cultivate the way of mind.
With the way of mind cultivated,
Learn to cultivate complete blessing and wisdom.
Once blessing and wisdom are complete,
You will attain perfect freedom.
With the learning of perfect freedom,
Let us march through the boundless heaven and earth.
All things in the wide world are the property of the enlightened,
Millions of years past and future are the property of the enlightened.
The innumerable changes are the creative transformation of the
    enlightened.
The fundamental principles of laws and morality are drawn up by the
    wise.
Such delight! Delight!
Such delight is here for the enlightened!
Once omniscient,
There should be no impediment.
They can be the parents of the world.
Upon delivering all sentient beings,
We will rejoice in longevity, happiness, and prosperity.
The principle of this is obvious, in front of our eyes,
Behold and see!
Be awakened and see!
With the good law of the Threefold Practice and the Eight Articles,
The way to know is illumined.
Let us hasten on the road to enlightenment!
With inquiry into all things,

Putting into practice what we learn,
Let us awaken ourselves from drunkenness,
Let us live the life of good measure.
Once what ought to be done is known,
Following the order of the innocent mind,
Following the order of self-nature,
Disciplining with spiritual cultivation,
We should carry it out,
And may the six roots be thwarted.
If we follow our nature and cultivate our spirit,
We can reach the highest good;
We will attain the great, consummate virtue of Irwŏn.
Good friends!
Let us preserve the great virtue of Irwŏn,
Taking a vow of permanent sincerity,
Let us rejoice in the common happiness forever.
How splendid! Splendid!
The law and principle of spring and autumn have been established!
(HH, 353–57)

Notes

Introduction

1. *Tonggyŏng taejŏn*, 33.
2. Ibid., 8; Yang Ŭnyong, "Han'guk chonggyo sasang esŏ pon sinchong-gyo" (New religions viewed in the context of the history of Korean religions), *HC* 23:164.
3. Ki-paek Lee, *A New History of Korea*, 258–59.
4. The third patriarch, Son Pyŏnghŭi (1861–1922), renamed Tonghak "Chŏndogyo" (Religion of Heavenly Way). For a brief history and doctrine of Tonghak and Chŏndogyo, see *SW*, 12–18.
5. King Kojong (1852–1919) renamed the Chosŏn kingdom "Taehan Cheguk" (Taehan dynasty) and assumed the title "emperor" with the approval of the world powers.
6. Approximately two million Koreans, 600,000 Chinese, 37,000 Americans, 3,000 Britons, and other UN armies.
7. See Yu Pyŏngdŏk, *Han'guk sinhŭng chonggyo*, 95–96. A survey records a half-dozen new religions, with 240 sects.
8. See *Taesun chŏn'gyŏng haesŏl*, 1:14, 15.
9. Ibid., 1:27.
10. Ibid., 2:1.
11. Ibid., 3:44.
12. For a brief history and theology of Chŭngsan'gyo, see *SW*, 18–26.
13. *Taesun chŏn'gyŏng haesŏl*, 5:3.
14. The Confucian cardinal moral virtues are benevolence (*ren*), righteousness (*yi*), propriety (*li*), wisdom (*zhi*), and faith (*xin*); the moral virtues of Tonghak are sincerity (*sŏng*), respect (*kyŏng*), and faith (*shin*).
15. For the details of the Buddhist reformation movement, see Chin Y. Park, ed., *The Makers of Modern Korean Buddhism*. Han Yongun's *Pulgyo taejŏn* (Compendium of Buddhism) was in the list of books Sot'aesan perused, and

273

Sot'aesan's *Chosŏn pulgyo hyŏksillon* (A treatise on the renovation of Korean Buddhism) agrees in spirit with Han Yongun's *Chosŏn pulgyo yusillon* (Treatise on the revitalization of Korean Buddhism).

16. Chŏngsan's biographical data used in this introduction is from *CCC*, which is an honest record of Chŏngsan's life.

17. *CCC*, 29–114. Chŏngsan's birth name was Song Togun; Song Kyu was his Won Buddhist dharma name, given by Sot'aesan in 1918; "Chŏngsan" was his Won Buddhist dharma title. Chŏngsan's birthplace is Sosŏng-dong, in Ch'ojŏn-myŏn, Sŏngju-kun, North Kyŏngsang province, Korea. Chŏngsan's genealogy can be traced back to Maengyŏng, who lived in the reign of the Koryo dynasty king Mokchong (998–1009). Chŏngsan was the thirtieth generation after Maengyŏng. Song Sŏnghŭm (1815–1900) married Yi Hyŏndŏk and they had one son, In'gi (1876–1951), whose Won Buddhist dharma name was Pyŏkcho and dharma title Kusan. Chŏngsan was his son.

18. The definitive eleventh-century history of China by Si Maguang (1019–1086); a synopsis of history from Zou dynasty onward.

19. *Lunyu* (The Confucian analects), *Zhongyong* (The doctrine of the Mean), *Daxue* (The great learning), *Mengzi* (The works of Mencius).

20. *CN*, pt. 2, ch. 4, sec. 1.

21. It is said that one night he saw light emanating from the mountain in front of the temple and he wondered what it was. Later, he was aware of its being gold and remembered a poem by Du Fu (712–770):

As the mind is devoid of desire,
I can discern the energy of gold and silver at night.
As ill will is gone far away,
I can see elks and deer disporting themselves nearby.

See *CCC*, 78.

22. *CCC*, 83.

23. See *SW*, 39–59, for a brief history of the foundation of Won Buddhism.

24. Sot'aesan first gave Chŏngsan the name Ch'u, the Chinese character of which means a pivot, cardinal point, an axis. The dharma name Kyu means "the stride made by a man"; the fifteenth constellation, which has sixteen stars, supposed to resemble a person's striding.

25. *SS* 1:2.

26. It was offered on the sixth, sixteenth, and twenty-sixth days of every month, with ten days of preparations. The nine disciples offered prayers separately on the nine mountain tops which surround Kilyongni, Sot'aesan's birthplace.

27. *DW* 1:6.

28. *SS* 1:13, 14.

29. *CCC*, 135.

30. *SS* 1:15

31. Ibid.

32. The central points of this work are summarized in *SS* 1:15–19.

33. For an analysis of Sot'aesan's renovation of Korean Buddhism, see Chung, "Sot'aesan's Creation of Won Buddhism through Reformation of Korean Buddhism," in *Makers of Modern Korean Buddhism*, ed. Jin Y. Park, 61–90.

34. See *HH*, 231–318. for the text.

35. The central points of this work are summarized in *DW*, ch. 11.

36. They cited his "bright countenance" as itself a source of inspiration. For examples, see *DW* 7:31.

37. *DW* 1:16.

38. For the dharma ranks, see *SW*, 163–64.

39. For a detailed analysis of the doctrine of Won Buddhism, see *SW*, 59–109; Chung, "Sot'aesan's Creation of Won Buddhism through the Reformation of Korean Buddhism," in Jin Y. Park, *Makers of Modern Korean Buddhism*, 74–86.

40. The term *fourfold beneficence* is not new with Won Buddhism; it can be found in other Buddhist scriptures with items different from those in the *Canon*. The *Xindiguan-jing* (*T* 159.3) includes parents, sentient beings, the sovereign, and the three treasures; the *Zhengfa nianchu-jing* (*T* 721.17) includes mother, father, the great teacher Tathāgatha, and preachers; the *Shishi yaolan* (*T* 2127.53) includes parents, teachers, the sovereign, and patrons; and Sōsan's *Sŏn'ga kwuigam* includes parents, the sovereign, teachers, and donors.

41. For a detailed history of the origination and development of the circular symbol, see Robert E. Buswell Jr., "Ch'an Hermeneutics: Korean View," in *Buddhist Hermeneutics*, ed. Donald S. Lopez Jr., 248–50.

42. See "On Irwŏnsang" in Part Three in this volume.

43. This title was changed to "The Vow to Irwŏnsang" in the *Canon* (1962).

44. For the three sections, see "Truth, Faith, Practice of Irwŏnsang" in Part Three. These three sections in the *Correct Canon of Buddhism* (1943) were altered in the *Canon* (1962) to the effect that Chŏngsan's reflections on the Mahāyāna Buddhist wisdom and practice were lost. In order to preserve Chŏngsan's original thought, these three sections are translated in Part Three in this volume.

45. "Buddha-nature" in Sot'aesan's original writing of 1938.

46. Sot'aesan does not explain what he means by "attaining the great power of Irwŏn" and "being unified with the noumenal nature of Irwŏn," leaving the impression that the circular form Irwŏn has such power. It was Chŏngsan who gave a reasonable interpretation to the two phrases as can be seen below.

47. In this section is summarized the chapter "Fourfold Beneficence" in the *Canon*; see *SW*, 124–31.

48. The entry "beneficence" in the *Shorter Oxford English Dictionary* quotes R. Niebuhr's expression "universal beneficence of nature."

49. See David Ross, *The Right and the Good*, 11–24, 28–41. Ross includes as prima facie duties: (1) fidelity and reparation, (2) gratitude, (3) justice, (4) beneficence, (5) self-improvement, and (6) nonmaleficence. A prima facie duty becomes a duty proper or an actual duty if it is not overridden by another duty. While the duties of beneficence and gratitude for Ross are limited to one's duty

to other humans, Sot'aesan includes heaven and earth, parents, brethren, and laws as the sources of beneficence to which one owes one's life.

50. According to Toulmin, "Ethics provide the reasons for choosing the 'right' course; religion helps us to put our hearts into it." See Toulmin, *An Examination of the Place of Reason in Ethics*, 219. In the doctrinal chart of the *Canon*, this injunction is stated as "Requite the beneficence as making an offering to the Buddha." See *SW*, 116.

51. See *SS* 6:24.

52. See *The Doctrine of the Mean* in *AGM*, 413: "Sincerity is the way of Heaven. The attainment of sincerity is the way of men. He who possesses sincerity, is he who, without an effort, hits what is right, and apprehends, without the exercise of thought; he is the sage who naturally and easily embodies the right way. He who attains to sincerity, is he who chooses what is good, and firmly holds it fast."

53. Here the Confucian view of heaven is clearly reflected. See *The Doctrine of the Mean* in *AGM*, 420: "The way of Heaven and Earth is large and substantial, high and brilliant, far-reaching and long-enduring."

54. See *SW*, 116. The ways of beneficence requital as moral imperative are spelled out in the doctrinal chart in the *Correct Canon of Buddhism* (*Pulgyo chŏngjŏn* [1943]). This cannot be found in the *Wŏnbulgyo kyojŏn* (Scriptures of Won Buddhism) (1962) as it was deleted during the redaction of the *Pulgyo chŏngjŏn* (*Correct Canon of Buddhism*[1943]). I have restored it in *The Scriptures of Won Buddhism* (2003).

55. *T* 2007.48:342b; Yampolsky, *The Platform Sutra of Sixth Patriarch*, 165: "The mind-ground, not in error, is the precept of self-nature; the mind-ground, undisturbed, is the meditation of self-nature; the mind-ground, not ignorant, is the wisdom of self-nature."

56. This way is called the Eightfold Noble Path, which consists of (1) right view, (2) right thought, (3) right speech, (4) right action, (5) right livelihood, (6) right effort, (7) right mindfulness, and (8) right concentration. The eight ways are summarized in the Triple Discipline as wisdom (1, 2), morality (3, 4, 5), and concentration (6, 7, 8).

57. Śīla, samādhi, and prajñā were put in the doctrinal chart by Sot'aesan in the *Correct Canon of Buddhism* (1943); they were deleted in the new doctrinal chart of the *Wŏnbulgyo kyojŏn* (1962). They are restored in *SW*, 116.

58. There are more than eighteen million people suffering from depression in the United States of America alone (December 2009).

59. The practice of inquiry into facts and principles reflects the Confucian teaching of investigation of things in *The Great Learning*: "Things being investigated, knowledge became complete." See *The Great Learning*, in *AGM*, 358.

60. For twenty "Essential Test Cases of *Ŭidu* (head of doubt)," see *SW*, pt. 3, chap. 5.

61. See "Translations," Part One, *The Canon of the World,* in this volume.

62. See *The Great Learning* in *AGM,* 357: "The ancients who wished to illustrate illustrious virtue throughout the kingdom, first ordered well their own States. Wishing to order well their States, they first regulated their families. Wishing to regulate their families, they first cultivated their persons. Wishing to cultivate their persons, they first rectified their hearts. Wishing to rectify their hearts, they first ought to be sincere in their thoughts. Wishing to be sincere in their thoughts, they first extended to the utmost their knowledge. Such extension of knowledge lay in the investigation of things."

63. *CW,* ch. 1.

64. The idea of prenatal influence goes back to King Wen's (r. 1184–1157 BC) mother, Tairen, who is said to have given moral teachings to the child in her womb.

65. While the chapter "Ailing Family and Its Remedies" in *CN* shows how to cure a morally sick family, Chŏngsan shows how to prevent a family from getting sick.

66. Chŏngsan's formulation of norms for a healthy family is a reformation of the Confucian moral codes for the five human relations: sovereign and vassal, father and son, husband and wife, old and young, and friends. See *DW* 4:35 for Chŏngsan's renovation of the Confucian moral codes.

67. Chŏngsan thinks, as Hobbes and Spinoza did, that "the state of nature" without a government is in "internecine war."

68. *CN,* pt. 3, sec. 4.

69. *DW* 10:31, 32, 22.

70. See the section "Truth, Faith, and Practice of Irwŏnsang" in Part Three in this volume.

71. *SS* 2:6.

72. The three sources are "On Irwŏnsang," *Hoebo* (Order's gazette) (1937); "Truth, Faith, and Practice of Irwŏnsang," in the *Correct Canon of Buddhism* (1943); and the chapter "Fundamental Principles" in *Dharma Words* (1972). See Part Three below for "On Irwŏnsang" and "Truth, Faith, and Practice of Irwŏnsang"; see *DW* 3:2–8 for Chŏngsan's elaborations of the tenet of Irwŏnsang.

73. "Shan, my doctrine is of an all-pervading unity." See *AGM,* 169 (*Analects,* bk. 5, ch. 15, sec. 1).

74. See Legge, *The Works of Mencius,* bk. 2, ch. 1, para. 11: "I am skillful in nourishing my vast, flowing passion-nature."

75. See Chan, *The Source Book in Chinese Philosophy,* 463–65, "An Explanation of the Diagram of the Great Ultimate."

76. See "On Irwŏnsang" in Part Three of this volume, esp. the section "The Truth of Irwŏnsang."

77. For the full text, see "Truth, Faith, and Practice of Irwŏnsang" in Part Three in this volume.

78. *WKC* 3:237–38; in *SS* 2:6, Sot'aesan says that Irwŏnsang is used to refer to the true Irwŏn, implying that Irwŏn has its identity apart from all beings in the universe.

79. In the *Wŏnbulgyo kyojŏn* (1962) (Scriptures of Won Buddhism), this statement was changed to "Irwŏn is the fundamental source of all things of the universe." This statement implies that all things in the universe spring from Irwŏn, just as, in Christian theology, all things in the universe are the creation of God.

80. The invisible Irwŏn seems to subsist between the visible Irwŏnsang and the inherent essence of all things, the original nature of all buddhas and patriarchs, and the Buddha-nature of all sentient beings, which are all invisible. If Irwŏnsang points to true Irwŏn as Sot'aesan says (*SS* 2:6), then a question remains unanswered of what the true Irwŏn is, even though he said that Irwŏnsang is the symbol of Buddha-nature or Mind-Buddha.

81. Those sutras that expound the Buddha-nature (tathāgatagarbha) are *Scripture of Perfect Enlightenment* (*Yuanjuejing*), *Srimāla Sūtra*, *Nirvāṇa Sūtra*, *Śūrāṁgama Sūtra*, and *Lotus Sūtra*. The treatises that expound the Buddha-nature are the *Awakening of Faith in Mahāyāna* and the *Treatise on Buddha Nature* (*Fo-hsing lun*), and *Ratnagotravibhāga*.

82. This characterization is quite similar to Nāgārjuna's middle path of eightfold negation: "(Therein every event is 'marked' by): non-origination, non-extinction; non-destruction, non-permanence; non-identity, non-differenti-ation; non-coming (into being), non-going (out of being)." See Inada, *Nāgārjuna*, 39.

83. *SS* 2:7.

84. This view reflects the Huayan Buddhist dictum that everything is the creation of mind. See *Dafangguang fo huayan jing, T* 278.9.466a.

85. *Dasheng qixin lun, T* 1666.32.577a; Hakeda, *The Awakening Faith*, 43–45.

86. Kant, *Critique of Pure Reason*, 111–14. Just as the concept of existence and nonexistence and that of causality belong to the phenomenal self as the forms of understanding for Kant, the differentiation of noumenon from phenomenon, existence from nonexistence, and causality appear in accordance with the light of numinous awareness for Chŏngsan.

87. Ibid., 82. "All our intuition is nothing but the representation of appear-ance; that the things which we intuit are not in themselves what we intuit them as being, nor their relations so constituted in themselves as they appear to us, and that if the subject, or even only the subjective constitution of the sense in general, be removed, the whole constitution and all the relation of objects in space and time, nay space and time themselves, would vanish. As appearances, they cannot exist in themselves, but only in us."

88. Cook, *Huayen Buddhism*, 104.

89. Presented here is the section "Practice of Irwŏnsang" as written by Chŏngsan in the *Correct Canon of Buddhism* (*Pulgyo chŏngjŏn* [1943]), which

was altered after Chŏngsan's death in such a way that Chŏngsan's teaching for right practice was lost in the 1962 edition.

90. *Susim kyŏl, T* 2020.48.1008c; Buswell, *KAZ,* 154: "Cultivation prior to awakening is not true cultivation."

91. *Xianzongji, T* 2076.51.458c. Shenhui (d. 760) writes that prajñā is the cause of nirvāṇa and nirvāṇa is the effect of prajñā. If we take "perfect, complete, utterly fair and unselfish mind" as nirvāṇa, then "perfect, complete, utterly fair and unselfish mind" as Irwŏn and "prajñā-wisdom" should not be identical. We should interpret the relation between the two as cause and effect; unless the light of prajñā-wisdom shines as the result of awakening to the truth of Irwŏnsang, one cannot have the "perfect, complete, utterly fair and unselfish mind" as Irwŏn in various adverse conditions. Just as Shenhui says a few lines later that nirvāṇa and prajñā are different names of the identical reality, Chŏngsan expressed the two as identical. The expression "like Irwŏn" means "like Buddha's pure and perfect mind."

92. *SS* 2:6. Sot'aesan does not explain what the true Irwŏn is.

93. *CPS,* 358.

94. *DW* 3:2, 4, 5, 8, 16, 23, 36, 37, 38, 39, 40.

95. *DW* 3:2.

96. *DW* 3:5.

97. See "On Irwŏnsang" in Part Three, the section "How to Model after Irwŏnsang."

98. See "Ode to the Consummate Enlightenment" in Part Three for Chŏngsan's moral inferences. Chŏngsan draws some moral implications from the *Book of Changes,* commentary on hexagram no. 1, *quian* (Heaven). See Legge, *Yi King,* 417: "The great man is he who is in harmony, in his attributes, with heaven and earth; in his brightness, with the sun and moon; in his orderly procedure, with the four seasons; and in his relation to what is fortunate and what is calamitous, in harmony with the spirit-like operations (of Providence)."

99. *DW* 3:28.

100. *DW* 3:39. See "Ode to Consummate Enlightenment" in Part Three below for illustrations.

101. See *DW,* ch. 6, for Chŏngsan's explanation of the essentials of moral culture.

102. See *CN,* pt. 3, ch. 11.

103. *DW* 6:45.

104. *DW* 6:50.

105. *DW* 6:18; *CN,* pt. 3, ch. 1. The first three articles state that the mind-ground is free from disturbances, delusions, and errors, which arise in mental spheres and that, hence, one should maintain the samādhi, prajñā, and śīla of the self-nature by keeping disturbances, delusions, and errors from arising respectively.

106. *DW* 3:25, 27, 28, 29; 6:44, 67, 69.

107. *DW* 4:27.

108. *Biyan lu*, case 65, *T* 2003.48.181c; Thomas Cleary and J. C. Cleary, *The Blue Cliff Record*, 2:318: "A monk asked Chao-chou, 'The ten thousand dharmas return to the One. Where does the One return?' "

109. For the original text, see *CN*, pt. 2, ch. 1, sec. 4.

110. See *CPS*, 402–403, for Chŏngsan's exegesis of "The Vow to Irwŏnsang" by Sot'aesan.

111. See *DW* 6:82 for the "Numinous Mantra" and "Purification Mantra."

112. *DW* 1:16.

113. See "The Great Sea of the Buddha-dharma" (*Pulbŏp taehae*) in *CPS*, 253–303, for Chŏngsan's interpretations of various Buddhist tenets.

114. See *DW*, ch. 4, "Exposition of Scriptures."

115. *DW* 4:30.

116. *DW* 10:28.

117. For the relevance of Chŏngsan's renovation of the Confucian ethics, see Chung, "The Relevance of Confucian Ethics," *Journal of Chinese Philosophy* 18, no. 2 (1991): 143–59.

118. See *DW* 3:31, 32, 33 for Chŏngsan's reformations.

119. *DW* 4:32.

120. *Pogyŏng yuktae yoryŏng* (Treasure scripture of six grand principles), in *WKC* 4:75–76.

121. *DW* 4:33.

122. This treatise is excerpted in *DW*, ch. 11, "On the Korean National Destiny."

123. For more on the disunity among political leaders, see Song Namhŏn, *Haebang samnyŏn sa* (Three-year history after liberation).

124. *DW* 10:31, 32, 33. In these sections, Chŏngsan elaborated the triple ethics that he briefly mentioned in *CW*, ch. 7, "The World." For the text of the *gāthā*, see the start of part 1 ("The Canon of the World"), in "Translations," in this volume.

125. Here Chŏngsan seems to endorse Chang Tsai's theory of vital force as the ultimate material principle of the universe. See Chan, *A Sourcebook in Chinese Philosophy*, 495–517.

Translations

Part One: *The Canon of the World*

1. *SS* 4:44.

2. *SS* 4:45.

3. *CN*, pt. 2, ch. 2, sec. 2.

4. *CN*, pt. 3, ch. 13, sec.3.

5. For the details of beneficence requital, see *CN*, pt. 2, ch. 2.

6. *CN*, pt. 3, ch. 13, sec. 4.

7. *SS* 1:18.

8. *DW* 6:64.

9. *SS* 9:3, 5.

10. See *Koryŏguk pojo sŏnsan susim kyŏl*, *T* 2020.48.1009b.

Part Two: *The Dharma Words*

1. See *SS* 1:13, 14.

2. Ch'oe Cheu (1824–1864), the founder of the Ch'ŏndogyo, is addressed as Ch'oe Suun and Kang Ilsun (1871–1909), the founder of the Chŭngsan'gyo, is addressed as Kang Chŭngsan.

3. *CN*, pt. 2, chs. 2 and 3 for the Fourfold Beneficence and the Four Essentials.

4. The way of Wŏn.

5. The religion of Wŏn.

6. *Daxue* (The great learning), by Confucius, sec. 7; see *AGM*, 357–59.

7. *Kŭmgang*, diamond, the least frangible of minerals, a synonym of hardness, indestructibility, power. The diamond is employed by the esoteric sects as a symbol of wisdom and power over illusion and evil spirit.

8. In March 1918 Grand Master Sot'aesan directed his nine disciples to construct an embankment along a tidal estuary to create a rice field; they completed it March 1919. See *SS*, 1:8, 9.

9. Kim Taegŏ (1914–1998), dharma title Taesan, was elected third head dharma master after Master Chŏngsan died in 1962.

10. It is not certain which sūtra Chŏngsan means; however, in the *Huayanjing* can be found the following: "If you wish to have a thorough knowledge of all the buddhas of the three time periods, then you should observe the nature of the universe (*dharmadhātu*) because all is only the creation of the mind." See *Dafang guangfo huayanjing*, *T* 279.10.102a-b.

11. The Won Buddhist Threefold Practice comprises cultivation of spirit, inquiry into facts and principles, and heedful choice in karmic action. See *CN*, pt. 2, ch. 4.

12. As large as an ox.

13. At the time of the admonition, the *Dharma Words of Master Chŏngsan* did not exist, which is now one of the two sacred books of Won Buddhism (as translated and redacted in this book).

14. *CN*, pt. 3, ch. 1.

15. See *Liuzi dashi fabao danjing*, *T* 2008.48.352a. "Not to stray from the self-nature is practice; to apply it with no infection is virtue."

16. *Biyanlu*, *T* 2003.48.146b. See Cleary and Cleary, *The Blue Cliff Record*, 37–45, case 6: "Yun Men's Every Day Is a Good Day."

17. *Book of History*, bk. 2, ch. 6, sec. 13; U Hyŏn-min, *Sŏgyŏng*, 391.

18. *Koryŏguk pojo sŏnsa susimgyŏl*, *T* 2020.48.1006b-c. See Buswell, *KAZ*, 143–44.

19. At the time of his death (1962), Master Chŏngsan left this line for his followers: "With your mind cultivation well done, be the minister to the New World." In referring to cultivation of the mind, Master Chŏngsan means the practice of the Threefold Practice of spiritual cultivation, inquiry into facts and principles, and heedful choice in karmic action, which will help one attain the three great powers of emancipation, enlightenment, and the Mean. By the mind, he means the three functioning aspects of the Buddha-nature, or Dharmakāya Buddha, by the perfection of which one attains buddhahood.

20. *CN*, pt. 3, ch. 17.

21. See *AGM*, 383, "What Heaven has conferred is called NATURE; an accordance with this nature is called THE PATH; the regulation of this path is called INSTRUCTION."

22. *SS* 2:7.

23. *SS* 1:14.

24. The Korean War started in 1950 and ended in 1953 (truce).

25. Longevity, wealth, health, love of virtue, peaceful death.

26. Cf. *Daodejing*, ch. 43: "The softest of all things overrides the hardest of all things."

27. Unidentified.

28. Unidentified.

29. An Chunggŭn (1879–1910) joined the Korean army, being outraged by the Japanese imposition of the Five Article Treaty in the year of *ŭlsa* (1905); he was arrested when he shot and killed Ito Hirofumi, the Japanese resident general, at the Harvin railway station in 1909, and was executed at the Lüshun prison.

30. For the whole text of *The Canon of Rites* (*Yejŏn*), see *WBC*, 533–719.

31. *Chŏnmu ch'ulsin*, a person who has left his or her home in order to devote his or her whole life to the missionary work of Won Buddhism.

32. *CN*, pt.1, ch. 1.

33. *CN*, pt. 2, ch. 1; a master plan of a building is not the building.

34. Ibid., ch. 2, sec. 1.

35. Ibid., ch. 6.

36. Ibid., ch. 2.

37. Ibid., ch. 3.

38. Ibid., ch. 3, sec. 1.

39. Ibid., sec. 4.

40. *CN*, pt. 3, ch. 4, sec. 2.

41. Ibid., ch. 17.

42. Ibid.

43. *T* 235.8.749a; Cleary, *The Sutra of Hui-neng*, 97, ch. 5, "Real Seeing in Accord with Truth."

44. *Jinggang boruo boluomi jing, T* 235.8.749a, "Furthermore, Subhuti, bodhisattvas should not dwell on anything as they practice charity"; See Mubi, *Kŭmganggyŏng ogahae*, 141, ch. 4. The "three wheels" are the giver, the receiver, and the gift; and the bodhisattva practices charity with purity of mind, without dwelling on any of the three wheels.

45. The five elements are water, fire, wood, metal, and earth.

46. Won Buddhism requires its followers to observe thirty precepts, divided into the three levels of "common faith," "unwavering faith," and "the struggle between good and evil"; there are ten precepts for each level. See *CN*, pt. 3, ch. 11.

47. The three moral virtues are based on the central tenets of the ethics of *Chŏndogyo*. See the *Tonggyŏng taejŏn*, 157.

48. Ibid, 154.

49. Ibid.

50. See *CN*, pt. 2, ch. 2.

51. On August 21, 1919 (WE 4), Sot'aesan's nine disciples pressed their bare thumbs under their names on a sheet of white paper on which was written "Sacrifice with no regret" before leaving for the nine mountaintops where they had agreed to sacrifice their lives all at the same time. Miraculously, there appeared nine bloody fingerprints. Seeing this, Sot'aesan called them back, telling them that the dharma realm was moved by their sincerity and devotion; hence, they did not have to sacrifice their lives. See *SS*, 1:14.

52. See *CN*, pt. 2, ch. 2, sec. 1. The eight ways of the heaven and earth as listed in the *CN* seems to reflect the Confucian thought on the moral character of heaven and earth in *The Doctrine of the Mean*, ch. 32. See *AGM*, 429–30. "1. It is only the individual possessed of the most entire sincerity that can exist under heaven, who can adjust the great invariable relations of mankind, establish the great fundamental virtues of humanity, and know the transforming and nurturing operations of Heaven and Earth;—shall this individual have any being or anything beyond himself on which he depends? 2. Call him man in his ideal, how earnest is he! Call him an abyss, how deep is he! Call him Heaven, how vast is he! 3. Who can know him, but he who is indeed quick in apprehension, clear in discernment, or far-reaching intelligence, and all-embracing knowledge, possessing all heavenly virtue?"

53. Unidentified.

54. The Fourfold Beneficence as the manifestation of the Dharmakāya Buddha in Won Buddhism comprises the beneficences of heaven and earth, parents, brethren, and laws. See *SW*, 124–31.

55. A pagoda tree; a Chinese scholar tree.

56. One of the Won Buddhist religious daily rituals, see *SW*, 156 (*CN*, pt. 3, ch. 9).

57. Or, the Way that signifies something like cosmic numinous, ubiquitous spirit.

58. One of the four Buddhist theories of causation; the other three theories are causation by *ālayavijñāna,* causation by true thusness, and causation by *dharmadhātu.*

59. For the view that the Vairocana Buddha is everywhere, see Francis H. Cook, *Hua-yen Buddhism,* 92: "The infinite universe is his body, and every particle of the universe, however minute or humble, constantly teaches the Dharma with his voice." Cook refers to *Huayan yicheng jiaoyi fenqui zhang, T* 1866.45.489c and 499a for Fazang's treatise on Vairocana Buddha.

60. See D. T. Suzuki, *Manual of Zen Buddhism,* 14: "However innumerable beings are, I vow to save them; However inexhaustible the passions are, I vow to extinguish them; However immeasurable the Dharmas are, I vow to master them; However incomparable the Buddha-truth is, I vow to attain it."

61. *Pulbŏp yŏn'guhoe ch'anggŏnsa, HH,* 229–318.

62. See *Jingde chuandeng lu* 10, *T* 2076.51.276c.

63. *CN,* pt. 3, ch. 17.

64. See *CN,* pt. 1, ch. 3 for "Four Pillars," the first of which is correct enlightenment and right practice. It means "for one to be enlightened to and model oneself on the truth of Irwŏn, namely, the mind-seal, which Buddhas and patriarchs correctly transmit from one to the other so that one can act perfectly without partiality, attachment, excessiveness, or deficiency when one uses the six sense organs: eyes, ears, nose, tongue, body, and mind."

65. *CN,* pt. 2, ch. 4.

66. *CN,* pt. 3, ch. 12, "The Essential Discourse on Following the Original Nature."

67. Huineng (AD 638–713), the sixth patriarch of the Chan Buddhist tradition in China.

68. For a detailed discussion on internal-external concentration and calmness, see the *Suyang yŏn'gu yoron,* in *WKC* 4:34–50.

69. For the nine articles of the Essentials of Daily Practice, see *CN,* pt. 3, ch. 1; the Glossary of Terms below.

70. *CN,* pt. 2, ch. 4, sec. 2.

71. *Confucian Analects,* bk. 12, ch. 1, sec. 1 (*AGM,* 250).

72. *CN,* pt. 3, ch. 1; See the *Confucian Analects,* bk. 12, ch. 1, sec. 1 (*AGM,* 250).

73. See *Biyanlu,* case 45, *T* 2003.48.181c; Cleary and Cleary, *Blue Cliff Record,* 2:318: "A monk asked Chao-chou, 'The Ten Thousand Dharmas return to one. Where does the One return?' The Master replied, 'While I was staying at Ch'ing Chou, I made a hemp that weighed seven pounds.'"

74. Chinul, *Koryŏguk pojo sŏnsa susimgyŏl*, T 235.48:1008b.
75. Ibid. See Yampolski, *The Platform Sutra of the Sixth Patriarch*, 149 and 164. For an English translation of Chinul's exposition, see Buswell, *KAZ*, pp. 151–54.
76. When Master Chŏngsan wrote the section "The Practice of Irwŏnsang" in *PC*, he used the expression "perfect and complete, and utterly fair and unselfish." He used it to describe the mind of prajñā-wisdom, but he did not make the distinction between the samādhi and śīla aspects of the Buddha-nature, Irwŏn, that he makes here. See *SW*, 121–22 (*CN*, pt. 2, ch. 1, sec. 3) for the text.
77. *CN*, pt. 3, ch. 17. "Dharma power's subjugation of *māra*."
78. There are six dharma stage ranks in Won Buddhism: (1) common faith, (2) unwavering faith, (3) battle between right and wrong, good and evil, (4) subjugation of evil, (5) transcendence, and (6) *tathāgata*. See *CN*, pt. 3, ch. 17.
79. *CN*, pt. 3. ch. 17.
80. An epithet of every buddha, *avaivartika*, never backsliding and always progressing; never retreating but going straight to nirvāṇa.
81. *CN*, pt. 3, ch. 8, "The Discourse on Repentance."
82. Ibid.
83. Ibid.
84. *CN*, pt. 3, ch. 11.
85. *Zhongyong*, ch. 1, sec. 3; *AGM*, 384.
86. *Jingang boruo boluomi jing*, T 235.8.749c; Conze, *Perfect Wisdom*, 126–27: "Therefore, then, Subhuti, the Bodhisattva, the great being, should produce an unsupported thought, i.e., a thought which is nowhere supported, a thought unsupported by sights, sounds, smells, tastes, touchables or mind-objects."
87. *Biyanlu*, case 45, T 2003.48.181c; Cleary and Cleary, *Blue Cliff Record*, 2:318: "A monk asked Chao-Chou, 'The ten thousand Dharmas return to the One. Where does the One return?' The master replied: 'While I was staying at Ching Chou I made a hemp rope that weighed seven pounds.'"
88. For Sot'aesan's exposition of the truth of Irwŏn in terms of "empty," "round," and "right," see *SS* 2:7.
89. *CN*, pt. 3, ch. 6.
90. *CN*, pt. 3, ch. 2, sec. 2.
91. *CN*, pt. 3, ch. 7, "When six sense organs are free from work, eliminate delusions and cultivate one-mind; and when the six sense organs are at work, eliminate injustice and cultivate justice."
92. The mantra is supposed to be chanted in its original sound. The Korean original sound is: *Chŏnji yŏnggi asim chŏng, mansa yŏŭi asim t'ong, chŏnji yŏa tong ilch'e, ayŏ ch'onji tong simchŏng.*
93. The Korean original sound is: *Pŏpsin chŏngjŏng pon muae, adŭk hoegwang yŏk puyŏ, t'aehwa wŏn'gi sŏng ildan, sama akch'wi cha somyŏl.*

94. Legge, trans., *The I Ching*, commentary on hexagram no. 1, *qian* (heaven), 417.

95. Chŏngsan's comments here allude to the founding motto of Won Buddhism: "Since material power is unfolding, let us unfold spiritual power accordingly." See *SW*, 114. The harmful consequences of this formidable material civilization are already apparent, as Sot'aesan predicted.

96. *CN*, pt. 2. ch. 2.

97. See *Susimgyŏl*, *T* 2020.48.1006c.

98. *CN*, pt. 2. ch. 2, sec. 3 for the principle of requiting the beneficence of brethren.

99. The "if" clause of the last sentence in the Korean original runs: "If thought and no thought is done as intended." The late Professor Ryu Kihyŏn told me that the editor of the Korean original copied it incorrectly.

100. Ch'oe Sihyŏng (1829–1898) was the second patriarch of Chʼŏndogyo, executed on July 20, 1898.

101. *CN*, pt. 3, ch. 1.

102. For the deliverance sermon, see *SS* 9:5.

103. Cf. Lao Tzu, *Tao Te Ching*, ch. 29: "Therefore, the sage avoids all extremes, excesses, and extravagance."

104. For requital of beneficence, see *CN*, pt. 2, ch. 2.

105. Ibid.

106. The triple mission of Won Buddhism is edification, education, and charity.

107. Just as the seven colors of light emerging from a prism all originate in white light, the different religions of the world all come from one source, which Chŏngsan identifies with the invisible Irwŏn (which can be envisaged as a unitary circle with no circumference).

108. The world was divided into the so-called free world and the Communist bloc when Chŏngsan proposed this system of morality.

109. The beneficence of heaven and earth, parents, brethren, and laws.

110. The Buddha, the dharma, and the sangha.

111. *Daxue*, "Text of Confucius," sec. 3; *AGM*, 357.

112. Unidentified.

113. This section reminds one of the seriousness of the question concerning karma. "An old man at the Buddha Kāśyapa a monk asked if a yogi who went through great spiritual training should be subject to the law of causation, and the monk told him, 'No, he is not subject to it.' For that wrong teaching, the monk received the body of a fox for 500 rebirths" (Suzuki, *Essays in Zen Buddhism*, vol. 2, 203–205); Ferguson, *Zen's Chinese Heritage*, 80.

114. The Korean original of this text uses two Chinese characters for "thought." Mencius used one Chinese character for "thinking." "To the mind belongs the office of thinking. By thinking, it gets the right view of things; by

neglecting to think, it fails to do this. These—the senses and the mind—are what Heaven has given to us. Let a man first stand fast in *the supremacy of* the nobler part of his constitution, and the inferior part will not be able to take it from him. It is simply this which makes the great man" (James Legge, *The Works of Mencius,* 418 (vi.a.15); emphasis in the original).

115. Song Tosŏng's dharma title.

116. Song Hyewan's dharma title.

117. Pak Chebong's dharma title.

118. Ch'oe Tohwa's dharma title.

119. See *Koryŏguk pojo sŏnsa susimgyŏl, T,* 2020.48.1009b.

120. Song Ch'anghŏ's dharma title.

121. *CN,* pt. 2, chs. 2, 3, 4.

122. Deliverance of sentient beings and curing the world of ills.

123. Unidentified. Cf. *The Confucian Analects,* bk. 3, ch. 3, "If a man be without the virtues proper to humanity, what has he to do with music?"; bk. 8, ch. 8, "It is from music that the finish is received."

124. The terms *three chiefs* (*samwŏn*) and *five successors* were coined in Won Buddhism, the former referring to Ch'oe Cheu (1824–1864), Kang Ilsun (1871–1909), and Pak Chungbin (1891–1943), the founders of Ch'ŏndogyo, Chŭnsan'gyo, and Wŏnbulgyo (Won Buddhism) respectively; and the latter to the five future sages.

125. The three sovereigns (*sanhwang*) are Fuxi, Shennong, Huangdi or Tianhuang, Dihuang, and Renhuang. The five emperors (*wudi*) are Taihao, Yandi, Huangdi, Shaohao, and Zhanxu.

Part Three: Other Selected Writings

1. See *WKC,* 4:99–104.

2. "Shan, my doctrine is of an all-pervading unity." See *AGM,* 169 (*Analects,* bk. 5, ch. 15, sec. 1).

3. See Legge, *The Works of Mencius,* bk. 2, ch. 1, para. 11: "I am skillful in nourishing my vast, flowing passion-nature."

4. See Chan, *The Source Book in Chinese Philosophy,* 463–65, "An Explanation of the Diagram of the Great Ultimate."

5. See Chu Hsi and Lü Tsu-ch'ien, *Reflections on Things at Hand,* 128, n. 17. Wing-tsit Chan's translation is "Never lack seriousness."

6. See *WKC,* 4:68–92.

7. *AGM,* 366.

8. Chŏngsan's own footnote in the Korean original. Chŏngsan calls the state of mind devoid of delusive thought the realm of Irwŏnsang.

9. *CN,* pt. 3, ch. 6, for the canonized section; *WKC* 4:82. The initial formulation of the rules for keeping a diary.

10. *CN,* pt. 3, ch. 2, sec. 2.

11. Ibid.

12. Ibid.

13. Chŏngsan's own footnote in the Korean original is "stupefaction."

14. These three sections are translations of Chŏngsan's own writing in the *Correct Canon of Buddhism* (*Pulgyo chŏngjŏn*) (1943). During the redaction process for *Wŏnbulgyo kyojŏn* (The scriptures of Won Buddhism) (1962), these three sections were altered to the effect that Chŏngsan's original thought was lost.

Chinese Character Glossary

An Chunggŭn (K) 安重根
Biyanlu (C) 碧巖錄
chagŏp ch'wisa (K) 作業取捨
chan (C) 禪
Changsu (K) 長水
chasŏng (K) 自性
Chesan (K) 齊山
chia-wu (C) 甲午
chil (K) 質
chin'gong (K) 眞空
chin'gong myoyu (K) 眞空妙有
Chinmuk (K) 震默
Chinsan (K) 晉山
chipsim (K) 執心
Chŏn Pongjun (K) 全琫準
Chŏnghwasa (K) 正化社
Chŏngjŏn (K) 正典
Chŏngjŏng yoron (K) 定靜要論
Chŏngsan (K) 鼎山
Chŏngsim yogyŏl (K) 正心要訣
chŏngsin suyang (K) 精神修養
chŏnmu ch'ulsin (K) 專務出身
Chogye (K) 曹溪
chongbŏpsa (K) 宗法師
chongsa (K) 宗師
Chosŏn (K) 朝鮮

Chosŏn pulgyo hyŏksillon (K) 朝鮮佛教革新論
Chu (C) 楚
Chŭngsan'gyo (K) 甑山教
Chusan (K) 主山
Ch'a Kyŏngsŏk (K) 車京石
Ch'anggŏnsa (K) 創建史
Chŏndogyo (K) 天道教
Chŏnjiŭn (K) 天地恩
Chŏngjŏngju (K) 清淨呪
Ch'oryang (K) 草梁
Ch'oe Cheu (K) 崔濟愚
Ch'oe Sihyŏng (K) 崔時亨
Ch'u (K) 樞
ch'ulga (K) 出家
Dafang guangfo huayanjing (C) 大方廣佛華嚴經
daiji dushuo (C) 太極圖說
dao (C) 道
Daodejing (C) 道德經
Dasheng qixin lun (C) 大乘起信論
Daxue (C) 大學
Dihuang (C) 地皇
Du Fu (C) 杜甫
Fahai (C) 法海
Fuxi (C) 伏羲
Gunlun (C) 崑崙
Haewŏl (K) 海月
Heduluoshu (C) 河圖洛書
Hoebo (K) 會報
Houying (C) 候瀛
huangdi (C) 皇帝
Huike (C) 慧可
Huineng (C) 惠能
hwadu (K) 話頭
ich'am (K) 理懺
irwŏn (K) 一圓
irwŏnsang (K) 一圓相
Ito Hirofumi (J) 伊藤博文
ixiang sanmei (C) 一相三昧
iixing sanmei (C) 一行三昧

Ji (C) 稽
Jingde chuandeng lu (C) 景德傳燈錄
Jingangjing (C.) 金鋼經
jingong miaoyu (C) 眞空妙有
junzi (C) 君子
kabo (K) 甲午
Kaesŏng (K) 開城
Kang Ilsun (K) 姜一淳
ki (K) 氣
Kim Taegŏ (K) 金大擧
Kongsan (K) 公山
Kŏn'gungnon (K) 建國論
Ko P'allye (K) 高判禮
kongjŏk yŏngji (K) 空寂靈知
kŭmgang (K) 金鋼
Kut'awŏn (K) 九陀圓
kwansim (K) 觀心
kyŏng (K) 敬
kyŏnsŏng (K) 見性
kyojŏn (K) 敎典
kyomu (K) 敎務
Kyu (K) 奎
li (C) 禮
lie (C) 烈
Liji (C) 禮記
Lunyu (C) 論語
Lushun (C) 旅順
Maenyŏng (K) 孟英
Mengzi (C) 孟子
munyŏm (K) 無念
musim (K) 無心
myŏngan (K) 明眼
myoyu (K) 妙有
naejŏngjŏng (K) 內定靜
naesuyang (K) 內修養
Namwŏn (K) 南原
Nanyang Huizhong (C) 南陽惠忠
nŭngsim (K) 能心
oejŏngjŏng (K) 外定靜

oesuyang (K) 外修養
Paek Hangmyŏng (K) 白鶴鳴
Pak Chungbin (K) 朴重彬
Panyaji (K) 般若智
P'alsan (K) 八山
pŏbŏ (K) 法語
pŏpki posal (K) 法起菩薩
Pochŏn'gyo (K) 普天教
Pogyŏng yukdae yoryŏng (K) 寶經六大要領
Pŏmnyurŭn (K) 法律恩
pul (K) 佛
Pulbŏp Yŏn'guhoe (K) 佛法研究會
Pulgyo chŏngjŏn (K) 佛教正典
Pulgyo taejŏn (K) 佛教大典
Pumoŭn (K) 父母恩
Qing (C) 清
Quian (C) 天
ren (C) 仁
Renhuang (C) 人皇
Ryŏ (K) 呂
sach'am (K) 事懺
sagwan (K) 四關
samdong yulli (K) 三同倫理
samwŏn (K) 三元
Sandong (K) 山東
sanfu (C) 三伏
sang (K) 相
sanhuang (C) 三皇
sariyŏn'gu (K) 事理研究
sasang (K) 四相
Sejŏn (K) 世典
Sengcan (C) 僧燦
Shaoxue (C) 小學
Shennong (C) 神農
Shenxiu (C) 神秀
shin (K) 信
Shishi yaolan (C) 釋氏要覽
shuai (C) 率
Shujing (C) 書經

Si Maguang (C) 司馬光
Sŏnga kwigam (K) 禪家龜鑑
Sŏnyo (K) 禪要
sŏng (K) 誠
Song Chunp'il (K) 宋浚弼
Song In'gi (K) 宋寅驥
Song Kyu (K) 宋奎
Shun (C) 舜
Sŏktuam (K) 石頭庵
Son Pyŏnghŭi (K) 孫秉熙
Sot'aesan (K) 少太山
Sugye (K) 水溪
Sunji (K) 順之
Sunzi (C) 筍子
Susim chŏnggyong (K) 修心正經
Suun (K) 水雲
Suyangyŏn'guyoron (K) 修養研究要論
Taegakchŏn (K) 大覺殿
Taehan (K) 大韓
Taejonggyŏng (K) 大宗經
Taesan (K) 大山
Taewŏnsa (K) 大原寺
Taihao (C) 太昊
Taiji dushuo (C) 太極圖設
Tairen (C) 太姙
Taisho shinshū daizōkyō (J) 大正新脩大藏經
Tianhuang (C) 天皇
todŏk (K) 道德
Tonggyŏng taejŏn (K) 東經大典
Tonghak (K) 東學
Tongp'oŭn (K) 同胞恩
Tosŏng (K) 道性
tot'ong (K) 道通
ŭmbu (K) 陰府
Wen (C) 文
Wŏlmyŏngam (K) 月明庵
wŏn (K) 圓
wŏnsang (K) 圓相
wŏnbulgyo (K) 圓佛教

wŏndo (K) 圓道
won'gwang (K) 圓光
wŏn'gyo (K) 圓敎
Wu (C) 禹
wudi (C) 五帝
Wudi (C) 武帝
wuji (C) 無極
Xianzongji (C) 顯宗記
xiao (C) 孝
Xiaohao (C) 少昊
Xiaoxue (C) 小學
xin (C) 心
Xindi guanjing (C) 心地觀經
xing (C) 性
yang (C) 陽
Yangshan Huiji (C) 仰山慧寂
Yao (C) 堯
Yejŏn (K) 禮典
yi (C) 義
Yi Ch'adon (K) 異次頓
Yijing (C) 易經
yin (C) 陰
Yin (C) 殷
Yinfujing (C) 陰府經
Yi Sunsin (K) 李舜臣
yŏng (K) 靈
yŏngdan (K) 靈丹
yŏngga (K) 靈駕
yŏngju (K) 靈呪
yŏngmowŏn (K) 永慕院
Yŏngsan (K) 靈山
Yongdam yusa (K) 龍潭遺詞
Yuanjuejing (C) 圓覺經
yuktae yoryŏng (K) 六大要領
yunyŏm (K) 有念
Yu Hujo (K) 柳厚祚
yuil (K) 唯一
Zhengfa nienchu jing (C) 正法念處經
zhong (C) 忠

Zhou (C) 紂
Zhou (C) 周
Zhuxi (C) 朱熹
Zizhitongjian (C) 資治通鑑
Zongyong (C) 中庸

Glossary of Terms

"C" stands for Chinese; "K" for Korean; and "S" for Sanskrit.

Amitābha (S): "Boundless light"; the Buddha Amitābha: the Buddha of measureless light.

asura (S): Fallen god or demon, being in one of the six realms of existence.

beneficence: The entry "beneficence" in the *Shorter Oxford English Dictionary* quotes R. Niebuhr's expression "universal beneficence of nature," which does not imply any sense of "divine grace." Just as ocean is the "universal beneficence of nature" for fish, heaven and earth, parents, brethren, and laws are "the universal beneficence of nature," which implies no sense of "divine grace." Thus, the word *grace* is avoided in this translation.

bhūtatathatā (S): Lit., "true thusness"; referring to pure Buddha-nature in one's mind devoid of worldly characteristics.

Bodhidharma (S): The first Chinese patriarch of Chinese Chan Buddhism.

bodhisattva (S): One who aspires to the attainment of buddhahood and devotes himself or herself to altruistic deeds, especially deeds that cause others to attain enlightenment.

bodhimaṇḍala (S): A circle, or place of enlightenment. A place for religious offerings. A place for teaching, learning, or practicing religion. Translated in Chinese as 道場.

brethren: An English rendering of the Chinese 同胞 meaning "brothers by the same mother or fellow countrymen." In Won Buddhism, fellow human beings, animals, and plants are brethren arising from the same womb of the universal beneficence of nature.

chagŏp chuisa (K) 作業取捨: Lit., "Heedful choice in karmic action." One of the threefold practice of Won Buddhism.

chin'gong (K) 眞空: See *chin'gong myoyu.*

chin'gong myoyu (K) 眞空妙有: The Korean reading of the Chinese *jin-gong miaoyou.* Rendered into English as "true emptiness cum wondrous existence." Emptiness of nonemptiness is true emptiness, and existence of nonexistence is wondrous existence. Basically, this term attempts to disillusion the Hīnayānas of their biased view of the immateriality of the phenomenal world and deluded beings of their wrong view of the existence of phenomenal reality. The compound term means that true emptiness is mysteriously existing: truly empty, or immaterial, yet transcendentally existing. Thus, true emptiness and wondrous existence are not two entities separated from each other; rather, they are two aspects of one and the same reality. What is not "the only nonexistence" of the biased Hīnayāna is called "true emptiness," which is the emptiness of nonemptiness; what is not "the existence of the phenomenal reality" of the deluded beings is called "wondrous existence." Therefore, this compound term means that all things arising through the dependent co-arising in the universe are ever clear because of true emptiness, and all the causal laws pertaining to all things in the universe are ever immutable because of "wondrous existence."

chipsim (K) 執心: Lit., "getting hold of the mind," meaning that, for beginning practitioners, one must get hold of the mind firmly so that one's mind should not be distracted to the object of desires or hatred. This requires constant watching over the mind's movements.

chŏng (K) 定: In this translation, this term stands for concentration (samādhi).

chŏngbŏp (K) 正法: Lit., "correct law"; by "law" is meant the doctrine or teaching of a sage, such as the Buddha. Thus, the teaching of the Buddha for the first one thousand years is regarded as the "true law."

Chŏngjŏng-yoron (K) 定靜要論: The title of a treatise meaning "Essentials of Concentration and Calmness," which expounds the principle of meditation used in the early stage of Won Buddhism.

Chŏngsan (K) 鼎山: Lit., "cauldron mountain." The dharma title Sot'aesan conferred on Song Kyu 宋奎 (1900–1962), implying that all the dharma or law of his order should be cooked in this cauldron before it could feed the followers of Won Buddhism. Chŏngsan succeeded Sot'aesan as the head dharma master of Won Buddhism in 1943 upon the death of Sot'aesan, its founder.

chŏngsin suyang (K) 精神修養: Lit., "Cultivation of spirit." One of the threefold practice of Won Buddhism.

chŏnmu ch'ulsin (K) 專務出身: One who has left home in order to devote his or her whole life to the missionary work of Won Buddhism.

chongbŏpsa (K) 宗法師: Lit. "head dharma master"; the title given to the leader of the Won Buddhist order, elected by the Supreme Council of the order and representing the order.

chongsa (K) 宗師: Lit. "ancestral master"; the title given to those who ascended the dharma stage of transcendence (the fifth level) in the dharma ranks of Won Buddhist order, who have the capacity and ability, among other things, to legislate a new dharma for the New World by comprehending the profound principle of heaven and earth.

Chŏndogyo (K) 天道教: Lit. "religion of the heavenly way"; a religion indigenous to Korea founded by Ch'oe Che-u 崔濟愚, teaching the unity of heaven and man.

Chŏnjiŭn (K) 天地恩: Lit., "Beneficence of heaven and earth." The first of the fourfold beneficence of Won Buddhism.

Chŏn'gang sŏng (K) 천강성: a star known in English as Arisaema Japonica.

Chŏngjŏngju (K) 清淨呪: Lit. "purification mantra"; the mantra composed by Chŏngsan.

cultivation: This refers to the longer expression "cultivation of spirit," one part of the threefold practice of Won Buddhism, the other two being "inquiry into facts and principles" and "heedful choice in karmic action."

dao (C) 道: Lit. "way"; central concept of Taoism and origin of its name; the Dao is also the central feature of the *Daodejing*. It also denotes "teaching." From earliest times the term has been used in the sense of human behavior and moral laws—the way of humanity; this certainly is its meaning in Confucianist texts.

Daxue (C) 大學: Lit. "great learning"; the title of one of the four Confucian classics.

deliverance sermon: The sermon delivered by a dharma master at the funeral service or deliverance service for the departed spirit.

deliverance service: The Buddhist service performed to deliver the departed spirit on every seventh day after death for forty-nine days.

deva (S): Lit. "god" or celestial being. Name of inhabitants of one of the good modes of existence who live in fortunate realms of the heavens but who, like all other beings, are subject to the cycle of rebirth. The celestial beings are allotted very long happy life as a reward for previous good deeds; however, precisely this happiness constitutes the primary hindrance on their path to liberation.

dharma (S): The teaching given by the Buddha; the moral principles; the truth; the all-encompassing principle that governs all manifestations of things and events, transcendental reality. In plural form, "dharmas" denotes things, phenomena, events, attributes, or beings. The expression "Buddha-dharma" in this work means the teachings of the Buddha as Sot'aesan originally intended to mean.

dharmakāya (S): See *Trikāya*. In Won Buddhism, Dharmakāya Buddha is the object of religious worship symbolized by a circle, Irwŏnsang, which is the sign pointing to it.

Dharmamodgata (S): The name of a bodhisattva supposed to be living in Mount Kŭmgang. The Korean name is *pŏpki posal,* meaning the bodhisattva who will let the dharma arise.

dharma stage: In Won Buddhism, practitioners are evaluated to measure the degree of their progress toward the final goal of attaining buddhahood; the degree of progress is ranked as: (1) common faith, (2) unwavering faith, (3) struggle between dharma and *māra,* (4) subjugation of *māra* with potent dharma, (5) transcendence, (6) tathāgata of great enlightenment.

dharmatā (S): The fundamental nature of the dharmas.

doubt: A technical term in Zen Buddhism used to refer to constant inquiry into the implications of a *hwadu* in order to arrive at an awakening. It has nothing to do with the mental state of skepticism.

dvadasanga pratītya-samutpāda (S): "Twelvefold dependent co-arising." The second of the Buddha's Four Noble Truths (existence of suffering, the cause of suffering, the cessation of suffering, the way). The causes of suffering are set out in the principle of twelvefold dependent co-arising: (1) ignorance; (2) action, activity, conception, disposition; (3) consciousness; (4) name and form; (5) the six sense organs; (6) contact, touch; (7) sensation, feeling; (8) thirst, desire, craving; (9) grasping; (10) being, existing; (11) birth; (12) old age, death.

earlier heaven: A term signifying the world of dark age in contrast with "later heaven," which signifies the world of highly civilized age. In *Chŭngsan'gyo* 甑山敎 this pair of terms take important place in their dogma, in which the year 1894 is alleged to be the point of demarcation.

Eight Articles: Prerequisites of the Threefold Practice: four articles to adopt: faith, zeal, doubt, and sincere devotion; four articles to forsake: disbelief, greed, laziness, and delusion.

emptiness: A translation of the Sanskrit term *śūnyatā,* meaning emptiness or insubstantial nature of all things; the central teaching of Buddhism.

Through realization of emptiness one attains liberation and perfection of buddhahood. Emptiness is not a nihilistic void, but a wondrous state wherein dynamic events can take place. True realization of emptiness is a state free of all types of clinging, a state encompassing all and unifying all.

essential ways of humanity: The way a human being ought to follow as a human being; Sot'aesan designated the tenet of Fourfold Beneficence and the Four Essentials as the way of humanity, distinguished from the way of practice.

essential ways of practice: The Threefold Practice and the Eight Articles. For the perfection of the three aspects of the Buddha-nature, viz., concentration (samādhi), wisdom (prajñā), and precepts (śīla), Sot'aesan suggests one must practice (1) cultivation of spirit, (2) inquiry into facts and principles, and (3) heedful choice in karmic action respectively.

Essentials of Daily Practice: The nine maxims that a Won Buddhist recites daily as moral guide: (1) The mind-ground is originally devoid of disturbances, but they arise in response to the mental spheres; hence, let us maintain the concentration (samādhi) of the self-nature by keeping disturbances from arising. (2) The mind-ground is originally devoid of delusions, but they arise in response to the mental spheres; hence, let us maintain the wisdom (prajñā) of the self-nature by keeping delusions from arising. (3) The mind-ground is originally devoid of errors, but they arise in response to the mental spheres; hence, let us maintain the precepts (śīla) of the self-nature by keeping errors from arising. (4) Remove disbelief, greed, laziness, and delusions by means of faith, zeal, doubt, and devotion. (5) Let us change the life of resentment into the life of gratitude. (6) Let us change the life of other power into the life of self-power. (7) Let us change those unwilling to learn into those who learn well. (8) Let us change those unwilling to teach into those who teach well. (9) Let us change those who do not have public spirit into those who have it.

evil: Transgression or violation of any of the thirty precepts by body, mouth, or mind in Won Buddhism.

evil path: Of the six realms of existence, the realms of beasts, hungry ghosts, and hells.

facts and principles: Facts are the right and wrong, gain and loss of human affairs; principles are the principles of noumenon and phenomenon, existence and nonexistence of all the things of the universe.

false notion: See "four false notions."

five components of a human being: (1) the physical form, (2) reception, (3) conception, (4) the functioning of mind, (5) mental faculty in regard to perception and cognition, consciousness.

five desires: the desires of wealth, sex, food and drink, fame, and sleep.

five relationships: The Confucian norms that dictate human relations: (1) There ought to be affection between father and son; (2) There ought to be justice between the sovereign and the subject; (3) There ought to be difference between husband and wife; (4) There ought to be orderliness between senior and junior; and (5) There ought to be trustworthiness between friends.

Four Essentials: The four maxims of social ethics of Won Buddhism: cultivation of self-power; the wise as the standard; education of the children of others, veneration for those dedicated to the public cause.

four false notions 四相: The four ejects of ego in the *Diamond Sūtra*: (1) the false notion (or illusion) that in the five skandhas there is a real ego; (2) that this ego is a person, and different from beings of the other paths; (3) that all beings have an ego born of the five skandhas; (4) that the ego has age, i.e., a determined or fated periods of existence.

Fourfold Beneficence: In Won Buddhism, the faith in Dharmakāya Buddha is the faith in heaven and earth, parents, brethren, and laws which are the manifestation of Dharmakāya Buddha. Since one cannot exist without their favors, they are identified as beneficence.

four forms of birth: Viviparous, as with mammals; oviparous, as with birds; moisture- or water-born, as with worms and fishes; metamorphic, as with moths from chrysalis, or with *devas,* or in hells, or the first beings in a newly evolved world.

Four Great Vows: Also known as the bodhisattva vows: However innumerable beings are, I vow to save them; however inexhaustible the passions are, I vow to extinguish them; however immeasurable the dharmas are, I vow to master them; however incomparable the Buddha-truth is, I vow to attain it.

Four Noble Truths: The fundamental teaching of the Buddha: suffering, cause of suffering, cessation of suffering, and the way toward nirvāṇa.

four pillars: the four pillars of Won Buddhism are (1) correct enlightenment and right practice, (2) awareness and requital of beneficence, (3) practical application of Buddha-dharma, and (4) selfless service for the public.

good path: Of the six realms of existence, viz., *devas* and humans.

Gṛdhrakūta (S): The Spirit Vulture Peak, a mountain in the central India where the Buddha Śākyamuni used to give sermons. The *Lotus Sūtra* was delivered there.

guest mind: The mind that is the opposite of the host mind. The mental attitude of the host who takes good care of the household, while a guest would not.

Hetuluoxiu (C) 河圖洛書: The Korean reading is *hado naksŏ;* the plan of the Yellow River and the book of the river Luo, mystic diagrams said to have been supernaturally revealed.

host mind: The mind of the owner, master, head of a household who takes care of the matter as one's own.

Huike (C) 慧可: The second patriarch of Chan (Zen) in China; he was the dharma successor to Bodhidharma and the master of Sengcan. According to tradition, Huike (487–593) came to Shaolin monastery in about his fortieth year to ask Bodhidharma for instruction. It is said that initially Bodhidharma did not acknowledge him and Huike stood for several days in the snow in front of the cave where the first patriarch was practicing seated meditation facing the wall. In order to prove his earnestness to the Indian master of buddha-dharma and to induce the latter to accept him as a student, Huike finally cut his own left arm off and presented it to Bodhidharma, who thereupon accepted him as a student.

hwadu (K) 話頭: Lit. "word head"; a point or key line of a *kongan* 公案, the word or phrase in which the *kongan* resolves itself when one struggles with it as a means of spiritual training.

ich'am (K) 理懺: Lit. "principle repentance," sometimes translated as "noumenal repentance," which means doing away with all roots of evil passions and transgression by being enlightened to one's Buddha-nature. This is one of the twofold repentance, the other being the phenomenal repentance, repentance done in front of the triple treasure, cutting off all the past transgressions and doing all good things.

inquiry: Part of the longer phrase "inquiry into facts and principles," which is one part of the Threefold Practice.

Irwŏn (K) 一圓: Unitary circle without circumference, thus invisible, referring to Dharmakāya Buddha, the noumenal essence of all things in the universe, the original nature of all buddhas and enlightened beings, the Buddha-nature of all sentient beings, nirvāṇa, and original enlightenment. In Won Buddhism, it refers also to the noumenal essence of the Fourfold Beneficence.

Irwŏnsang (K) 一圓相: Lit. "form of the unitary circle." A sign of the unitary circle, it is visible. Like a finger pointing at the moon, it plays the role of a sign signifying Dharmakāya Buddha, which is called Irwŏn in Won Buddhism. The Irwŏnsang is enshrined in the temples of Won Buddhism as the object of religious worship and as the standard of practice.

junzi (C) 君子: Lit. "princely man"; the ideal personality of Confucian moral system; a gentleman.

kabo (K) 甲午: The thirty-first year of the sexagenary cycle, the year of the horse. Chŏngsan refers to AD 1894 as the demarcation point between earlier heaven and later heaven.

kalpa (S): A Sanskrit term meaning aeon; a day of *Brahmā* or a period of 432 million years of mortals.

karma (S): Lit. "action" or "deed." It also means the effect of a deed or deeds that survives death and contributes to the formation of one's next life. The "law of karma" asserts that virtuous or evil deeds of body, mouth (speech), and mind (volition) will inevitably bring corresponding results to the doer, in this or future life.

Kŏn'gungnon (K) 建國論: Lit. "treatise on founding a nation"; the title of a short treatise of the moral guideline Chŏngsan wrote in 1945 for founding the nation of Korea upon the liberation from Japanese colonial occupation.

kongan (K) 公案: Lit. "public notice"; the Chinese *gongan* originally meant a legal case constituting a precedent. In Zen a *kongan* is a phrase from a sūtra or teaching on Zen realization, an episode from the life of an ancient master.

kŭmgang (K) 金鋼: Lit. "diamond." The adamantine nature of this stone is used as the symbol of the unremitting and unwavering faith and integrity.

Kŭmgangdan (K) 金鋼團: Lit. "diamond association." The name was given by Chŏngsan to the youth association of the young devotees in the headquarters of Won Buddhism.

kwansim (K) 觀心: Lit. "observing the mind"; upon getting hold of the mind against adverse conditions, the practitioner should observe the mind to see how it responds to the internal and external conditions, and thereby one nourishes the One Mind.

kyojŏn (K) 教典: Lit. "canon of the order." In Won Buddhism, this term stands for *The Scriptures of Won Buddhism*.

kyomu (K) 教務: Lit. "one who devotes oneself to the mission of the Won Buddhist religious edification." In Won Buddhism, this title is conferred on the person who becomes a minister upon completing all the required education and spiritual training.

lie (C) 烈: Chastity.

Maitreya (S): Lit. "the kind one," a great Bodhisattva, the future Buddha after Śākyamuni Buddha, who will come to this world to teach the Dharma.

mantra (S): A power-laden syllable or series of syllables that manifests certain cosmic forces and aspects of the buddhas, sometimes also the name of a buddha. Continuous repetition of mantras is practiced as a form of meditation in many Buddhist schools. Here mantra is defined as a means of protecting the mind. In the transformation of body, speech, and mind that is brought about by spiritual practice, mantra is associated with speech, and its task is the sublimation of vibrations developed in the act of speaking.

māra (S): Lit. "murder, destruction"; although actually the embodiment of death (personified as *Māra*), *māra* symbolizes in Buddhism the passions that overwhelm human beings as well as everything that hinders the arising of the wholesome roots and progress on the path of enlightenment.

Mind-dharma: The way of using one's mind well as Buddha-bodhisattvas use their mind.

Mind-ground: A technical term in *Chan* Buddhist tradition, signifying the original nature or Buddha-nature, which is originally devoid of evil passions.

mind seal: the seal that certifies the Buddha-mind.

muguk (K) 無極: The Korean reading of the Chinese *wuji,* meaning the ultimate of nonbeing, which is the ontological basis of *daiji* 太極 (supreme ultimate) in the Confucian and Daoist metaphysics.

munyŏm (K) 無念: Lit., "no-thought or thoughtlessness." It is used in the sense of harboring no false thought, e.g., if you do not abide by the idea of having rendered a favor to someone after rendering it, you practice the virtue of *munyŏm.*

musim (K) 無心: Lit., "no mind." In Chŏngsan's moral system, this term is used to refer to one of the four stages in Spiritual Cultivation expounded in the *Susim chŏnggyŏng* (Correct canon of mental cultivation): *chipsim, kwansim, musim,* and *nŭngsim. Musim* is the state of mind that is devoid of all passions, discriminations, and the worldly thought comparable to samādhi.

mutual benefit: Or benefiting oneself by benefiting others; one of the four essential ways of beneficence requital, namely, the beneficence of brethren.

myoyu (K) 妙有: See *chin'gong myoyu*.

nature: English rendering of the Chinese *xing* 性, used to refer to the original nature of human mind as well as the ultimate principle of the universe.

Nirmāṇakāya (S): See *trikāya*.

nirvāṇa (S): In early Buddhism, it is departure from the cycle of rebirths and entry into an entirely different mode of existence. It requires complete overcoming of the three unwholesome roots—desire, hatred, and delusion—and coming to rest of active volition. It means freedom from the determining effect of karma. Nirvāṇa is unconditioned; its characteristic marks are absence of arising, subsisting, changing, and passing away. In Mahāyāna, nirvāṇa is conceived as oneness with the absolute, the unity of saṁsāra, and transcendence. It is also described as dwelling in the experience of the absolute, bliss in cognizing one's identity with the absolute, and as freedom from attachment to illusions, affects, and desires.

noumenal repentance: See *ich'am* 理懺.

numinous awareness: Gnosis

numinous consciousness: Chŏngsan gives the name "numinous consciousness" to the consciousness that is the third feature in twelvefold dependent co-arising, and which enters the womb of the new mother.

nŭngsim (K) 能心: Lit., "omnipotent mind"; the last phase of the spiritual cultivation expounded in the *Susim chŏnggyŏng*. This is the spiritual realm where the mind is always with the self-nature and one's response to the external environment and conditions is always in accord with the principle of the self-nature and yet absolutely free with prajñā-wisdom always shining.

Other-power: In Won Buddhism, this term refers to two things. One is to the Fourfold Beneficence as the object of religious worship, since one's life is impossible without it. The other is to the power of other people on whom one can depend for living. The latter practice, in which many people did not work but expected to be supported by others, was widespread in Korean society until the turn of the twentieth century.

own nature: The Sanskrit *svabhāva* rendered in Chinese as *zixing* 自性, meaning inherent nature, often rendered in English as "self-nature."

pŏbŭn (K) 法恩: Lit. "the beneficence of dharma"; refers to the charitable foundation Chŏngsan established for the health care of the devotees of the Won Buddhist order.

pŏmnyurŭn (K) 法律恩: Lit., "Beneficence of laws." The fourth of the fourfold beneficence of Won Buddhism.

pŏpsa (K) 法師: Lit., "dharma teacher"; an epithet conferred on the practitioner who has conquered all *māras* in one's mind in Won Buddhism; a highly regarded teacher of dharma.

prajñā (S): Wisdom; a central notion of the Mahāyāna referring to an immediately experienced intuitive wisdom that cannot be conveyed by concepts or in intellectual terms. The definitive moment of prajñā is insight into emptiness (*śūnyatā*), which is the true nature of reality. The realization of prajñā is often equated with the attainment of enlightenment and is one of the essential marks of buddhahood. Prajñā is also one of the "six perfections" actualized by a bodhisattva in the course of his or her development.

public service: What one gives in terms of spiritual, corporeal, and material contributions to the public (the order). This is one of the dual tasks of the religious life in Won Buddhism; the other being religious practice. The dictionary meaning of the Korean of this term is an enterprise or a business; this has nothing to do with its meaning as used in Won Buddhism.

pumoŭn (K) 父母恩: Lit., "Beneficence of parents." The second of the fourfold beneficence of Won Buddhism.

ren (C) (仁): Rendered in English as benevolence, kind-heartedness, humanity, or love; one of the two most important moral virtues of Confucianism, the other being *yi* (righteousness).

rūpa (S): Physical body made from earth, water, fire, and air.

sach'am (K) 事懺: Lit. "factual repentance"; Repentance done in front of the triple treasure, cutting off all the past transgressions and doing all good things. This is one of the two kinds of repentance, the other being "principle repentance."

sagwan (K) 四關: Lit. "four gates"; four acupuncture points.

Śākyamuni (S): Lit. "Sage of *Śākya* clan"; epithet of Siddhārtha Gautama, the founder of Buddhism, the historical Buddha, who belonged to *Śākya* clan.

Salāpralāpa (S) 常啼菩薩: Name of a bodhisattva who wept while searching for truth.

samādhi (S): Concentration; composing the mind; intent contemplation; perfect absorption of thought into the one object of meditation.

Sambhogakāya (S): See trikāya.

samdong (K.) 三同: Lit. "triple identity"; Chŏngsan's metaphysical bases of the ethics of triple identity. The original source of all religions is identical; all sentient beings are related by an identical biological energy; and the goals of all enterprises and ideology are identical.

sanfu (C) 三伏: Lit., "three surrenders"; the (three 10-day periods of) "dog days."

sangha (S): Lit. "crowd, host"; the Buddhist community. In a narrower sense the sangha consists of monks, nuns, and novices. In a wider sense the sangha also includes lay followers.

sari yŏn'gu (K) 事理研究: Lit., "Study of facts and principles." One of the threefold practice of Won Buddhism.

sasang (K) 四相: The four false notions in the *Diamond Sūtra*: the notion of ego, the notion of personality, the notion of a being, the notion of life.

śastra (S): Lit., "instruction, text book"; treatises on dogmatic and philosophical points of Buddhist doctrine composed by Mahāyāna thinkers that systematically interpret philosophical statements in the sūtras.

Sejŏn (K) 世典: Lit. "canon of the world." The title of Chŏngsan's treatise, which lays out the Ways to be followed for a perfect life in this and eternal life. Part 1 of this book.

self-nature: See "own nature."

self-power: See "other-power."

Shaoxue (C) 小學: A book widely used during the Sung dynasty China for moral cultivation. Recorded in the book are the Confucian moral thought and the sayings of various sages.

Shun (C) 舜: Name of a legendary Chinese ruler, said to have ruled from 2255 to 2205 BC.

śīla (S): Lit., "Obligations, precepts"; refers to the ethical guidelines that in Buddhism determine the behavior of monks, nuns, and laypersons and that constitute the precondition for any progress on the path of awakening. The ten *śīla*s for monks, nuns and novices are: (1) refraining from killing, (2) not taking what is not given, (3) refraining from prohibited sexual activity, (4) refraining from unjust speech, (5) abstaining from intoxicating drinks, (6) abstaining from solid food after noon, (7) avoiding music, dance, plays, and other entertainment, (8) abstaining from the use of perfumes and ornamental jewelry, (9) refraining from sleeping in high, soft beds, (10) refraining from contact with money and other valuables. In Won Buddhism there are three sets of ten precepts, totaling thirty precepts.

six paths: The six realms of existence into which a sentient being is to be born: *deva*, humans, *asuras,* animals, hungry ghosts, and hells.

six roots: Or six bases of consciousness: eyes, ears, nose, tongue, body, and volition.

skandha (S): Lit. "heaps, aggregates." In early Buddhism a human being is analyzed away in terms of body, sensation, conception, volitional activities, and consciousness.

Sot'aesan (K) 少太山: Dharma title of Pak Chungbin 朴重彬 (1981–1943), the founder of Won Buddhism.

spirit of the deceased: See *yŏngga*.

susimgyŏl (K) 修心訣: Lit. "Secret on Cultivating the Mind"; the title of Chinul's work on Zen practice. This book is included in the *Essential Scriptures of Ancient Buddha and Patriarchs* used in Won Buddhism as reference source book.

śūnyatā (S): See "emptiness."

Susim chŏnggyŏng (K) 修心正經: Lit. "correct scripture of cultivating the mind"; a reference book frequently used during the beginning stage of the Won Buddhist order's history; author and publication data unknown, believed to have been originated in Chŭngsan'gyo 甑山敎. The content consists of the explication of the principle and method of spiritual cultivation, in which some tenets of Buddhism, Confucianism, and Taoism are mixed.

sūtra (S): Lit., "thread"; discourses of the Buddha, the sūtras are collected in the second part of the Buddhist canon, the *sūtra pitaka,* or "Basket of the Teachings."

Suyang yŏn'gu yoron (K) 修養研究要論: Lit. "Essentials of Spiritual Cultivation and Inquiry into Facts and Principles"; the title of a canonical text used during the beginning stage of the history of Won Buddhism published in 1927. In this book Sot'aesan explicates the principles of spiritual cultivation, inquiry into facts and principles, and heedful choice in karmic action.

svabhava (S): See "own nature."

Taejonggyŏng (K) 大宗經: Lit. "great ancestral scripture"; the title of the *Scripture of Sot'aesan.*

Tairen (C) 太姙: The name of King Wen's mother, who is said to have taught him while he was in her womb.

tathāgata (S): Lit. "the thus-gone (thus-come, thus-perfected) one"; refers to one who on the way of truth has attained supreme enlightenment. It is one of the ten epithets of the Buddha, which he himself used when speaking of himself or other buddhas.

three great powers: The powers of great emancipation, great enlightenment, and great Mean as the result of cultivation of spirit, Inquiry into facts and principles, and heedful choice in karmic action respectively, which are the Threefold Practice of Won Buddhism.

Threefold Practice: The way of practice in Won Buddhism consists of cultivation of spirit, inquiry into facts and principles, and heedful choice in karmic action; equivalent to the Buddhist triple discipline of samādhi, prajñā, and śīla (concentration, wisdom, and precepts).

three worlds: Translation of the Sanskrit *tridhātu* that literally means "three worlds, three spheres." The three worlds are: (1) The desire-world (*kāmadhātu*); here sexual and other forms of desire predominate. The world of desire includes the realms of existence of hell beings and of the *asuras*. (2) The material or form world (*rūpadhātu*); here desire for sexual and food falls away, but the capacity for enjoyment continues. This world contains the gods dwelling in the dhyāna heaven. Rebirth in this sphere is possible through practice of the four absorptions (dhyāna). (3) The immaterial or formless world (*ārūpyadhātu*); this realm is a purely spiritual continuum consisting of the four heavens in which one is reborn through practice of the four stages of formlessness.

todŏk (K) 道德: Lit. "way and virtue"; translated as "morality"; Chŏngsan's aspiration was to build one household under heaven with *todŏk* or the "Way and its virtue."

Tonggyŏng taejŏn (K) 東經大典: Lit. "great canon of Eastern learning"; the title of the Chŏndogyo canon.

tongp'oŭn (K) 同胞恩: Lit., "Beneficence of brethren." The third of the fourfold beneficence of Won Buddhism.

tot'ong (K) 道通: Lit. "mastery of the way"; refers to the mastery of facts and principles as the result of practice of inquiry into facts and principles.

trikāya (S.): Lit. "three bodies"; refers to the three bodies possessed by a buddha according to the Mahāyāna view. The basis of this teaching is the conviction that a buddha is one with the absolute and manifests in the relative world in order to work for the welfare of all beings. The three bodies are as follows. (1) Dharmakāya ("body of the great order"); the true nature of the Buddha, which is identical with transcendental reality, the essence of the universe. The Dharmakāya is the unity of the Buddha with everything existing. At the same time it represents the "law" (dharma), the teaching expounded by the Buddha. (2) *Sambhogakāya* ("the body of delight"); the body of buddhas who in a "buddha-paradise" enjoy the truth that they embody. (3) *Nirmā-*

ṇakāya ("body of transformation"); the earthly body in which buddhas appear to men in order to fulfill the Buddha's resolve to guide all beings to liberation.

Tripitaka Koreana (S): Lit., "three baskets of Buddhist canon published during Koryŏ dynasty" 高麗大藏經; Canon of Buddhist scriptures, consisting of three parts: *vinaya-pitaka* (rules of discipline), *sūtra-pitaka* (sermons), and *abhidharma-pitaka* (a compendium of Buddhist psychology and philosophy).

twelvefold dependent co-arising: See *Dvadasanga pratītya-samutpāda.*

ŭmbu 陰府 (K): Lit. "the place of the departed"; the Korean reading of the Chinese *yin-fu,* which refers to Hades.

vijñāna (S): The six kinds of consciousness (i.e., those of the five sense organs and mental consciousness), each of which arises from contact of an object with the organ corresponding to a given sense. *Vijñāna* is the fifth of the five *skandhas* and the third link in the chain of dependent co-arising.

vipaśyanā (S): Insight, clear seeing; intuitive cognition of the three marks of existence, namely, the impermanence, suffering, and egolessness of all physical and mental phenomena. In Mahāyāna Buddhism, *vipaśyanā* is seen as analytical examination of the nature of things that leads to insight into the true nature of the world—emptiness (*śūnyatā*). Such insight prevents the arising of new passions. It is one of the two factors essential for the attainment of enlightenment (*bodhi*); the other is *śamatha* (calming the mind).

way: See *dao.*

way and its virtue: See *todŏk.*

Wŏlmyŏngam 月明庵 (K): A Buddhist temple on Mount Pyŏn, in Puan county, North Chŏlla province, where Sot'aesan met Zen monk Paek Hangmyŏng and Chŏngsan stayed for five years as the Zen monk's chief disciple.

wŏn (K) 圓: Lit. "circle" refers to Dharmakāya Buddha that is enshrined in the circular form Irwŏnsang (unitary circular form) as the object of religious faith in Won Buddhism.

Wŏnbulgyo (K) 圓佛教: Lit., "circle or 'consummate' Buddhism"; the name of the Won Buddhist order.

Wŏn'gwang (K) 圓光: Lit., "the light of circle"; the title of the Won Buddhist monthly publication.

Yao (C) 堯: A celebrated Chinese emperor who is said to have reigned 2257–2255 BC.

Yejŏn (K) 禮典: Lit., "the canon of rites"; the title of the Won Buddhist *Canon of Rites.*

yi (C) 義: Righteousness, one of the Confucian constant virtues.

yin and yang (C) 陰陽: Lit., "shade and light"; the dual principle of the universe: the negative or female principle of nature and its opposite, the positive or male principle.

yŏngdan (K) 靈丹: Lit., "spirit decoction, or elixir"; the Korean reading of the Chinese *ling-tan,* which means "elixir of immortality." A practitioner of spiritual cultivation gains this spiritual elixir after sufficient practice; with it one attains the power to go and come freely through the six paths.

yŏngga (K) 靈駕: Lit., "spirit vehicle"; refers to the departed spirit after death and before rebirth; or the departed spirit of the intermediate existence between death and rebirth, a stage varying from seven to forty-nine days, when the karma-body will be reborn.

Yŏngju (K) 靈呪: Lit., "numinous mantra"; refers to the chanting formula composed by Chŏngsan.

yŏngmo (K) 永慕: Lit., "eternal admiration, longing for."

Yŏngmowŏn (K) 永慕院: The name of the shrine where the tablets of the ancestral founders of Won Buddhism, all sages, devotees, and parents are enshrined in the headquarters of Won Buddhism.

yŏngt'ong (K) 靈通: Lit., "mastery of spirit"; refers to the spiritual realm where, on account of one's spiritual gate being open, one can know the transformation of all beings in the universe and the principle of karmic retribution of human beings without study; this mastery is mainly the result of the cultivation of spirit (samādhi).

yuil (K) 唯一: Lit., "only one"; part of the name of the first learning institute in Won Buddhism, which later grew to be what is now Won Kwang (Wŏn'gwang) University.

yulli (K) 倫理: Lit., "principle of human relations"; refers to ethics.

yunyŏm (K) 有念: Lit., "guarding the thought"; refers to the mental practice of "taking care of" the mind before saying or doing something, before, say, writing a bad check or protecting one's clothes from catching fire.

Zongyong (C) 中庸: The title of one of the four Confucian classics, *The Doctrine of the Mean.*

Selected Bibliography

I. Chŏngsan's Writings and Analects

Chŏngsan chongsa pŏbŏ 鼎山宗師法語 (Dharma words of Master Chŏngsan). Iksan: Wŏnbulgyo Ch'ulp'ansa, 1972.

Chŏngsan chongsa pŏpsŏl 鼎山宗師法說 (Master Chŏngsan's dharma discourses). Comp. O Sŏnmyŏng. Iksan: Wŏlgan Wŏn'gwangsa, 2000.

Chŏngsan chongsa pŏpsŏljip 鼎山宗師法說集 (Collected sermons of Master Chŏngsan). Iri: Wŏnbulgyo Wŏn'gwangsa, 1962.

Hanuran hanich'ie 한울안한이치에 (With one truth within one fence). Comp. Pak, Chŏnghun. Iri: Wŏnbulgyo Ch'ulp'ansa, 1982.

Kŏn'gungnon 建國論 (A treatise on the national foundation). Iri: Pulbŏp Yŏn'guhoe, 1945.

Pulbŏp yŏn'guhoe ch'anggŏnsa 佛法研究會創建史 (The founding history of the Society for the Study of Buddha-dharma). Iri: Pulbŏp Yŏn'guhoe, 1938.

Pulgyo chŏngjŏn 佛教正典 (Correct canon of Buddhism). Seoul: Pulgyo Sibosa, 1943.

Sejŏn 世典 (The canon of the world). In *CP*. Iri: Pulbŏp yŏn'guhoe, 1972.

Susim chŏnggyŏng 修心正經 (Correct scripture on cultivating the mind). Iri: Pulpŏp Yŏn'guhoe, ca. 1950.

Wŏnbulgyo kyosa 圓佛教教史 (A history of Won Buddhism). Iksan: Wŏnbulgyo Chŏnghwa-sa, 1975.

Wŏnbulgyo yejŏn 圓佛教禮典 (Book of rites of Won Buddhism). Iksan: Wŏnbulgyo Chŏnghwa-sa, 1968.

II. Works Cited

Biyan lu. In *T* 2003.

Buswell, Robert E. Jr., trans. *The Korean Approach to Zen: The Collected Works of Chinul.* Honolulu: University of Hawaii Press, 1983.

Chan, Wing-tsit. *A Sourcebook in Chinese Philosophy.* Princeton: Princeton University Press, 1963.

⸻, trans. *Reflections on Things at Hand: The Neo-Confucian Anthology.* Compiled by Chu Hsi and Lü Tsu-chien. New York: Columbia University Press, 1967.

Chinul. *Koryŏguk pojo sŏnsa Susimgyŏl* 高麗國普照禪師修心訣. In *T* 235.48:1008.

Chung, Bongkil. *The Scriptures of Won Buddhism: A Translation of the* Wŏnbulgyo kyojŏn *with Introduction.* Kuroda Institute for the Study of Buddhism and Human Values. Hawaii: University of Hawaii Press, 2003.

⸻, trans. *The Dharma Words of Master Chŏngsan.* Iksan: Wŏn'gwang Publishing, 2000.

⸻. "The Relevance of Confucian Ethics." *Journal of Chinese Philosophy* 18, no. 2 (1991): 143–59.

⸻. "Beneficence as the Moral Foundation in Won Buddhism." *Journal of Chinese Philosophy* 23 (1996): 193–211.

⸻. "The Moral Philosophy of Master Chŏngsan." *Wŏnbulgyohak* 圓佛教學 (Studies of Won Buddhism) 6 (2001).

Cleary, Thomas. *The Sutra of Hui-neng: Grand Master of Zen with Hui-neng's Commentary on the* Diamond Sutra. Boston: Shambhala, 1998.

⸻, and J. C. Cleary. *The Blue Cliff Record.* 3 vols. Boulder: Shambhala, 1977.

Conze, Edward. *Perfect Wisdom.* London: Luzac, 1973.

Cook, Frances H. *Hua-yen Buddhism.* University Park: Pennsylvania State University Press, 1977.

Dasheng qixin lun 大乘起信論. In *T* 1666.

Ferguson, Andrew. *Zen's Chinese Heritage.* Boston: Wisdom Publications, 2000.

Hakeda, Yoshito, trans. *The Awakening of Faith.* New York: Columbia University Press, 1966.

Han'guk chonggyo 韓國宗教 (Religions of Korea). Vols. 1–18. Iksan: Wŏn'gwang Taehakkyo Chonggyo Munje Yŏn'guso.

Huayan yicheng jiaoyi fenqui zhang 華嚴一乘教義分齊章). In *T* 1866.

Inada, Kenneth, trans. *Nāgārjuna: A Translation of His Mūlamadhyamaka-kārikā*. Tokyo: Hokuseido Press, 1970.

Jingang boruo boluomi jing 金鋼般若波羅密經. In *T* 235.

Jingde chuandenglu 景德傳燈錄. In *T* 2076.

Kant, Immanuel. *Critique of Pure Reason*. Trans. Norman Kemp Smith. New York: St. Martin's, 1965.

Lao Tzu. *Tao Te Ching*. Trans. John C. H. Wu. New York: St. John's University Press, 1961.

Lee, Ki-baik. *A New History of Korea*. Trans. Edward W. Wagner with Edward J. Shultz. Cambridge: Harvard University Press, 1984.

Legge, James, trans. *Confucian Analects, The Great Learning, and The Doctrine of the Mean*. Oxford: Clarendon Press, 1893.

———, trans. *The Works of Mencius*. Vol. 2 of *The Chinese Classics*. Oxford: Clarendon Press, 1895.

———, trans. *The I Ching*. Vol. 16, pt. 2, of *The Sacred Books of the East, The Yi King*. Oxford: Clarendon Press, 1899.

Liuzi dashi fabao danjing 六祖大師法寶壇經 (The Platform Sūtra of Dharma Treasure of the Sixth Patriarch). In *T* 2008.48.347c–362b.

Makra, Mary Lelia, trans. *The Hsiao Ching* 孝經. New York: St. Johns University Press, 1961.

Mubi 無比. *Kŭmganggyŏng ogahae* 金鋼經五家解 (Interpretations of the *Diamond sūtra* by five masters). Seoul: Pulkwang Ch'ulp'anbu, 1992.

Nagao, Gadjin M. *Madhyamika and Yogacara*. Trans. Leslie S. Kawamura. Albany: State University of New York Press, 1991.

Pak Chŏnghun 朴正薰. *Chŏngsan chongsa chŏn* 鼎山宗師傳 (A biography of Master Chŏngsan). Iksan: Wŏnbulgyo Ch'ulp'ansa, 2002.

Park, Jin Y., ed. *Makers of Modern Korean Buddhism*. Albany: State University of New York Press, 2010.

Pak Chungbin. *Chosŏn pulgyo hyŏksillon* 朝鮮佛教革新論 (Treatise on the renovation of Korean Buddhism). Iksan: Pulbŏp Yŏn'gu-hoe, 1935.

Pogyŏng yuktae yoryŏng 寶經六大要領 (Six essential principles of treasury scripture). In *WKC* 4:75–76.

Pulgyo chŏngjŏn 佛教正典 (Correct canon of Buddhism). Seoul: Pulgyo Sibo-sa, 1943.

Ross, David. *The Right and the Good*. Oxford: Clarendon Press, 1930.

Ryu Pyŏngdŏk. *Han'guk sinhŭng chonggyo* 韓國新興宗教 (Korean new religions). Iksan: Wŏn'gwang Taehakkyo Ch'ulp'an'guk, 1974.

The Scriptures of Won Buddhism. See Chung, Bongkil.

Shishi yaolan 釋氏要覽. In *T* 2127.53.

Sŏsan Hyujŏng. *Sŏn'ga kuigam* 禪家龜鑑 (Paragon of Zen), ed. Sŏ Cheha. Seoul: Poyŏn'gak, 1978.

Sŏngchŏl 性澈. *Sŏnmun chŏngno* 禪門正路 (Correct path to Zen tradition). Seoul: Changgyŏng-gak, 1981.

Song Namhŏn 宋南憲.*Haebang samnyŏnsa* 解放三年史 (Three-year history after liberation). Seoul: Tosŏ ch'ulp'an kkach'i, 1983.

Susim chŏnggyŏng 修心正經 (Correct scripture of cultivating the mind). In *WKC* 4, appendix 9.

Susimgyŏl 修心訣 (Secret on cultivating the mind). In *T* 2020.48.

Suyang yŏn'gu yoron 修養研究要論 (Essentials of spiritual cultivation and inquiry). Iri, South Korea: Pulbŏp Yŏn'guhoe, 1927.

Suzuki, D. T. *Essays in Zen Buddhism:* 2nd series. London: Rider, 1949.

———. *The Manual of Zen Buddhism.* New York: Grove Press, 1960.

Taesun chŏn'gyŏng haesŏl 大巡典經解設 (An explanation of the scripture of the great itinerancy). Kimje, South Korea: Chŭngsan'gyo Ponbu, 1984.

Taisho shinshū daizōkyō 大正新脩大藏經. Tokyo: Daizō shuppan kabushiki kaisha, 1914–1922.

Tonggyŏng taejŏn 東經大典 (Great canon of eastern learning). Seoul: Ŭryu Munhwasa, 1973.

Toulmin, Stephen Edelston. *The Place of Reason in Ethics.* Cambridge: Cambridge University Press, 1950.

U Hyŏnmin 禹玄民. *Sŏgyŏng* 書經 (Book of history). Seoul: Ŭryu Munhwasa, 1976.

Wŏnbulgyo chŏnsŏ 圓佛教全書 (Complete works of Won Buddhism). Iksan: Wŏnbulgyo Ch'ulp'ansa, 1977.

Wŏnbulgyo kyogo ch'onggan 圓佛教教故叢刊 (Comprehensive collection of Won Buddhist earlier publications). 6 vols. Iksan: Wŏnbulgyo Chŏnghwasa, 1968–1974.

Wŏnbulgyo kyosa 圓佛教教史 (History of Won Buddhism). Iksan: Wŏnbulgyo Chŏnghwasa, 1975.

Xindiguan jing 心地觀經. In *T* 159.3.

Yampolski, Philip B. *The Platform Sutra of the Sixth Patriarch.* New York: Columbia University Press, 1967.

Zhengfa nienchu jing 正法念處經. In *T* 721.17.

Index

317

traces remaining in empty space, 205
traitors, 225
transcending fate, 205
transmigration of the soul, 233–34
treasure: of faithfulness, 185; seven
 treasures, 198;true for human beings,
 104–5
A Treatise on National Foundation
 (Kŏn'gungnon), 13, 43, 220–24
trees, 186
triple discipline of Irwŏnsang, 18
triple identity, ethics of (samdong yulli),
 216–18
triple yielding (san fu), 123
triumph, 187
true emptiness. See emptiness
true-heartedness, 93
true life, 129
true thusness (bhūtatathatā), 36, 122,
 148
truly empty/truley nonempty, 32
truth, retribution of, 124
truthful human of great public spirit,
 211
truthfulness, indestructibility of, 90
truthful religion, 63–64
twelve apostles, 162
twelve-fold dependent co-arising, 126,
 140

uniformity of initial aspirations and
 later minds, 177
unimpeded functioning, 36
United Nations, 221
unity of mind, 94–95
universal harmony, 214
universal mentor, 110
upright mind, 127

Vairocana Buddha, 284 n 59
vein of dharma, 189
victory, law of, 191
virtue: love of, 190; word signifying
 greatness, 204
virtuous person, 183, 204
vital force: all life related by, 45–46,

118–19, 217; and clarity and purity
 of the mind, 146; and formation of
 human being, 233; Mencius's theory
 of nourishing, 256
void, 31
vow to attain buddhahood, 102
vow to deliver sentient beings, 102
Vow to Irwŏnsang, 29, 39

war, escaping calamity of, 197
warm influence, 200
watch the mind (kwansim), 162, 169
water, 187
waxing and waning, 266
way of humanity, 11–12
ways correct for each stage of life, 53
weak and strong, way of, 53, 66
Wen, mother of, 56
"Western Way," 1
wisdom (prajñā): and ability, 93; great
 power, 39; in practice of Irwŏnsang,
 264; seeking of, 98–99; of self-nature,
 22, 103, 166; as food of spirit, 201;
 for subjugating māra, 40
Wisdom Sūtras (Prajñāpāramitā), 38
wives, 59–60
Wŏlmyŏngam, 10, 11
women: and men, way of, 53, 65; as
 wives, 59–60; in world affairs, 249
wŏn: meaning of, 12, 90; origin of all
 dharmas, 88
Wŏnbulgyo. See Won Buddhism
Wŏnbulgyo kyojŏn, 251
Won Buddhism (Wŏnbulgyo):
 administration of, 92–93; Chŏngsan's
 development of, 47; destiny of, 219;
 early name for, 12; founding motive
 of order, 135; founding of, 5, 7–11,
 88–89; Fourfold Beneficence (See
 under main heading); four pillars
 of, 16–17; in Korean reconstruction,
 226–27; naming of, 13–14, 88;
 offerings to the Buddha, 19–20,
 22; order's constitution, 102–3;
 propagation of, 89, 91; Śākyamuni
 Buddha as grandfather, 116; selfless